Sebr. Kneipp

MY WATER-CURE

TESTED FOR MORE THAN 35 YEARS

AND PUBLISHED FOR THE CURE OF DISEASES
AND THE PRESERVATION OF HEALTH

BY

SEBASTIAN KNEIPP
SECRET CHAMBERLAIN OF THE POPE, PARISH PRIEST OF WÖRISHOFEN (BAVARIA)

TRANSLATED FROM HIS 36th GERMAN EDITION.

With 100 Illustrations and a Portrait of the Author.

THIRD EDITION.

JOS. KŒSEL PUBLISHER
KEMPTEN (BAVARIA)
MDCCCXCIV.

PRINTED BY JOS. KOESEL AT KEMPTEN (BAVARIA)
PUBLISHER OF SEB. KNEIPPS WORKS.

Preface to the first Edition.

Being a priest, the salvation of immortal souls is the first object for which I wish to live and to die. During the last 30 or 40 years, however, the care for mortal bodies has absorbed a considerable portion of my time aud my strength. This work I have never sought after; on the contrary every patient coming to me is (naturally speaking) a burden to me. Only the thought of Him who came down from Heaven to heal all our infirmities, and the remembrance of His promise: "Blessed are the merciful; for they will obtain mercy," — and: "Even a cup of cold water given in My name shall not be unrewarded," was able to detain me from refusing every petition, no matter who the petitioner might be. The temptation to do so was the more natural, because not profit, but incalculable loss of time, not honour, but often calumny and persecution, not gratitude, but in many cases ingratitude, scorn and insults, were my reward. But God allowed it to be so, and I shall not complain of it. It is easy to be understood that after such precedences I feel not much inclined to write, especially now that I am feeling the oppression of old age, and both mind and body long for rest.

Only the constant and impetuous urging of my friends who call it a sin against charity if I do not write down before my death what I have learned by experience, the innumerable petitions of those who have been cured, and most of all the entreaties of poor, abandoned patients in the country, could induce me to take the resolution to write, almost against my will.

I have had a peculiar affection and care for the poorer classes, the sick country-people who are so often neglected and forsaken, and to them especially I dedicate my little book; therefore the language is plain and clear. I have purposely tried to use familiar language, instead of giving a dry, inefficacious skeleton. If one or other story is somewhat long, or if repetitions occur, I trust the reader will overlook it on account of my good intention.

It was by no means my intention to oppose any of the existing medicinal systems, or to attack any individual, or his science and reputation, in the least point.

Of course I am aware that only professional men are called upon to publish such things; but I am sure that just such men will be glad to see that even a layman imparts his knowledge obtained by long years' experience. Everyone will be welcome to me who with a sincere heart wishes to give corrections or useful hints; but I shall leave unregarded those who criticise out of party-spirit, and call me a bungler and quack.

My earnest wish has been that a professional man, a physician, would release me of this heavy burden and oppressive work, and I should feel so happy if at last these professional men would begin to study the system of hydropathy thoroughly and put it in practice under their inspection; this little work of mine could then be of some use to them. I can give assurance that notwithstanding my sometimes repulsive demeanour, the sick and suffering people who came to me, could be numbered by thousands and tens of thousands, and I could easily have become rich, and very rich, if I had accepted only part of the sums offered to me for cures.

Many came saying: I will give you £ 5 or £ 10 if you cure me. The sufferer looks out for help, wherever he can find it, and he is happy to pay the physician who has healed him, whether it be by the medicine bottle or by the water jug.

There have been celebrated physicians who practised the water-cures with energy and great success; but they died, and their hints, counsels and experiences were buried with them. May now at last the aurora be followed by a full and lasting morning!

All names given or indicated in this book I can answer for, and on application will be ready to give the addresses in full. It may be that sometimes my expressions are a little harsh; but that springs from my somewhat austere and rough disposition. With it I have grown old, and separation or concealment would be hard now to both of us.

I trust the blessing of Almighty God may accompany my little book on its travels. And when one day my friends of the water-cure are told that I have departed this life, I beg of them to send me a refreshing "Our Father" to the place where the physician of physicians heals and purifies the souls in the fire-cure for eternal life.

Wörishofen, Railway Station Türkheim in Suabia.
October 1st, 1886.

The Author.

Preface to the 5th Edition.

Every father is glad when from time to time he is able to settle a son or a daughter in life, and I too feel happy to have sent out 4 editions of my book in all directions, as advisers and helpers in the manifold troubles of life. Go then also, my 5th edition of 6000 copies, and enter the dwellings of the rich and the poor as a well meaning friend.

I have received a very great number of letters, and I regret that I am unable to answer them all. It is indeed a great pleasure to me to find that many have chosen themselves the right remedies out of my book, and so have been restored to health. But my greatest pleasure would be to find that physicians practise this system and thus help mankind in such a simple way. Several of them have already been here to learn by experience the most simple way of putting it into practice. Although it had never been advertised that a medical establishment had been erected here, and no invitation had been given to any one, many came from every direction to ask for help which they also found. To make this plain system as useful as it can be, it is first of all necessary to erect new bathing places.

Therefore I heartily welcome the new water-cure-establishment in Jordanbad near Biberach in Württemberg which is arranged entirely according to my system and will be opened early in 1889 under the direction of Sisters of Charity and of a practitioner, who, during the last two years, has acquired such a perfect knowledge and practice of my system that I place my entire confidence in him. Therefore I recommend the institution in Jordanbad as heartily as possible.

That it may be multiplied like my little book, and restore to health many who are sick and weary of life, is the wish of my heart.

Wörishofen, October 27th, 1888.

The Author.

Preface to the 6th Edition.

To my great surprise the 5th edition of 6000 copies has been sold in 5 weeks, a success I never dreamed of. As I have said many times, both by word of mouth and by letter, it is always my greatest delight to see physicians taking the trouble of studying my system, and I am always ready to explain it to them.

But I must oppose those who, without having acquired a thorough knowledge of it, pretend to be representatives of my system. If by incorrect appliance of my remedies the results are evil consequences, it is simply the fault of misuse and ignorance.

I, therefore, embrace this opportunity to recommend once more the Jordanbad near Biberach in Württemberg which is to be opened next May under the direction of a practitioner J. Stützle M. D. who has acquired a solid knowledge and experience of my system, and in whom I have entire confidence.

I am quite sure that such physicians will obtain their own satisfaction as well as the welfare of their patients from my system.

Begin then thy travelling too, thou my 6th 6000 fold edition, and bring to all poor sufferers advice and help, and also kind regards and best wishes from their friend.

Wörishofen, New-year's day 1889.

The Author.

_____

Preface to the 7th Edition.

The 1st edition of my "water-cure" I called a son whom I was sending out into the wide world; very quickly five more of such sons followed, and just now the 7th is preparing to go with the same intention to be a helper in need to as many as possible. — As the children who have left their home generally cause parents much anxiety, so these editions of my widely known water-cure published in so short a time are causing me much trouble in so far as they deprive me of every leisure hour from early morning to late at night. I am deluged with letters full of inquiries; every day 30 or 40 arrive asking for particulars about the applications, although the book itself gives sufficient explanations for most diseases, and in order to prevent harm, one need only be careful, and not make use of too many applications at once; the effects produced by small applications of water are often marvellous. Most of the letters adressed to me relating to water-cures are generally so detailed that a fourth or sixth part of them would be sufficient; moreover the hand writing is sometimes very bad and neither name nor residence of inquirer written legibly. — Much as I should like to gratify every sufferer it has become entirely impossible to me to answer all the inquiries contained in these letters, and therefore, I find myself forced to declare that I cannot promise an answer to any one writing to me about water-cure, and I beg of them not to be displeased at this. So then I also sent out into the world the 7th edition of 6000 copies, with the hearty wish that God's blessing may accompany them.

Wörishofen, April, 1889.

The Author.

Preface to the 12th Edition.

Already 11 editions of my "water-cure" have been sent out into the world as advisers and helpers in diseases and the different troubles of this life, and it gives me great comfort that suffering humanity obtains help from the remedy everywhere to be found, the water. What gives me the greatest comfort is the erection of new hospitals in different countries in order to spare long journeys to the sufferers who wish to use the water-cure. The "Jordanbad" in Biberach has been opened; a great many patients have gone there, and the establishment can show forth many successful cures. Another opportunity presents itself at Immenstadt; of this establishment also honorable reports only are given, and therefore we have a good prospect that in future it will continue progressing more and more.

The third institution has been opened at Ulm. There the establishment has begun in a smaller style, so as to suffice for the environs of the town.

In Rosenheim an establishment upon my system
has been opened lately at the general request of the
citizens, and, as I have been informed, with good success; for Dr. Bernhuber has been with me in Wörishofen as physician to my patients, and has great
talent for his profession. He is not only a good physician, but also a good operating surgeon. He has
often declared to me: "By application of water, diseases
can be cured in cases where other remedies are of
no avail." Therefore I have reason to hope this
establishment especially will be a source of blessing
to many.

Dr. George Wolf has opened a new establishment
in Traunstein. Dr. Wolf is of a quiet, thougthful and
noble character, has studied and practised my whole
system in Wörishofen for a long time, and I am sure
I can highly recommend this physician to all patients
who wish to use my water-cure. Thus my numerous
friends and guests near and far, especially those in
Austria, have a favorable opportunity of experiencing
the wholesome effects of my water-cure under his
direction; for exactly patients from Austria and Hungary, so far off from here, have visited my own bathing-
establishment with great delight, and after returning
home have made known my system in grateful remembrance of the results produced by it.

It is a comfort to me to give evidence of the increasing number of physicians favorably disposed
towards my system; by these means the whole will
gradually pass over to professionists, and this will be
my greatest consolation. Go then out thou, too,
12th edition, not without the blessing from Heaven, and
continue the work of thine eleven brothers, seek out

the sick and bring them help; but to the healthy be a preservative against sickness.

Wörishofen, December 3rd, 1889

The Author.

Preface to the 27th Edition.

The number of physicians adopting my method of curing by water has considerably increased during the two last years. I mention especially Dr. Bergmann and Dr. Tacke who are assisting me in my work in this place.

Of late two new establishments based on the principle of water-cure have been opened, one at Aistersheim (Upper Austria), and the other at Brixen (Tyrol). The former is under the direction of Mr. Otto Ebenhecht, a disciple of mine whom I can heartily recommend to every one; head of the latter is Dr. Otto de Guggenberg, one of the most learned men who ever came hither to study the water-cure.

In January 1891 Dr. Lœser opened an establishment conducted according to my method at Veitshöchheim near Wuerzburg. Dr. Lœser is a quiet thinker and will certainly do honour to the undertaking.

Wörishofen, February 26th, 1891.

The Author.

Preface to the 33rd Edition.

I am a priest and hence bound to work for the salvation of souls. How happy should I be if no other burden were weighing on my shoulders! But compassion for the helpless sick has induced me to act also as physician, and this compassion still urges me to carry a double burden and to imitate the merciful Samaritan alleviating the sufferings of my fellow-men through word and deed. I hope that this work of mercy will obtain mercy for me according to the words of Holy Scripture.

Of the book "My Water-cure" to which many owe the restoration of their health, a new life, as it were, 33 editions in German language have now been published. I am far from thinking highly of my book, but the many editions, the translation in several foreign languages, the numerous successful cures, and the innumerable letters of thanksgiving reaching me every day, give testimony of the value of its contents. This is a comfort for me and, at the same time, an encouragement to make my simple method of curing diseases always more known.

When I began to write this work, my only motive in doing so was the love of my Creator and the welfare of my fellow-creatures. May God regard this edition also as an act of charity for the performance of which I fervently implore His blessing.

Wörishofen, August 14th, 1891.

The Author.

Preface to the 50th Edition.

Had a stranger passed through Wörishofen six years ago, counting the house-numbers as he went along, he might have said to himself: "This is not a bad place, it has a good many buildings". Now, in the year 1894 going again through the same Wörishofen, and counting the old houses as they stood when he last saw them, and the new ones which had sprung up since, he might exclaim full of astonishment: "Well! how has it come about that the new houses have almost outnumbered the old ones? What can have influenced these people so powerfully as to cause them to build so much?" To this he could not obtain a better answer than the following: "Father Kneipp has written a book called: "*My Water Cure*", and has sent it out into the world, as a father sends his son. This book has taught and enlightened young and old, rich and poor, high and low, as to how they should make use of water, and how they can by its various applications be cured of disease and be delivered from many ills, or at the very least find relief. On account of this book invalids have come to Wörishofen in increasing numbers from year to year, so that, at last, the available houses became insufficient for their accommodation, — and that is the reason why so much has been built."

The "Water Cure" has now lived out its fiftieth edition and would like to celebrate its

Jubilee

and to cry out to men, especially to the sick: "Learn ye to know water, its application and its effects, and it will bring you help where help is possible!"

As to me, I can only rejoice and wish from my heart that, in times to come, all the sick may find this relief and help. I particularly wish that medical practitioners would hasten to make proper use of water, this gift of the Creator, and to vouchsafe this step-child a place in their households and among their store of remedies.

To the fiftieth edition I give the mission: Take care of the sick that they may be cured! Be a good friend to the healthy that they may not fall ill! And as I, a priest, offer daily the Holy Sacrifice, so shall all those who come to Wörishofen, together with those who employ the cure at home, be included in the Holy Sacrifice of the Mass, that they may obtain the blessing of Heaven for their recovery.

Wörishofen, Candlemas-day, 1894.

The Author.

Translator's Preface.

Scarcely ever has a book found its way through Europe and the whole civilised world in so incredibly short a time as the little volume of which this is a translation.

The author in the brief and plain sketch of his life at once endears himself to the reader. From the humble place of his birth we follow him through the toils of his early life: with him we feel grateful to the kind friend under whose hospitable roof the poor traveller found not only shelter but also the longed-for teacher. We, then, accompany him through his college years and witness his indefatigable zeal in the pursuit of his studies, but alas! when about to congratulate him on their prosperous termination, we are suddenly grieved at the saddening aspect of his failing health. Certainly the shortsightedness of human understanding with regard to the plans of Divine Providence cannot be more sorely tried than it was in the poor student's case; but thus it had to be in order to make his life that wonderful illustration of the Apostle's word: "To them that love God, all things work together unto good." Rom. VIII. 28.

Finding help nowhere and lacking both physical and mental strength to achieve what he had commenced, the young man was left to spend his time in the royal library. Here one day an old little book attracts his curiosity, he opens it, it treats of water-cures. This was the moment was to be a turning-point in his life. The contents of the small unsightly volume were to be the rough outline of a plan which, in its completion, has become a blessing for numbers of his fellow-creatures who, labouring under more or less grievous disease, were restored to the full possession of bodily health and mental vigour; for as soon as the author in this early period of his life had experienced the salutary effects of water, it seemed but natural to his noble heart to make as many as possible partakers of the benefit he then enjoyed in the sense of undisturbed health. Since his endeavours in this respect had for their sole objects the glory of God and the good of poor sufferers, since he sought neither honour nor any other earthly reward, he was well armed against the temptation to give up a work which, besides adding considerably to the exertions imposed on him by his sacred office, earned for him much contradiction and ingratitude.

For many years had he continued to attend to the cure of human bodies without neglecting the least of his obligations to the immortal souls, before he yielded to the entreaties of thousands who urged him to write down the results of his study and experience of the water-cure and render them thus useful also to those who were unable to profit by his oral advice. His book obtained for him what he had neither aimed at, nor wished for: his name, always pronounced with love and veneration within the limited sphere of his activity as parish-priest, has since acquired more than European fame. The eyes of the whole civilized world look with admiration on the aged pastor of the humble Bavarian village and, attracted by the wisdom of his counsels and the kindness of his heart, numbers of invalids are daily seen to gather round him for help and advice.

I myself have had the enviable fortune of living for nearly two years on most confidential terms with the venerable man. The look of his eyes so penetrating and yet so full of compassion, the unpretentiousness and simplicity of manners displayed in his personal intercourse with all classes of men, the noble disposition of his heart, the disinterestedness in all his attempts for the good of others, act like as many charms delighting and fascinating everyone that approaches him. The rich and the poor, the prince and the beggar, are all welcomed by the same kindly look, the same loving heart. The artless, I should almost say, the rustic style which characterizes his oral counsels is a peculiar feature also of „My Water-cure". I should consider it a want of filial piety and affection for my fatherly friend and master, were I in my translation to deviate from his principle of simplicity by turning his words into elegant periods.

Moreover was it expressly desired by the author that translations of his book should be complete, correct, and, as much as possible, literal. He wrote "My Water-cure" chiefly for the lower classes, for poor country people who lack either means or convenience to have recourse to medical aid in their maladies, and this circumstance particularly made him fear that want of correctness in translating might be of fatal consequences. Since there has already been edited another English translation which cannot claim to be either correct or complete, I myself thought it especially advisable to produce a literal translation of the 33rd. German edition which has been quite recently thoroughly revised by the author.

This translation has the additional advantage of numerous illustrations representing the medicinal herbs and their essential parts, which will, besides imparting knowledge about the plants, facilitate the work of the gatherer.

The consideration that the master having all means of greater elegance at his command, chose nevertheless simplicity to be the prominent feature of his style, and the fact that in spite of this, two hundred thousand copies of his book have been published, was apt to confirm me in my resolution at the risk of doing even more violence to the English language than the author did to his native tongue.

These are the grounds on which I base the hope that my readers will judge kindly about my work. I shall consider it the most desirable compensation for my toils if it will prove of real and lasting profit to all who wish to follow its advice. If they are Christians the venerable person of the author will increase their confidence in his counsels; if they are not Christians they may remember that his heart beats warm for all and that, by making "My water-cure" known to the world, he wished to benefit all without exception.

For any explanation or detail respecting the contents of this book, apply to the Editor.

St. D.

Contents.

—•—

Introduction.

s on a tree no leaf resembles perfectly to another, so also do men's destinies differ one from the other. If every man were to write a sketch of his own life, we should have as many different biographies as there are men. Intricate are the ways twisting themselves in our life in every direction, sometimes like an inextricable ball of silk, the threads of which seem to be laid without plan or purpose. So it frequently seems; but it never is so in reality. Faith darts its enlightening beam into the confused darkness, and shows how all these entangled paths serve wise purposes, and how all of them lead to one end designed and fixed by the all-wise Creator from the beginning. The ways of Providence are wonderful.

When, from the high watch-tower of old age, I look back on the past years of my life and all the complications of my paths, they seem to wind themselves sometimes on the brink of the abyss; but they lead against all expectation to the glorious heights of vocation, and finally attain them, and I have every reason to praise the tender and wise ruling of Providence, the more so as the paths which, according to human ideas, seemed to be sad and leading to death, showed to me and numberless others the opening to a new life.

I was more than 21 years old when I left my home as a weaver seeking employment; but, since the days of my childhood, something else had occupied my mind. With unspeakable pain and longing desire for the realization of my ideal, I had awaited this departure for long, long years, as my sole wish was to become a priest.

I went away then, not as was expected to throw the weaver's shuttle, but I hurried from place to place seeking for some one who would provide me with the means for studying. The now deceased prelate Matthias Merkle († 1881) at that time chaplain in Grönenbach, took me under his care, gave me private instructions during two years, and with indefatigable zeal tried to prepare me for the gymnasium, so that I was able to be received there at the end of that time. It was no easy task and its effects on my body and mind seemed to render all my efforts utterly useless. After five years of the greatest exertions and privations my strength both physical and mental was broken. Once my father came to town to fetch me, and even now the words of the innkeeper, at whose inn we stopped, seem still to be ringing in my ears. „Weaver,“ he said, „this is the last time you will come to fetch your student.“ A physician in the army, a celebrated man, who at that time was known as a benevolent and generous helper of poor patients, visited me in the second last year of my studies 90 times, and in the last one more than a hundred. He wished so much to help me, but my increasing debility rendered his medicinal knowledge and devoted charity unavailable. I myself had given up all hope long ago and was expecting my end with quiet resignation. To procure a little amusement and dissipation of mind, I used to run over the pages of many books. By chance — I only use this customary but insignificant word, because it is customary; for things never happen by chance — an unsightly little book fell into my hands; I opened it; it treated of the water-cure. I perused the book and found in it descriptions of various diseases and the wonderful effects obtained by the use of the water-cure. At last this was the thought which struck me: You may find your own state described in it. And so it was; my state was represented to a hair's breadth.

What joy! What comfort! New hopes electrified my withered body and my still more withered mind. At first this little book was the straw to which I clung; soon afterwards it became the staff which supported the sufferer; to-day I acknowledge it to be the life-boat sent to me by a merciful Providence at the right time, at the hour of extreme need. This little book treating of the healing power of fresh water, is written by a physician; the applications are most of them extremely rugged and rigid. I tried them for 3 months, for 6 months; no real improvement ensued, but at the same time I did not grow worse and that gave me new courage. I spent the winter of 1849 in Dillingen. Two or three times a week I went to a solitary spot to bathe in the Danube for some moments. Quickly I ran to the spot; more speedily I hastened back to my warm room at home. This cold exercise never hurt me, but, as I thought, it was of no great use either. In 1850 I came to the Georgianum in Munich. And there I found a poor student who was in a much more miserable state than myself. The physician of the institution refused to give him the certificate of health necessary for his ordination, declaring that he would not live much longer. Now I had a dear companion whom I initiated into the mysteries of my little book, and we tried to surpass each other in the practice of the various water applications. In a short time my friend got the wished for certificate, and at the present day he is still alive. I myself grew continually stronger, became a priest and am living as such over 38 years. My friends tell me that they admire the power of my voice and are amazed at the bodily strength I enjoy at the age of 70. The water remained my well tested friend, and who can blame me, if I remain faithful to it also?

He who has been in want and misery himself, knows how to sympathise with the want and misery of his neighbour.

Not all patients are alike unfortunate, and surely he who has the means of regaining health, can easily reconcile himself with a short time of suffering. Such patients I have refused by hundreds and thousands during the first years. But the poor man, who is needy and abandoned, given up by the physicians and no longer helped by medicaments and remedies, has every right to our sympathies. Great numbers of this kind of people are my favourite patients; such poor and entirely forsaken people I have never sent away. It would seem hard, unconscientious, and ungrateful to shut my door upon such poor sufferers, or to deny them the resources which brought me health and strength in my necessity.

The great number of sufferers, the still greater difference of their sufferings, urged me to enrich my experience in the use of water and to perfect the method of applying it.

To my first adviser, the well-known little book, I am always indebted for the introductory lessons I learned from it, but I soon found out that many applications were too rigid, too strong and discouraging for human nature. For this reason people called at first the water-cures „horse-cures“, and up to this day many who abuse that which they do not understand, like to give the name of swindle and quackery to everything connected with the water-cure.

I willingly grant that many applications and exercises of the primitive and still undeveloped water-cure were more suited to a muscular and strong-limbed horse than to a human skeleton clothed with soft flesh and stringed with tender nerves.

In the life of the celebrated F. Ravignan S. J. the following incident is recorded: „His complaint, a disease in the throat, was increasing on account of too great exertion, (he was a celebrated preacher who practised his sacred office with apostolic zeal in Paris, London. and many other large towns) and soon became chronical....His windpipe was simply one wound, his voice was entirely gone. He had to spend two whole years (1846—48) in a state of inactivity and suffering; and cures tried at several places, change of air in the south, were of no result. In June 1848, F. Ravignan was living with Doctor K.

R.. in his country-house in the vale at B... One morning
after Mass, the doctor looked anxious and announced
to the assembled family that F. Ravignan felt worse
and could not come to breakfast. Then he himself disappeared and went to the patient saying: „Arise and
follow me!" „But where to?" the latter replied. „I am
going to throw you into the water." „Into the water?
said Ravignan, with my fever and my cough? But never
mind, I am in your hands and must obey." A so-called
shower-bath was meant, a violent but efficient remedy,
as the biographer says. The effect was evident. At dinner
time that same day, the doctor triumphantly brought his
patient, then remarkably better; and he who was voiceless
in the morning, told the tale of his recovery at night.

This, I too, call a little „horse-cure" which, notwithstanding the good result, I should not like to imitate or
to recommend for imitation.

Here I must state that I do not approve of all the
applications now in use in the water-cure hospitals; of
some of them I even strictly disapprove. They appear
to me too strong, and, pardon the expression, too partial.
Too many things are treated exactly alike, and much too
little difference is made, in my opinion, between the various patients, their greater or lesser weakness, their
more or less obstinate illness, the more or less advanced
devastations and consequences, etc. etc.

It is just in the variety of the applications and in
their proper choice, that the master-hand will and must
be recognised.

Patients of the different hospitals came to me complaining bitterly: „It is beyond endurance, it is killing
me." But thus it ought not to be. Once a healthy man
presented himself to me, asserting that he had been injured
by washing himself in the morning. „How did you do
that?" I asked him. „I put my head under the pump,
and let the icy water run over it, for a quarter of an
hour!" It would certainly be a miracle, if such an unreasonable man did not entirely ruin himself. We mock
and deride such a foolish proceeding, and yet, how many
who must be supposed to know how to apply the water

reasonably, have acted just as foolishly, in my opinion
even more foolishly, and thereby made the patients start
with horror from the water for ever. I could give numerous instances which would be just as many proofs
of my assertion.

I warn against every too strong or too frequent
application of water, for that which otherwise would be
an advantage of the curing element, is thereby turned to
injury, and the hopeful confidence of the patient is changed into fear and horror. For 30 years, I have tried
every single application upon myself. Three times —
this I acknowledge openly — I found myself induced to
change my system, to loosen the strings, to descend
from strictness to softness, from great to still greater
softness. According to my present conviction, now fixed
for 17 years and tested by innumerable cures, he who
knows how to apply the water in the plainest, easiest,
and most simple way, will produce the most profitable
effects and the safest results. The various modes in
which I use the water as a remedy, are told in the third
part of this book, treating of the different diseases. In
the second part (see the particular preface), I have given,
especially for country people, some remedies to make a
family chemistry, which, applied interiorly, tend to the
same purposes as the water; either to dissolve, to evacuate, or to strengthen.

To every patient consulting me I put some questions
so as not to act too hastily and to my disadvantage.

In like manner this little book is bound to answer
shortly the following questions:

1. What is sickness, and what is the common
source of all sickness?

The human body is one of the most marvellous
structures of God's creative hand. Every joint agrees
to joint, every accurately measured limb to the har-
monious whole, combined to an astonishing unity. More
remarkable still is the conjunction of the organs, and
their activity within the body. Even the most disbeliev-
ing physician and naturalist, who, „has not found a
soul with his lancet and his dissecting knife," cannot

refuse his most just and highest admiration to the inimitable wisdom displayed in the structure of the human body. — This euphony and harmony, called good health, is disturbed by different causes, which we call „diseases". Such diseases of the body, interior and exterior, belong to the daily bread which most human creatures must eat, willingly or unwillingly. All these diseases whatever their names may be, have their cause, origin, root and their germ in the blood, or rather in disturbances of the blood, whether it be only disturbed in its circulation, or corrupted in its ingredients by humours not belonging to it. The net of blood-vessels spreads its red vital spirit through the whole body, in its suitable way. Order consists in proportion; every too much or too little in the tempo of the circulation of the blood, every penetration of foreign elements, disturbs the peace, the concord, causes discord, changes health to sickness.

2. How is the healing to be effected?

By the tracks in the snow the expert hunter discerns the game; he follows these tracks according as he wishes to hunt a deer, a chamois, or a fox. An able physician soon knows where the disease is, in what it has originated, what progress it has made. The symptoms show him the disease, the latter indicates the remedies to be chosen. Some would say: This procedure is most plain. Yes, sometimes it is, but sometimes it is not. If someone comes to me with frozen ears, I directly know that this has been caused by severe cold; if a person sitting at the millstone suddenly screams, having his finger crushed, I need not ask what is the matter with him. But it is not so easy even with ordinary headache or with diseases of the stomach, the nerves, or the heart, which originate not only in several or manifold causes, but very often in diseases of the neighbouring organs, which diseases injure the action of the stomach, the heart, or the kidneys. A straw stops the pendulum of the largest clock; a mere trifle is able to disturb the heart most painfully. But it is precisely in finding this trifle that the difficulty consists, for the examination is often very complicated and mistakes of many kinds are likely to occur. Many of such instances are to be found in the third part of this book.

If I strike the trunk of a young oak-tree with my foot or an axe, it will tremble; every branch, every leaf moves. How mistaken I should be, if I were to conclude that because the leaf trembles, it must have been attacked, touched by something. No, it is because the trunk trembles, that the branch and the leaf, as part and particle of the trunk, do the same. The nerves are such branches on the trunk of our body. „He suffers with his nerves; the nerves are attacked." What does this mean? No, the whole organism has received a shock, has been weakened, therefore the nerves are trembling too.

Cut one thread of the skilful cobweb of a spider, running from the centre to the periphery very cautiously, and the whole net shrinks, the quadrangles and triangles, spun with a wonderful accuracy and seeming to be measured out with compasses, suddenly form the most irregular and inordinate figures. How foolish it would be to think that this time the spider must have made important mistakes in weaving its silken house. Put the little thread in its place again, and instantly the former wonderful order is restored. The art consists in finding out this single diminutive thread; to fumble about in the cobweb, would be to destroy it entirely. I leave it to everyone to make the application himself, and conclude with the true answer to our question: How plain, uncomplicated, and easy the cure is, how it almost excludes every possibility of mistake, as soon as I know that every disease is caused by disturbances of the blood. The work of healing can only consist in one of the two tasks: either to lead the irregularly circulating blood to its normal course, or endeavour to evacuate the bad juices, the morbid matter, which disturb the right combination of the blood. There is no further work to be done except the strengthening of the enfeebled organism.

3. In what way does the water effect the cure?

The ink-blot on your hand is quickly washed off by the water · the bleeding wound is cleansed by it. If in summer-time after the day's exertions you wash the sweat off your forehead with fresh water, you feel quite revived; it refreshes, strengthens, and does you good. The mother perceiving scurf on her baby's little head takes warm water, and by it the scurf is dissolved.

Dissolving, evacuating (washing off, as it were) strengthening, these three qualities of the water are sufficient for us, and we make the assertion:

The water, in particular our water-cure, heals all diseases in any way curable; for the various applications of water tend to remove the roots of the disease; they are able;

    a) To dissolve the morbid matters in the blood,

    b) to evacuate what is dissolved,

    c) to make the cleansed blood circulate rightly again.

    d) finally, to harden the enfeebled organism, i. e. to strengthen it for new activity.

4. What is the cause of the sensibility of the present generation, of the striking susceptibility for all possible diseases, of which even the names were scarcely known in former days?

Of course, many people would like to dispense me from this question. Nevertheless it appears to me to be of great importance, and I state, without hesitation, that these evils arise from a want of hardening. The effemination of the people living now-a-days has reached a high degree. The weak and delicate, the poor of blood and nervous, the sick of heart or stomach, almost form the rule; the strong and vigorous are the exception. People are affected by every change of weather; the turn of seasons does not pass by without colds in the head and chest; even the too quickly entering a warm room, when coming from the cold street, does not remain unrevenged, etc. etc. 50—60 years ago it was quite different, and where shall we come to, if, according to the general complaint of the thoughtful, mankind's strength and life are decreasing so rapidly, if decay begins even before man has reached maturity? It is high time to see what is wanting. As a small contribution towards remedying such distress we offer the few simple and safe remedies for hardening the skin, the whole body and single parts of the body. These may be added to the water-applications. These remedies have already been accepted by numbers of persons of all conditions, first by some of them with ridicule, but afterwards practised with trust and with visible success. Vivant sequentes!

Treatises, as important as that about hardening, could be written on food, clothing and airing; this will perhaps be done later on. I am quite aware that my particular opinions will be strongly contradicted; nevertheless I keep to them; for they have been ripened by an experience of long years. They are not mushrooms sprung up in my brain during the night; they are precious fruits, hard and severe perhaps to incarnate prejudices, but extremely relishing to a sound mental digestion. I only want to give some hints regarding the food.

My chief rule is: Dry, simple, nourishing household-fare not spoiled by art or by strong spices; the drink should be the genuine beverage offered by God in every well. Both taken moderately are the best and most wholesome nourishment for the human body. (I am not a Puritan and allow gladly a glass of wine or beer, but without regarding them as important as they are commonly believed to be.) From a medicinal view, after illness for instance, these beverages may sometimes play a part; but for healthy people I prefer fruits.

As regards clothing, I follow the maxim of our forefathers: (Self-spun and self-made is the best country garb.) First I oppose the striking inequality or rather unequal distribution of clothing, especially in winter time which is a great injury to health. The head has its fur cap, the neck its tight collar, covered with a **woollen** scarf a yard long; the shoulders wear a 3 or 4 fold cover; for walks a wadded cloak or even a fur-cape; only the feet, the poor neglected feet, are covered as in summer, with socks or stockings, with shoes or boots. What are the consequences of such an unreasonable partiality? The upper girdings and wrappers draw up blood and warmth to the upper story, while the lower parts are suffering from want of blood and from cold; head-ache, congestions, enlargement of the arteries of the head, hundreds of indispositions and miseries become solved problems.

Further I oppose thick woollen clothing worn next to the skin, but I approve of the clothing made of firm, dry, strong linen, or hemp-cloth. The latter is to me the best skin on the skin which never effeminates it, but does the good service of a rubber. The many-branched, hairy greasy texture of the wool on the bare body (how the wool serves my purposes, is said in the general explanations of my water applications) I look upon as a sucker of fluids and warmth, as a concurring cause of the dreadfully spreading want of blood in our weak miserable generation. The newest method of wool-wearing in the revised style will not remedy this want nor aid the blood either. Younger people may live to experience this and to outlive the method. —

Now to the airing. — We prefer by far fish obtained from spring-water, or trout from the mountain streams, to all others; fish from rivulets are inferior; those from ponds in moors and marshes, with their disgusting taste, we leave to any one. There is likewise moor and marsh air, and whoever inhales it, feeds his lungs with pestilential vapour. A celebrated physician says that the air, when inhaled for the third time has the effect of poison. Indeed, if people would understand how to provide their sitting- and especially their bed-rooms, with pure, fresh air, they would prevent many indispositions and many diseases. The pure air is spoiled mostly by breathing. We know very well that 1 or 2 grains of incense strewn on the glowing fire, fill a whole room with perfume, and we know likewise that 15—20 puffs from a cigar or pipe are sufficient to make a large room smell of the smoke. Often the most insignificant thing is enough to spoil the pure air in one way or the other, agreeably or disagreeably. Is not breathing similar to such a smoke? How many breaths do we take in a minute, in an hour, during the day, the night? How much must the air become spoiled, though we do not see the vapour? And

if I do not air, i. e. purify the bad atmosphere spoiled
by carbonic acid, what infected air, what miasms, are
streaming into the lungs? The consequences cannot,
and will not, be other than injurious.

Like breathing and exhalation, too much heat is pre-
judicial to the wholesome pure vital air, especially too
much heating of rooms. By it the air becomes bad, as
they consume and destroy the oxygen, they render it unfit
for maintaining life and therefore injurious to breathing.
12—14 degrees R. are sufficient, 15 degrees should never
be exceeded.

Care should be taken to air thoroughly all the sit-
ting- and bed-rooms, day by day, in such a way that
without trouble to anyone each one's health may draw
benefit from it. Above all great attention must be given
to the airing of the beds.

Now I have stated what I considered necessary to
be said on these points. It is sufficient to give a picture
of the stranger who knocks at your door, and whether you
admit him friendly or dismiss him unheard, he is prepared
for both, and shall be contented with either.

Part the first.

Applications of water.

—◆—

Aquae omnes . . . laudent nomen Domini.
All ye waters . . . praise the name of the Lord.

General remarks.

The applications of water used in my establishment and described in this first part, are divided into:

> Wet sheets,
> Baths,
> Vapour baths,
> Shower baths,
> Ablutions,
> Wet bandages,
> Drinking of water.

The subdivisions of each application are given in the first index. The name and the meaning of strange sounding practices are explained in their proper place.

According to the nature of all diseases by which they originate in a disordered circulation of the blood, or in corrupted and heterogeneous ingredients mixed with the blood, and in morbid matters, the applications of water tend to the triple aim:

> To dissolve,
> to evacuate the morbid matters, and
> to strengthen the organism.

In general it may be said that the dissolving is brought about by the vapours and the hot baths of medicinal herbs; the evacuation by the water bandages and partly by the shower baths and wet sheets; the strengthening by the cold baths, the shower baths, partly by the ablutions, and finally by the entire system of hardening.

I cannot and will not give particulars here in order to avoid misunderstanding.

As every disease originates in the above named disorders of the blood, it is evident that in every case of disease all the respective applications must be used more or less dissolving, evacuating and strengthening; further, that not only the suffering part, foot, or hand, or head, as the case may be, is to be treated, but always the whole body through every part of which the bad blood is flowing: of course the diseased part with preference, the rest of the body only as fellow-sufferer. It would be partial and wrong to act otherwise with regard to these two important points. Many instances in the third part will justify my statement.

Whoever uses the water as a remedy, according to my ideas and wishes, will never think the applications to be for his own whims, i. e. he never will use an application just because he likes to do so; he will never, like a fool, take pleasure in being able to „handle, and boast of, and to rave about many things, about vapours and shower-baths and bandages." To a sensible man the applications will always be only the means for the purpose, and if he can attain it by the mildest water-application, he will be happy; for his task is only this: to help nature struggling for health i. e. for her own and independent activity; to obtain this activity, to loosen the fetters of illness, the chains of suffering, and to enable nature to do the work herself again, unprevented, gaily and cheerfully. Is this task finished, the treatment must cease. This remark is important, more important still to observe it. For there is nothing which so greatly brings the water as healing element into miscredit and bad reputation, as to make applications in an indiscreet way without measure and reason, a sharp, strict, rugged proceeding. Those, and only those, I cannot repeat it enough, who consider themselves to be competent in the system of water-cures, but frighten every patient by their endless bandages, their vapours almost driving out the blood, etc. are causing the greatest harm, which it is very difficult to amend. I do not call this using the water for healing, but such outrages — I beg pardon for the expression — I call putting the water to shame.

Whoever has a knowledge of the effects of water, and knows how to use it in its extremely manifold ways, is in possession of a remedy which cannot be surpassed by any other, whatever its name may be. There is no remedy more manifold in its effects, or as it were, more elastic than the water. In creation it begins in the invisible globule of air or steam, continues in the drop, and finally forms the ocean filling up the greater part of the globe.

This ought to serve as a hint to every hydropathist, to show him that every application of water, whether it be dropping or aeriform, can be raised from the gentlest to the highest degree, and that in each case it is not the patient who ought to accommodate himself to the bandage, the vapour, etc., but every application is to be accommodated to the patient.

It is in the selection of the applications to be used that the masterhand shows itself. The one who undertakes the cure will carefully examine the patient, but not in a startling way. At first the subordinate sufferings will come under his notice, i. e. those diseases which like toad-stools spring up from the interior ground of disease. By them one can, in most cases, easily conclude, where the hearth of the disease, the principal evil, is to be found. By means of questioning and searching he will find what progress the disease has already made, what mischief it has done; then it must be taken into consideration, whether the patient is old or young, weak or strong, thin or stout, poor of blood, nervous, etc. All these points, and others besides, give to the mind of him who undertakes the cure, the right picture of the diseased; and it is only then, when this is clear and complete, that he goes to the water-apotheca and prescribes according to the principle: The gentler and more sparing, — the better and more effective.

A few general remarks may be given here, regarding the whole of the water-applications. —

No application whatever can cause the least harm, if it is made according to the directions given.

Most of them are to be made with cold water, either from the spring, well, or river. In all cases where warm water is not expressly prescribed, the word „water" means cold water. I follow my principle founded on experience: The colder, the better. In winter-time I mix snow with the water for shower-baths when they are for healthy people. Do not accuse me of ruggedness; for, think of the very short duration of my cold-water-applications. He who has once ventured to make a trial has conquered for ever; all his prejudices are entirely removed.

But I am not, nevertheless, inexorable. To beginners in the water-cure, to weak persons, especially very young or very old ones, to sick people who are afraid of cold, to such as have not much warmth in their blood, whose blood is poor, or who are nervous, I gladly allow, especially in winter-time, a warm room for their baths and shower-baths (14—15 degr. R.) for the beginning, and lukewarm water for every application. Flies are to be attracted not by salt and vinegar, but by honey.

There are special prescriptions for every warm-water application respecting the degree of warmth, the time, etc. The degrees marked R. are according to Réaumur.

Regarding the cold-water applications, we must briefly give some hints for regulating the course of action observed before, during, and after the application. (In the third part this point is often dwelt upon

No one should venture to make any cold application, whatever, when feeling cold, shivering, etc. unless it is expressly allowed in the prescription relating to his case. The applications are to be made as quickly as possible, but without agitation and haste; also with dressing and undressing no delay should be caused by slowness in buttoning or tying up, etc. All this secondary work can be done, when the whole body is properly covered. To give an instance: a cold whole-bath, including undressing, bathing and redressing, should not exceed 4—5 minutes.

It only needs a little practice to accomplish this. If with an application the time „one minute" is given, the shortest time possible is meant; if it is said 2—3 minutes, the cold is intended to be of more enduring, but not of longer, influence.

After a cold application the body must never be wiped dry, except head, and hands as far as the wrist (the latter in order not to wet the clothes when dressing). The wet body is at once covered with dry underlinen and other articles of clothing; this is to be done quickly, as before remarked, so that as soon as possible all wet spots may be closed hermetically. This proceeding will seem strange to many, even to most people, because they will imagine that they are thereby obliged to remain wet all the day long; but let them try it only once before judging, and they will soon experience what this not-wiping is good for. Wiping is rubbing, and, as it cannot be done quite equally on every spot, it produces disproportionate natural warmth, which is not of much consequence with healthy people, but of very great moment with sick and weak ones. The not-wiping helps to the most regular, most equal, and most speedy natural warmth. It is like sprinkling water into the fire; the interior warmth of the body uses the water clinging to the exterior as material for speedily bringing forth greater and more intense warmth. As before said, it all depends upon a trial.

On the other hand we strictly prescribe exercise to be taken (either by working or walking) as soon as the patient is dressed after the application, and this must be continued, until all parts of the body are perfectly dry and in normal warmth. At the beginning one may walk somewhat swiftly, but the speed must be slackened when the patient gets warm. Every one feels best himself when the bodily warmth has become normal, and when the exercise may cease. People who easily become hot and perspire freely, ought to walk more slowly from the beginning, and for them it is better to walk a little longer, but by no means to sit down in perspiration or

2*

when overheated, even in a warm room; a catarrh would be the inevitable consequence.

As a rule for all it may be said that the shortest time for exercise after an application ought to be at least 15 minutes. The kind of exercise taken, whether working, walking, etc., is of no consequence.

Concerning those applications which require the patient to be in bed, especially the wet sheets and bandages, instructions are given in their proper place, as well as particulars for every special practice. If a patient falls asleep during such an application, he should not be disturbed, even if the prescribed time has expired; for nature itself is the best and most exact alarm here, as in every other great or small need.

If sheets are ordered, they are not meant to be of fine linen, but strong, and if possible, of coarse hempen cloth. Poor people might use instead of these a worn out bed-tick, a hempen flour-sack, or such like.

For washing the body, which is prescribed often, the best thing is also a rather coarse piece of linen or hemp.

For reasons which I have mentioned briefly in the introduction, I oppose woollen clothing next to the skin; but I prefer woollen material for covering, with the icy water-bandages, for example. It produces speedy and abundant warmth, for which purpose it is unsurpassed. For the same reason I recommend feather-beds as coverings with such applications.

The violent rubbing or brushing is entirely excluded from my system; its first purpose, the producing of warmth, is accomplished in a more proportionate and equal way by the not-wiping; its second purpose, the opening of the pores, the increasing of the activity of the skin, is effected by the coarse linen or hemp, and with the advantage that it works not only for minutes like a brush, but day and night without cost of time and labour. When „vigorous washing" is spoken of, it is simply meant a quick washing of the entire part under treatment. The main point is to get wet, not to get rubbed.

There is still another point which I should like to mention here. Most people do not like the applications at night before going to sleep, because they get excited, and, as it were, roused from the first sleep by them; others, on the contrary, feel as if rocked to sleep by gentle applications. In general, I do not recommend such applications, but would advise every one to act in this respect according to his own discretion and experience, because every one has to bear the consequences himself.

Regarding the particular instructions for every kind of application, reference may be made to the first part of this book, and for the use of them in special cases to the third part. It is also said there which applications are complete in themselves, and which are only part-applications, i. e. to be used in connection with others; likewise which of the applications (vapours) are to be used with great precaution.

I conclude these general remarks with the wish that by the applications of water many healthy people may become more healthy still, and many who are sick be restored to health. I will now proceed to give a short list of the means of hardening, and then a short treatise on the applications of water in use at my establishment.

Means of hardening.

— ◆ ◆ —

As means of hardening we name:

1. Walking barefooted,
2.   „   „   in wet grass,
3.   „   „   on wet stones,
4.   „   „   in newly fallen snow,
5.   „   „   in cold water,
6. Cold baths for arms and legs,
7. The knee-shower (with or without upper shower).

~~~~~~~~~~~~~~~~

1. The most natural and most simple means of hardening is **walking barefooted.**

This can be practised, according to the different conditions of life and age, in the most manifold ways.

Babies, who are still entirely dependent on others, who are always shut up in the rooms, ought to be, if possible, always without shoes or stockings. Would that I could imprint this as a settled, irrefragable rule on all parents, especially on the all too anxious mothers! Parents who are too strongly prejudiced to agree with this, may, at least, have mercy on the little helpless creatures, and provide for them such coverings for their feet as will permit the fresh air to penetrate easily to the skin.

Children who are able to stand and walk know well how to manage for themselves.   Heedless of all human respect they throw away the troublesome, tormenting shoes and stockings and are quite in their delight, particularly at spring time, if they are allowed to run about freely without them.   Sometimes a toe is hurt; but never mind, that does not prevent them from trying again. Children do this quite by instinct, following a certain natural impulse, which grown-up people also would feel, if the over-polished, moulded, nature-destroying civilisation, had not oftentimes deprived them of all common sense.

The children of the poor are seldom disturbed in their pleasure; but the children of parents who are rich, or of rank, are less fortunate, and yet they feel the want no less than the poor ones.   Once I watched the boys of a high stationed and distinguished officer, and saw how, as soon as they thought themselves out of range of the penetrating eyes of their strict Papa, the elegant little shoes and stockings were thrown over the hedges, and away they ran galloping over the green meadow.   Their mamma, a sensible lady, was not displeased at their proceedings, but if, by chance, papa saw his little lords in such an unbecoming attire, at once long lectures were given about duties of rank, about refinement and unrefinement, about feeling and behaving in a manner conformable to one's rank.   The children were so deeply impressed by these lectures that the next day they were jumping barefooted in the grass more lively than ever.   Once more I say: at least, let the children who are not yet spoiled by refinement, have their enjoyment!

Sensible parents who would willingly allow this to their children, but who, living in town, have no remote garden or lawn, may sometimes allow them to walk barefooted in a room or in a passage, if only their feet as well as their face and hands may sometimes be exposed to the fresh air to their feet's content, and to move about in their element.

Grown-up people of the poorer classes, especially in the country, do not want any admonition; they are used to going barefooted and do not envy the richest towns-man his elegant, high, or low, varnished, buttoned boots, torturing, pinching and fettering his feet, nor his fine stockings either.

Foolish country-people with townish manners, who are ashamed to do the same as their equals, punish them-selves enough by their self-conceit; let the old-fashioned conservatives cling firmly to the good traditions. In my youth every one in the country went barefooted: children and adults, father and mother, brother and sister. We had to walk miles to school and church; our parents gave us a piece of bread and some apples to eat on the way, and also shoes and stockings for our feet; but these were hanging on our arms or over our shoulders, until we ar-rived at school or at church, not only in summer, but also in the colder season. No sooner had spring arrived, and the snow had begun to disappear from the hills, than our bare feet trod the ground soaked with its water, and we felt merry, bright, and healthy in our exercise.

Grown-up people in towns, especially those who be-long to the better, or even to the highest classes, cannot make use of this practice, — that is quite clear, and if their prejudices have reached such a degree that they fear to draw rheumatism, catarrh, sore throat or such like upon themselves, if for a moment, when dressing, their tender feet should stand on the bare floor instead of on warm soft carpets, I shall not trouble them at all. But if any really wish to do something in the way of hardening, what is there to prevent them from taking such a prome-nade in their room, for 10, 15, or 30 minutes at night before going to sleep, or in the morning when rising? At first, to begin gently, they could do so with their stockings on, then barefooted, and at last, after dipping their feet up to the ankles in cold water for some moments before the walk.

Every one, even the highest in rank, the most occu-pied in his office, could with good arrangement, good will, and true care for the preservation of his health, save time enough to bestow such a benefit upon himself.

I knew a priest who went every year to stay for a few days with a friend who owned a large garden, and there his morning walk was always taken barefooted in the wet grass. He has many times spoken in glowing terms of the excellent effects of this kind of promenade; and I could name a number of persons of the higher and highest ranks of society, who did not despise his well-meant advice, but tried to harden themselves in the better season, by going barefooted during their morning walks in the solitary wood, or on a remote meadow.

One of this comparatively still small number, has owned to me that in former times he seldom spent a week without a catarrh, if it were only a slight one, but this simple practice had entirely cured him of this susceptibility.

One word I dedicate to mothers in particular. I need not say much; for I have already promised them to give some particular hints for a good education chiefly concerning the body, if God spares me life and health. It is mothers, before all, who are charged with the bringing up of a stronger generation capable of greater endurance, and with helping to remove the ever increasing effemination, debility, poverty of blood, nervousness, and all such miseries, which enervate and shorten life, and make such great gaps in the human race. This is to be done by hardening, by making the child accustomed to hardening from its tenderest years. Air, food, clothes, are necessaries for the suckling as well as for the old man; they form the territory for hardening. The purer the air which the child inhales, the better the blood. In order to accustom the frail little creature as soon as possible to staying in the fresh air, those mothers do well, who, after the daily warm bath, dip the baby in colder water, at such a warmth as if it had been warmed by the sun, or wash it quickly with cold water. The warm water in itself relaxes and effeminates; the cold washing at the conclusion of the bath strengthens, hardens and secures a healthy development of the body. The first signs of an inclination to cry will cease of themselves at the third or fourth application. This kind of hardening protects the babies from frequent colds and their consequences, and

is a relief to mothers who are anxious to prevent these
miseries by muffling and wrapping the little creatures in
woollen or other hermetical materials, which are enough
to terrify all reasonable people. In this way dreadful
harm is done to the health of the little ones. The delicate little body is inclosed, as it were, in burning wool-
ovens, and gasps under the burden of bandages and coverings; the little head is wrapped up in such a way that
hearing and seeing is impossible; the neck which, above
all, ought to be hardened, wears in addition to the others,
its own special means of warming, and is by them quite
closed to the outer air. Even then, when nurse is ready
to take baby out for a walk, properly wrapped up, faddling
Mamma comes to examine, if not a little corner still remains to be closed to the air. Is it to be wondered
at under these circumstances, with this want of every
particle of understanding for rational hardening, that the
number of feeble little creatures snatched away every year
by croup, etc. is innumerable? that many families are
crowded with weaklings? that mothers are deploring the
hectic, spasmodic, or other complaints formerly not known,
even by name, but now so common especially with girls?
And who could number all the mental infirmities, these
empty blossoms and rotten fruits of a body which begins
its slow decay even before it has attained its normal
development and strength. Mens sana in corpore sano.
A healthy soul resides only in a healthy body. A principal condition for the development of enduring health,
is hardening in the earliest age. Would that mothers
would understand early enough and profoundly enough
this their task and responsibility, and then not neglect
any opportunity of taking good advice from good sources!

2. A special and extremely efficacious kind of walking
barefooted is the **walking in the grass,** * no matter if
it be wet with dew, rain, or watering. In the third part

---

* Walking in wet grass is far preferable to walking on
wet stones.

his means of hardening is mentioned very often, and I
an highly recommend it to young and old, healthy and
ick, no matter what other applications they may be
.sing. The wetter the grass, the longer one perseveres
n the exercise, and the oftener it is repeated, the more
erfect will be the success.

This exercise is generally taken for 15 to 45 minutes.

After the promenade all the improper adherents, such
s leaves or sand, are quickly wiped off the feet; yet the
eet are not to be dried, but in statu quo i. e. as wet as
hey are, at once provided with dry stockings and shoes.
The walking in the grass is followed by walking with
overed feet on a dry path, first more quickly, by and by
n the ordinary measure. The time of so walking depends
on the feet becoming dry and warm, but should not be
less than 15 minutes. I urgently call attention to the
words „dry stockings and shoes;“ for wet or damp stockings
must never be worn after an application. The consequences would soon be felt in head and neck; this would
not be building up, but pulling down. It may not be out
of place to remind young, quick, and thoughtless people,
not to throw their shoes or stockings into the wet grass,
when they take them off, but to secure a dry spot for
them, in order that they may bring the damp and cold
feet to their proper warmth, later on. This exercise, likewise the walking barefooted generally, may be taken even
when the feet are cold.

3. About the same effect as that produced by the
walking in wet grass, is produced by **walking on wet
stones**, which is more convenient and easy for many
people. Every house or cottage has, either on the ground
floor in an upper story, in the wash-house, or in the bake-
house, etc. a more or less spacious pavement; which will
be sufficient for our barefooted promenade on wet stones
In a stone passage of good length one can run quickly
to and fro; on a little spot of 4—5 stone squares one
must tread the stones like the vine-dresser does the grapes,
or like, at some places, the baker's apprentice treads the
dough. The main point consists in the stones being wet,

and the patient not standing quietly on them, but walking at a rather quick rate. To wet the stones, it is best to take a watering-can, or a jug, and make a water-line which is then extended by treading. If the stones dry too quickly, the watering is to be repeated once or even oftener; the coldest water is the best.

In cases where this means of hardening is employed as a remedy, it ought not to exceed 3 to 15 minutes; but the condition of the patient must decide the length of time, whether he is stronger or weaker, poor of blood, etc.; generally 3 — 5 minutes will be sufficient. When taken simply as a means of hardening by healthy people, this exercise can be extended to 30 minutes and longer still, without doing any harm, and I can sincerely recommend it to all those who wish to begin a solid hardening. Even the weakest and most sensitive need not be afraid to try it.

Persons who are suffering from cold feet, who are inclined to sore throat, catarrh, congestion in the head, and head-ache caused by it, may try this promenade on wet stones. It would be advisable to mix a little vinegar with the water to be used.

As regards shoes and stockings, and exercise, the same rules are to be observed as with the walking in the grass. Like the latter, it can also be undertaken even when the feet are cold before beginning the exercise.

4. **Walking in newly fallen snow** produces even greater effect than that of the two preceding practices. We distinctly remark in newly fallen, fresh snow, which forms into a ball or clings to the feet like dust, not in old, stiff, frozen snow, which almost freezes the feet and is of no use whatever. Moreover this promenade must never be made in cold, cutting winds, but in spring when the snow is being melted by the sun. I know many people who have walked through such snow-water for half an hour, an hour, even $1^{1}/_{2}$ hours with the best result. The first minutes only caused a little struggle; later on they felt no uneasiness or special cold. The regular duration of such a walk in the snow is 3 — 4 minutes. I em-

phatically remark, there must be no stand-still but constant walking.

Sometimes it happens that all too tender toes, which are quite unaccustomed to outer air, cannot bear the snowy cold and get snow-fever, i. e. become dry and hot, burning and painful, and swell. But there is no cause for fear, it is of no consequence if the dry toes are bathed in snow-water or rubbed with snow, they will heal directly.

In autumn the snow-walk can be replaced by walking in the grass covered with hoar-frost. The feeling of cold is much more painful then, because at that time, at the change of season, the body is still accustomed to the warmth of summer. Even in winter the snow-walk is replaced by walking on stone-squares, soaked with snow-water. The rules for covering the feet, and exercise are the same as in the preceding numbers.

Generally, the verdict upon this means of hardening is: „Nothing but folly and nonsense“, — because people are afraid of catching colds, of rheumatics, sore throat, catarrh, and every possible complaint. Everything depends on a trial and a little self-conquest; one will soon become convinced how groundless prejudices are; and that the dreadful snow-walk, instead of causing any harm, brings great advantage.*

Many years ago, I became acquainted with the wife of a higher officer. This energetic mother set a high value on the hardening of her children; daintiness in eating and drinking was by no means tolerated; complaints about the weather, heat, cold, etc. were always censured. As soon as the first snow-fall came, she promised her boys a reward, if they ventured to go in the snow barefooted. This she did for many years; her children, in consequence, became strong and vigorous, and all their life long they were grateful for this by no means soft way of education. That mother was fully expert in her task.

---

* I know many physicians who approve entirely of this practice, provided that it is done with due precaution. Those who are inclined to call it too rugged, I wish to remind of the much more rugged use of ice.

This, then, is the snow-walk for healthy people; we shall mention two cases to show with what success it can be practised in many complaints.

A person was suffering for many years from chilblains, which opened, formed ulcers and gave her great pain. According to my advice she began her snow-walks with the first snow-fall in autumn, repeated them frequently, and the troublesome tumours ceased to torment her.

Not long ago a girl of seventeen came to me complaining of dreadful tooth-ache. „If you would go through the newly-fallen snow for 5 minutes," I said to her; „your tooth-ache would soon vanish." She followed my advice instantly, went to the garden, and 10 minutes afterwards she came back, joyfully exclaiming that her tooth-ache was gone.

The snow-walk ought never to take place, unless the whole body be perfectly warm. When feeling cold or shivering, it is necessary to procure normal warmth, by working or exercise. Persons who are suffering from perspiring feet, wounded feet, open or suppurating chilblains, are, of course never allowed to walk in the snow until the feet have first been healed. (See foot-baths or foot-vapours.)

5. **Walking in water.** As simple as it may appear to walk in water reaching as far as the calf of the leg, yet even this application serves as a means of hardening: (a) it has influence on the whole body, and strengthens the whole system; (b) it operates on the kidneys; by this many complaints, originating in the kidneys, the bladder and the bowels, are prevented; (c) it operates powerfully on the chest, facilitates breathing and carries gases out of the stomach; (d) it operates especially against head-ache, congestion, and other sufferings of the head. This means of hardening can be employed by moving the feet in a bath of cold water, reaching over the ankles. It is more efficacious for hardening, if one goes into the water up to the shins, and most efficacious of all, if the water reaches the knees.

As to the duration, one can begin with 1 minute, then longer, up to 5 or 6 minutes. The colder the water, the better. After such a practice exercise is necessary, in winter time in a warm room, in summer in the open air, until the body is completely warm. In winter, snow may be mixed with the water. With weaklings, warm water may be used in the beginning, then by and by, colder, and lastly quite cold water. (See fig. 1.)

Fig. 1.

6. For the special hardening of the extremities, arms and legs, the following practice is excellent: To stand in cold water up to the knees or over them, for not longer than one minute; then, when the feet have been covered, to put the bare arms up to the shoulders in cold water for the same length of time. It is better still to put arms and legs into the water together; in a larger bath, this is easily done. But one can just as easily stand in the bath and put the bare arms and hands in another vessel, standing on a chair. I like to prescribe this practice after diseases, in order to increase the flow of the blood to the extremities.

To those who are suffering from chilblains and cold hands, this dipping in of the arms is of very good service; but one has to be careful, that the hands (not arms) be directly well dried, as they are exposed to the air.

It is essential that before this practice the body be in normal warmth (not shivering). If the feet are cold up to the ankles (but not the shins), the arms up to the elbows, this need not prevent the application.

~~~~~~ ~~~

7. As a last means of hardening I name the **knee shower.** How it is to be applied, can be seen where the shower-baths are spoken of. It is of especial service to the feet, inducing the blood to come to their bloodless veins.*

Here I have only to say that the shower-bath on the knees is to be given in a stronger way, if healthy people use it for hardening. This can be done, e. g. by the water-jet coming from a height, by mixing snow and ice with the water in winter time, etc.

This practice can only be undertaken, if the body is warm (not shivering); but cold feet up to the ankles are no impediment. The shower-bath on the knees ought not to be used for more than 3 or 4 days, unless it is taken in connection with other practices. If undertaken for a longer time, it must be used alternately with the upper shower-bath, or the dipping in of the arms (No. 6), the one in the morning, the other in the afternoon.

The means of hardening here mentioned, may suffice. They can be practised at every season, and continued in winter and summer. In winter, it would be well to shorten the application itself a little, but to prolong the exercise after it somewhat. For those who are unaccustomed to them, it would be well not to begin with them in winter, more especially those who are suffering from poverty of blood, interior cold, and who are faddled, effeminated, and made sensitive by woollen clothing. I do not say this, as if I were afraid of any harm, but only to prevent people from becoming frightened of such an excellent remedy.

Healthy, as well as weak people, may without hesitation make use of all the applications, both of them observing care and following strictly the directions given.

---

* With a gentleman of high condition instead of nails on the toes a soft mass had formed. The shower-baths on the knees were sufficient to induce the blood to give to the nails what belonged to them; they became as firm as they had been before.

If bad consequences ensue, they are never to be attributed to the applications, but always to some greater or lesser imprudence. Even to consumptive people, with whom the disease had made considerable progress, I have applied No. 1, 2, 3, 6 with great success. Those people to whom my little book is especially dedicated, need not to be encouraged to hardening. Their state in life, their daily duties, bring of themselves, every day, and in many cases every hour, one or other of the means of hardening here mentioned, besides numerous others. They may persevere quietly and not envy others who seem to be more fortunate than they are; for these are illusions, and very often, even mostly, great illusions.

I invite those of my honoured readers who perhaps have never yet heard even the name of these things, to give them a small, the very smallest, trial before condemning them. If it turns out in my favour, I shall be glad, not for my own sake, but on account of the importance of the matter. Many storms break out in life upon man's health; happy he who has its (the health's) roots well fastened, deepened and grounded by hardening

Applications of water.

—◆◆—

The water-applications which I make use of are divided in:

A. Wet sheets.
B. Baths.
C. Vapours.
D. Shower baths.
E. Ablutions.
F. Water bandages.
G. Drinking of water.

A. Wet sheets.

1. Covering with wet sheets.

A large, coarse piece of linen (such as used for straw-mattresses does very well) is folded 3, 4, 6, 8, or 10 times lengthwise, wide and long enough to cover the whole body, beginning at the neck. The sheet ought not to end on both sides as if cut off, but hang down a little on the right and left of the body. The so prepared sheet is dipped in cold water (in winter, warm water may be used) well wrung out and then put on the patient lying in bed, in the way described above. A woollen blanket or a piece of linen doubled 2 or 3 times, is laid upon it, in order to close the wet covering hermetically, to thoroughly prevent the entry of the air; the whole is covered with a feather-quilt. As a rule I lay a rather large piece of woollen material round the neck, to prevent the air entering from above. Care must be taken about the covering, otherwise the patient would easily take cold.

The wet sheet is applied from forty-five minutes to an hour; if a longer duration is prescribed, in order to operate by cold, the sheet having become warm, must be wetted again in cold water.

As soon as the prescribed time has expired, the wet sheets are taken away; the patient dresses himself and takes some exercise, or remains in bed for a short time.

This application operates especially on the expelling of gases shut up in stomach and bowels.

This practice, like the following ones, demands that the body be warm.

2. Lying on wet sheets.

To the covering with wet sheets corresponds the lying on wet sheets, which, in case both applications are used alternately, must be applied first. The following remarks are to be made regarding it.

As this application is also to be made in bed, a piece of linen, and over it a woollen blanket, are laid upon the mattress, to prevent it from getting wet. Then the same piece of coarse linen, as used for the preceding application (doubled 3 or 4 times), dipped in water and wrung out, is placed lengthwise upon the woollen blanket, so that it reaches from the last cervical-vertebra to the end of the back-bone, i. e. the whole length of the back. The patient lies down on his back, wraps himself in the extended blanket from both sides, in order to prevent the air coming in, and then covers himself with a blanket and feather-quilt. This lying on wet sheets is also to be applied for three quarters of an hour; if longer, the wetting of sheets with cold water must be repeated, because its effect, like that of the covering with wet sheets, is produced only by cold. The same rules as given above are to be followed.

This application is especially efficacious for strengthening the back-bone and the spinal-marrow, for pain

3*

in the back and for lumbago. I know many cases in which lumbago was entirely removed by two applications of wet sheets made on the same day.

Also against congestions, in the heat of fever, this lying on wet sheets is of very good effect. In which individual cases it is to be used, and how often it is to be repeated, is said where the diseases are spoken of.

3. Covering with, and lying on wet sheets taken together.

The two applications can be taken one after the other or both together.

The sheet for lying on is prepared as given in No. 2; that for covering, likewise prepared, is laid at the bedside. The patient lies down undressed on the one wet sheet and covers himself with the other. The covering with blanket and feather-bed is easily done. If there is another person attending, it is well to tuck in both blanket and feather-bed on both sides, to prevent the entry of the outer air. It is important that the blanket lying under the wet sheet broadwise, be large enough to wrap up both the wet sheets like a bandage.

The duration of this application ought not to be less than three quarters of an hour, and not more than an hour.

Against great heat, gases, congestions, hypochondriasis, and other sufferings it is of very great service.

4. Compress on the abdomen.

The patient lies in bed. A piece of linen, folded 4 to 6 times, dipped in water, and thoroughly wrung out, is laid upon the abdomen (from the stomach downwards) and covered carefully with blanket and feather-bed.

The application may be made for three quarters of an hour to 2 hours; in the latter case, it must be renewed after an hour, i. e. wetted anew.

This application is of good service against indigestion, cramps, also where the blood is to be led away from the chest and heart.

For wetting the linen vinegar is very often used instead of water, also decoctions of hay-blossoms, shave-grass, oat-straw, etc.

In order to save the vinegar, a twofold piece of linen may be dipped in a mixture of vinegar and water and laid on the body, and over it another piece of linen doubled 2 or 4 times, which is dipped only in water. The covering is done as given above.

I have been asked many times what principles I followed with regard to coverings with ice, bleeding, etc. These I will briefly state.

Whoever wishes to reconcile himself with an enemy, and for this purpose offers him his hand with knitted brows, will find greater difficulty in succeeding than if he met him with a bright face and a joyful heart. It is something similar to this with ice and water. I have always esteemed the application of ice, especially on the nobler parts of the body, (head, eyes, ears, etc.) to be among the most rugged and violent remedies ever used. They do not help nature to recommence its work; they force it with violence to do so, and that must revenge itself. Ice-cloth and ice-bag, or whatever the names of those things may be, are entirely excluded from my department. Only imagine these colossal counter-parts: inside the body a burning heat, outside a mountain of ice, and between them a suffering member, the organ of tender flesh and blood, worked on by both. I have always waited with great anxiety for the result of such work, and in most cases my anxiety was justified.

I know a gentleman who was ordered to have ice laid upon one of his feet day and night, for a whole year long, without any interruption. It would surely take nothing less than a miracle to prevent this flake of ice from taking away not only all heat, but also the indispensable natural warmth! Nothing was to be seen of the healing of the foot.

But, some one will reply, in many cases it has really done good. Yes, for it may be that the disease could not withstand the means of compulsion. However, what

were the consequences? Innumerable persons have come
to me who had partly lost their eye-sight, become more
or less deaf, others with rheumatics of every kind, especially in the head, or with great sensibility of the head,
etc. What was the cause of all this? „Yes, there, and
then," I was answered, „the tiresome ice-bag did it;
I have been burdened with this complaint for so and so
many years." Certainly, and most of them will be burdened
with it to their last breath.

I repeat again that I oppose absolutely any application of ice, and I assert, on the contrary, that water,
applied in the right way, is able to soften and to extinguish any heat even the most violent, in whatever part or
organ of the body it may be raging. If a fire can no
longer be extinguished by water, ice will do just as little
for it; that is easily understood by every one.

I said just now that a regular application of water
will bring help. But I do not mean that, e. g. with an
inflammation on, or in the head, it would be advisable
to use as many wet bandages as there were ice-bags formerly used; 100 ice-bags and bandages will not stop
the blood streaming to the inflamed spot and thereby
increasing the heat. I must try to lead the blood away,
to distribute it to the different parts, i. e.' I must use
applications on the whole body, besides those on the
suffering part. I shall e. g. attack the enemy in, or on
the head, first of all at the patient's feet, and then gradually proceed to the whole body.

Nevertheless, the ice is of good service to my water-
cure by indirect use. In summer it cools the water, when
it is about to get luke-warm.

What is my opinion with regard to bleeding, leeches,
and all the different kinds of blood-extractions? Fifty,
forty, thirty years ago there was seldom a woman who
was not bled 2, 3 or 4 times a year; the half-holidays and,
of course, the most favorable signs were faithfully chosen
for this end in the beginning of the year and marked in the
calendar with red or blue strokes. The country-physicians,
the surgeons and barbers, themselves, called their own work

in this way, a real butchery. Institutions and convents, too, had their appointed time for bleeding and the strictly regulated diet above all. Congratulations were made to one another after having endured the bloody toils, which may have been no small ones sometimes. A priest of that time assured me that he had undergone this bleeding for 32 years, the process being repeated 4 times every year, and each time he lost 8 oz. of blood, making in all $8 \times 4 \times 32 = 1024$ oz.

Besides this bleeding, leeches were used, and scarifying and other processes practised. Young and old, high and low, men and women, were all well provided for.

How times are changing! For a long time these doings were looked upon as the only and absolutely necessary means of being and remaining healthy! And what is thought of them now-a-days? We smile at and ridicule this false opinion of the old, this false natural-science, to imagine that any man should have too much blood. About two years ago a foreign physician, who was also an active literary man, and who was following a new school, told me that he had never in his life seen leeches.

Many physicians attribute the poverty of blood in the present time, to the former misuse of bleeding. They may be right; however this is not the only cause of it.

But to the subject! My conviction is this: In the human body everything corresponds so wonderfully, the particle to the part, and every part to the whole, that one cannot help calling the organism of the body an incomparable work of art, the idea of which could only originate in the creative mind of God, and the execution of which was only possible to the creative power of God. The same order, the same measure, the same harmony exists between increase and consumption of the ingredients necessary to the support of the body, provided man himself, reasonable and independent as he is, co-operates with the will of God by rightly using what is given to him, provided he does not overturn the order by misusing it, and so bringing dissonances into the harmony. As this is the state of the case, I cannot imagine how the for mation of blood alone, this most important of all processes in the human body, should go on without order, without number and measure, unarranged and immoderately.

Every child, so I imagine, receives as a heritage from its mother, together with the life, a quantity of stuff for formation of blood, call it what you will, which is, as it were, the essence without which no blood can be prepared. If this essence is exhausted, the formation of blood, and with it life itself, ceases. Fading away, decaying, I do not call „living". By every loss of blood, however, whether it be caused by a fall, an accident, or by bleeding, leeches, or scarifying, a particle or part of this substance of blood, of this essence of life, is lost, and in the same measure the body's life is shortened. Every extraction of blood means nothing less than a shortening of life; for life resides in the blood.

The objection to this will be: Nothing is more speedily accomplished than the formation of blood; losing blood and gaining blood is almost one and the same thing.

Yes, the formation of blood takes place with an incredibly wonderful speed; I quite agree with this argument. But excuse me, if I give another one based on experience: it will interest my readers who are engaged in farming, and they will be obliged to confirm it. If a farmer wishes to fatten cattle quickly, he draws a good quantity of blood from them, and after having done so, he feeds them well. In a short time plenty of fresh new blood is formed, and the cattle progresses and fattens. After three or four weeks, the bleeding is repeated, then good and nourishing food, as well as many strengthening potions, are given. The progress is excellent, and even with old cattle, as much and as nice blood will be found when the animal is killed, as with young cattle. But let us look more closely at this blood. The blood produced artificially, is only watery, weak blood without vitality. The cattle has no longer any strength or power of endurance, and if not soon killed, will get dropsy.

Should it be otherwise with man? Having lived more than 70 years and gained some experience and knowledge of human life, I know that precisely the immoderate bleeding of our ancestors has influenced the capacities, talents, and duration of life, of their posterity. The gentleman mentioned in the beginning of our treatise, who had lost so many ounces of blood, died in the best years of manhood, of dropsy. And if a woman (I state facts only) had been bled 150, another 200 times, and had thereby become unspeakably weak and ill, must not the following generation be sickly and frail, inclined to cramps, and other sufferings?

I willingly acknowledge that there can be cases, but only exceptional ones, where an immediate danger is removed by bleeding, other quickly operating remedies not being at hand.

But otherwise I ask every reasonable, impartial person: Which is preferable, to have the thread of life extorted from you piece by piece, or to have the blood distributed by proper water-applications, in such a way that even the most full-blooded has not a too great quantity of blood? How, and by which applications, this distributing is to be done, I have discussed several times in the proper place.

It is generally said that in cases of impending strokes, bleeding is the only means of escape. But I remember, just now, a case in which a stroke had taken place; the first physician quickly bled the patient; the second one, however, declared that precisely in consequence of this bleeding the patient would die, which indeed was verified It is not fulness or profusion of blood which generally leads to a stroke, as people erroneously think, but poverty of blood. „He died of a stroke" generally means that the blood being consumed, life was consumed also The oil ceased its flowing and nourishing; therefore the glimmering wick was extinguished. Of what useful service the water is immediately after strokes, can be seen in the third part of this book. I will only state here that my predecessor in the office of curate, had a stroke three times, and after the third time, the physician declared that he could not live any longer; but the water has not only saved his life for the moment, but it has preserved him to his congregation for several years.

B. Baths.

I. Foot-baths.

The foot-bath can be taken cold or warm.

1. The cold foot-bath

consists in standing in the cold water as far as the calves of the legs or higher, for 1 to 3 minutes.

In diseases they serve principally for leading the blood down from head and chest; but they are generally taken in connection with other applications, sometimes in cases in which whole or half-baths cannot be endured by the patient for different reasons.

When taken by healthy people, they aim at giving freshness, and strength; they are especially advisable for country-people in summer-time, if after a hard and fatiguing day's work, they are unable to sleep at night. These baths take away weariness, bring on rest and good sleep.

2. The warm foot-bath

can be taken in different ways.

a) A handful of salt and twice as much wood-ashes are mixed with warm water of 25 to 26° R. Then the foot-bath is taken for about 12 to 15 minutes.

Sometimes, but always by special order, I give such a foot-bath with a temperature as high as 30° R.; but then a cold foot-bath of half a minute's duration must always follow.

The foot-baths are very useful in all cases where vigorous and cold remedies cannot well be used on account of weakness, fragility, want of vital warmth, etc.; as little or no reaction takes place, i. e. the cold water cannot produce sufficient warmth for want of blood.

These foot-baths are suitable for weak, nervous people, for those who have poor blood, for very young, and very old people, mostly for women, and are efficacious against all disturbances in the circulation of the blood, against congestions, complaints of head or neck, cramps, etc.

They lead the blood to the feet, and have an appeasing effect. But I do not recommend them to people who suffer from sweating feet.

With our country-people these warm foot-baths are well noted, and their effect acknowledged by the general use of them.

b) A sanative foot-bath is that made from hay-flowers.

Take about 3 to 5 handfuls of hay-flowers,* pour boiling water upon them, cover the vessel, and let the whole mixture cool to the warmth of 25 to 26° R., the most comfortable for a foot-bath.

It is of no consequence, whether the hay-flowers remain in the foot-bath, or whether the decoction only is used. Poorer people use the whole to save time and trouble.

These foot-baths operate by dissolving, evacuating, and strengthening; they are of good service for diseased feet, especially sweating feet, open wounds, contusions of every kind (whether arising from a blow, a fall, etc. or bleeding or black and blue with blood), for tumours, gout in the feet, gristle on the toes or putridity between them, for whitlows and hurts, caused by too narrow shoes, etc. In general, it may be said that these foot-baths are of excellent service for all feet the juices of which are more morbid, and more inclined to putridity, than safe and sound.

A gentleman suffering to a great extent from gout in his feet, was freed from pain in an hour by one of these foot-baths, together with a foot-bandage dipped in the decoction.

c) The foot-bath with oat-straw is closely connected with the preceding one.

The oat-straw is boiled for half an hour in a kettle, and a foot-bath of 25 to 26° R. is prepared with the decoction, which is to be taken for 20 to 30 minutes.

According to my experience these foot-baths are unsurpassed as regards the dissolving of every possible obduration on the feet. They are useful against gristle,

* What I call hay-flowers are all the remains of hay such as stalks, leaves, blossoms and seeds, even the hay itself.

knots etc.; against results of gout, articular disease, podagra, corns, nails grown in and putrid, and against blisters caused by walking. Even sore and suppurating feet, or toes wounded by too sharp foot-sweat, can be treated with these foot-baths.

A gentleman had cut his corn, and the toe became inflamed; a poisonous ulcer seemed to threaten with pi-aemie. The foot was healed in four days by taking daily 3 foot-baths with oat-straw, and applying bandages, dipped in the decoction, reaching to above the ankles.

A patient was in danger of having all his toes rotted off; they were swollen and of a dark blue colour; he, too, got frightened about piaemie; but the foot-bath and foot-bandages cured him in a short time.

In many cases I prescribe these foot-baths to be taken like the warm whole baths, (See respective passage on „The warm whole-bath" page 60) changing three times, and concluding with the cold bath.

A constant exception to this rule, however, is made with regard to the „warm foot-bath" of 25 to 26° R. with admixture of ashes and salt, (mentioned under a). The object of this is, to draw the blood more powerfully downwards, and there to distribute it. But, if after this warm foot-bath a person were to apply a cold bath or ablution, to end with, he would thereby drive the blood which had been strongly led down to the feet, back again; and it would by no means flow again so plentifully to the feet as it had done by means of the warm water with ashes and salt. The first desired effect would in this manner be, at least partly, destroyed, and the aim frustrated. Therefore the warm foot-bath with ashes and salt is never followed by a cold one.

d) I wish to mention here a special kind of foot-baths which are more of a solid than a fluid nature. If there is a possibility of using them, do not reject them! I have used them often, very often, with great success. Take malt grains, when still warm, and put them into a foot-bath. The feet penetrate easily into them and soon feel comfortable in the salutary warmth. This bath can last for 15 to 30 minutes. Those who are suffering from

rheumatism, gout, and such like, will best find out its sani-
tary power.

There is one remark to be made concerning all the
foot-baths. For persons affected with varixes, the foot-
bath ought never to reach higher than the beginning of
the calf, and never exceed the temperature of 25° R.

Foot-baths with warm water only, without anything
being mixed with it, I never take or prescribe.

II. Half-baths.

In general when speaking of half-baths, I mean such
as wash the body, at the utmost, up to the stomach, but
very often do not go so far. I wanted to have something
between the whole-baths which offer too much, and the
foot-baths which offer too little. I take the liberty of calling them half-baths.

Their application is threefold:

1. To stand in the water so that it reaches above
   the calves or above the knees;
2. To kneel in the water so that the whole of
   the thighs is covered with it;
3. To sit in the water. This third application alone
   fully deserves the name of half bath; it reaches
   to about the navel.

These three applications, which are always made with
cold water, rank first among the means of hardening.
They are, therefore, suitable for healthy persons who wish
to become stronger still, for weaklings who wish to become strong, and for those in a state of convalescence
who desire to get entirely well and strong.

In diseases they should only be taken when especially
and expressly prescribed; experiments ought not to be made
with them; for in some circumstances they might do harm.

Whenever they are applied, be it by healthy or sick
people, it must be always in connection with other applications, and they should never be taken for longer than
from one half minute to 3 minutes.

I have practised No. 1 and 2, standing and kneeling
in the water, and always with great success, upon such
persons who, from different causes, were in thorough de-

cline; with this application they began the water-cure.
I will not name these causes, but only indicate that there
are many who, in the beginning, cannot bear the pressure
of the water in whole baths, without the most disagreeable consequences. It is just such patients as these that
have led me (by their great weakness and wretchedness)
to these two applications; their condition required this
discrete, moderate and considerate application of water,
sometimes for long weeks, until they got stronger and
were able to endure more.

With these two practices the dipping in of the arms
up to the shoulders (see means of hardening page 31), is
generally connected, as a second means of hardening. But
in addition to this manner of hardening, I use this whole
application (consisting of two part-applications) especially
against cold feet.

No. 3, the real half-bath, is well worthy of attention;
I recommend it most impressively to all healthy persons.
The disorders and diseases of the lower part of the body
— and their number is legion; their cause in reality but
one, want of hardening, effemination — are by this bath
suffocated in the germ, or removed where they are already settled. These half-baths strengthen the bowels, and
preserve and increase their strength. Thousands and thousands of persons wear one, two, or even more bandages
and similar things. Do they get help from them? Many
times quite the contrary; by them the effemination, the
fragility, is even as it were, forced into the poor body.

Only once try our half-baths, slowly, but decidedly,
and the complaints of hemorrhoids, wind-colic, hypochon-
dria, hysteria, will soon greatly diminish; these diseases
which now make their bewildering sport in the diseased
and weakened body.

I should advise healthy people to wash the upper
part of their body when rising in the morning, and then
in the afternoon or evening to take our half-bath. If
there is no time for the early washing, they may wash
their chest and back in the half-bath.

A few incidents may show how the one or the other
of these three applications is to be made in diseases.

A young man had been so much weakened by typhus, that he was quite unable to work. He tried the kneeling in the water every second or third day, first for 1 minute, later on for 2 or 3 minutes After having done so for some time, he improved from week to week, and became as strong as he had been before.

A person was suffering from violent congestions, which originated in the body (as is often the case). The upper part of the body was washed one day, and the next day the kneeling in the water was undertaken. This was repeated for some time, and the congestions ceased.

Pains in the stomach, caused by retained wind, are cured in the same way.

The evacuation of such gases, which are so very troublesome after diseases, is quite a special effect of our half-bath.

III. Sitting-baths.

The sitting-baths are taken both cold and warm.

1. The cold sitting-bath

is taken as follows. The vessel made expressly for these baths (fig. 2) or in default of it, the wide, but not deep vessel of wood, tin or zinc (fig. 3) is filled to the fourth or fifth part with cold water. The patient sits down undressed in this bath as on a chair; the lower part of the body up to the kidneys, and the upper part of the legs being in the water (fig. 4).

Fig. 2.

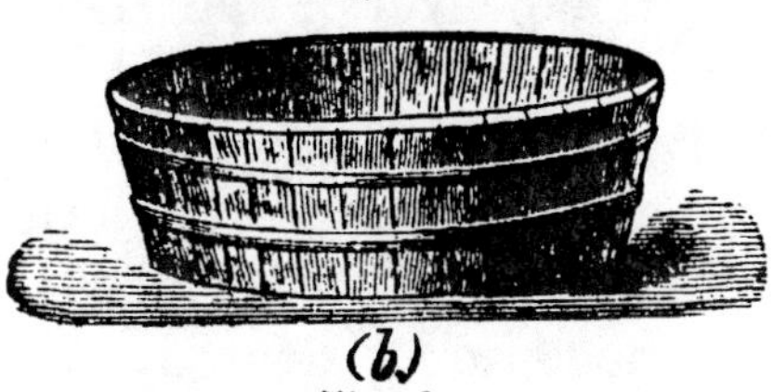

Fig. 3.

It is not necessary to undress entirely. This bath is to be taken for half a minute to three minutes.

These cold sitting-baths belong, next to the half-baths, to the most important and efficacious applications for the bowels. They eva-cuate the gases, help the weak digestion, regulate the circulation of the blood, and strengthen,; therefore they cannot be sufficiently recom-mended against green-sick-ness, bloody flux and such like complaints, against dis-orders in the lower part of

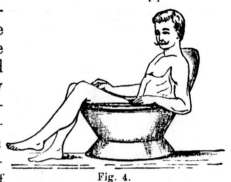

Fig. 4.

the body of the most delicate kind. No one need be frightened at the cold application lasting only for one to two minutes. If taken according to prescription, it can never do any harm.

To prevent colds, to become steeled and strengthened against the change of temperature, often so hurtful, it is advisable to take such sitting-baths often, but best of all at night. When awakening at any hour, spring quickly from bed and into the sitting-bath, then at once without drying go back to bed again. I wish, however, to caution against a too frequent repetition of this sitting-bath, be-cause by it the blood is too strongly led to the lower parts, and hemorrhoids are caused thereby; 2 or 3 times a week may be allowed.

Whoever is in want of a sound, quiet sleep at the beginning of the night, who, suddenly awakening at night, cannot go to sleep again, every one in general, who is suffering with sleeplessness, may frequently use this sitt-ing-bath, taking it for one to two minutes. It removes excitement and produces agreeable repose.

A patient, for a long time, could seldom sleep for more than 1 or 2 hours, and, tossing about in bed, he became more and more excited with thougths of every kind. These baths brought back to him the longed for guest (sleep).

This application is especially recommended to those who rise in the morning with a confused and heavy head, or more tired than when they lay down; also to all healthy persons it is once more recommended most heartily.

2. The warm sitting-bath

is never prepared only with warm water; it is always made either with

    a. Shave-grass,
    b. Oat-straw, or
    c. Hay-flowers.

All these baths are prepared in the same way; boiling water is poured upon the herbs, and the mixture is put on the fire to boil for some time; then the vessel is taken away, and the mixture allowed to cool to the temperature of 24 — 26° R. (in few cases 30°), when the whole is poured into the prepared bath. Such a bath may last for a quarter of an hour; in order not to waste the herbs, I use them for two more applications. The one is made 3 to 4 hours after the first, the other an hour after the second, but both in the cold mixture, for 1 to 2 minutes each.

Such sitting-baths with herbs I allow 2 to 3 times a week at the utmost, many times only alternately with cold baths, in cases where a deep-rooted complaint is to be cured, e. g. bad hemorrhoids, fistulas at the rectum, disorder of the blind gut and such like. Those who are troubled with ruptures, need not be prevented from the use of these baths on their account.

a. The sitting-bath with shave-grass serves especially and chiefly for spasmodic, rheumatic disorders, of the kidneys and the bladder, and for gravel and stone complaints.

b. The sitting-bath with oat-straw is an excellent bath for all complaints of gout.

c. The sitting-bath with hay-flowers is of more general influence and may be used instead of the two others against all the complaints named above, but with less effect. It has always been of good service to me for the evacuation of stagnant matters in the bowels, for exterior swellings, ulcers (erysipelas), constipation, hemorrhoids, spasmodic and colic-like symptoms (caused by wind).

IV. Whole-baths.

These baths also are divided into cold and warm whole baths. Both kinds are useful for healthy as well as for sick persons.

1. The cold whole-bath

can be taken in two different ways, either by the patient standing or lying with his whole body under the water; or, to prevent the perceptible pressure of the water on the lungs, (although there is never any danger attached to it,) he may go into the water up to the armholes, so that the top of the lungs remains free; then the upper part of the body is quickly washed with the hand or with a coarse towel.

The shortest time for such a cold whole-bath is half a minute, the longest, which should not be exceeded, 3 minutes.

I shall be obliged to speak of this, my particular view, several times hereafter. Here I will only remark that, about 20 years ago, I was of another opinion myself, that I advised baths of a longer duration, and supposed that water-cure-institutions could not deviate from the best method.

My experience of long years and my daily practice upon myself and others have long since taught me better. These, my teachers, brought me to the firm conviction that regarding cold-water-baths the right and true principle is this:

The shorter the bath, the better the effect. To remain one minute in the cold-water-bath is wiser and safer than to remain there for 5 minutes.

Whether it be for the use of healthy or sick persons, I reject every bath of more than 3 minutes duration.

This conviction to which innumerable facts have brought me, and which have since then confirmed me in it, explains my own opinion on the rugged applications used in hydropathic establishments, as well as on the oftentimes thoughtless bathing in summer time.

As regards the latter point, there are people who once, or even twice a day, remain for half an hour and more in the water. If this is done by able swimmers who move about vigorously during the time, and who can take good, nourishing food after bathing, I have less objection. Their robust nature will soon make up for that which the bath has taken. But to land-rats, who, without real movement, creep about in the water for half an hour like toilsomely moving tortoises, such a tormenting bath is not only of no use, but it injures, and if often, too often repeated, it injures much; such baths are relaxing and fatiguing. Instead of being useful to nature, to the organism, they harm it; instead of strengthening and nourishing, they consume.

a. The cold whole-bath for the healthy.

I have many times received admonitions at known and unknown hands, telling me that I ought to consider how the applications of cold water were synonymous with extraction of warmth, how such an extraction was very hurtful to persons who are poor of blood, and how much nervousness was being increased by it.

I agree with every word, if the too rugged applications described above are meant; but my applications of which we are now speaking, the cold-water-baths, I recommend to all healthy persons at every season, summer and winter, and I assert that precisely these baths contribute in a substantial manner to the maintaining and strengthening of health; they purify the skin; they increase the action of the skin; they refresh, vivify and strengthen the whole organism. In winter these baths ought not to exceed the number of two a week; one is sufficient every week, in some circumstances, every fortnight.

There are still two more points to be mentioned here.

The hardening against the different influences, the changes of temperature, (weather, seasons), plays an important part in keeping healthy. Unhappy he whose lungs, neck or head are injured by every wind, every breeze, who is obliged to consult the vane the whole year

4*

round, to see what kind of wind is about. It is a matter of indifference to the tree in the open air, whether there is storm or calm, heat or cold. It braves wind and weather; it is hardened. Let a healthy man try our bath and he will resemble the strong tree.

One cause of fear and anxiety on account of the cold-water-applications, cannot easily be taken away from many; I am inclined to call it a fixed idea of extraction of warmth. The cold weakens and must weaken, they say, unless a feeling of warmth immediately follows the application. Quite true; I agree with them. But on the other hand I assert that, not to speak of the amount of exercise, which according to our principles is regularly and strictly prescribed after every application of cold water, our cold-water-baths do not deprive nature of warmth, but on the contrary they support and foster it. Let me only ask one question: If a weak man, effeminated by a continual sedentary life, and afraid to venture out in winter time except in case of utmost need, is by the baths and ablutions all at once so hardened, that he takes walks in every weather without fear, if he scarcely feels even the sharpest cold, must not the natural warmth have increased in him? Should all that be nothing but imagination and deception?

One instance out of many may be given here.

A gentleman of high position, who was more than 60 years of age, had an excessive aversion for water. When going out, every care was taken not to forget one of his indispensable wrappers; all possible and impossible colds, etc. could of course be the consequences of such a forgetfulness.

But above all other parts of his body, this gentleman's neck was so sensitive, that he scarcely knew how to take enough care of it or to wrap it up sufficiently. At last the „Barbarian“ came upon him, and with a certain mischievous joy prescribed our cold whole-baths. The gentleman obeyed. And the consequences? They were exceedingly favourable. Even after a few days the first woollen shirt was stripped off: soon the second followed the first, and by and by the woollen wrappers for the neck shared the same fate. He felt himself so steeled against climate and weather by these baths, that the day on which he was prevented from taking one seemed to him but incomplete. And he took them not only in a non-heated room, but, even in October, during his daily walk, he took them in a river, the cold water of which was more welcome to him than that in the bath prepared for him at home.

The chief questions we have to answer are these:

1. In what condition, in what disposition must a healthy person be, to make use of such cold whole-baths with good effect?

2. How long is a healthy person allowed to remain in the bath?

3. Which season is the best to begin this cure for hardening?

The good disposition for the cold whole-bath requires chiefly that the whole body be perfectly warm. Therefore a person, who, by staying in a warm room, by working or walking is thoroughly warmed, is in the right condition.

The cold whole-bath should never be taken when a person is cold, suffering from cold feet, or shivering; he must beforehand thoroughly warm himself by walking etc. On the contrary, when in a state of perspiration, when heated (I am speaking of healthy persons,) as it were bathed in perspiration, our whole-bath may be taken without the least fear.*

There is scarcely anything so much feared, even by quiet, thoughtful and intelligent men, as going into the cold water, when heated or perspiring freely. And yet, nothing is more harmless. Yea, I venture deliberately to assert, according to my experience of long years, that the greater the perspiration, the better, the more efficacious the bath.

---

* Whoever is wet through rain, ought not to have anything to do with water; it would do him harm. I also warn against putting on wet clothes after such a bath; they must be quite dry.

Countless persons, who beforehand had thought that with such a „horse-cure" they must immediately get a stroke, have lost all fear, all anxiety, all prejudice after the first trial.*

What man, when coming home from work with his face and hands bathed in perspiration, would have the least fear to wash them, perhaps even his chest and feet as well? Everyone does so; for it is very refreshing and comforting. Should not the effect on the whole body, as a necessary conclusion, be the same? Should a thing which is of excellent effect for single parts of the body, which is a benefit to them, be a disadvantage, an injury to the whole?

I believe that the fear of the bad effect of cold baths when taken in perspiration, proceeds from the facts that many persons, who, bathed in sweat, have suddenly come into the cold, or into the fresh air, especially into draught, have sometimes entirely ruined their health for life.

That is quite true. I own still more, namely that many persons in a state of perspiration, have got the germs of serious sufferings by the cold water. But which was to blame, the perspiration or the water? Neither! As with everything else in life, here also it depends before all not upon the „What", but upon the „How", i. e. in our case, how people in perspiration use the cold water. A delirious man can do unspeakable harm with a simple knife. Unreasonable application can turn the best gift to the greatest evil. It is only remarkable that in such cases, it is always the good gift which is condemned, and not the blamable misuse made of it. The whole then depends upon the „How" in application. If any one is headstrong in this matter, he may also bear the consequences, which he has frivolously caused.

Now we come to the reply to the second question: How long may a healthy person remain in the cold whole-bath?

A gentleman to whom I had ordered two such baths a week, came to me a fortnight afterwards, lamenting

* See the treatise on „perspiration" in the third part.

that his state had become much worse; he was like a lump of ice. His appearance was that of a great sufferer, and I could not understand how the water should, all at once, have left me in the lurch. I asked him, if he made the application strictly according to my prescription. His answer was: „Most strictly; I have even done more than what you ordered me to do; instead of one minute, I have remained in the water for five minutes; but then I could not possibly get warm again." During the following weeks he made use of the baths in the right manner, and soon got back his former natural warmth and freshness.

This single case represents all the cases in which it is supposed that the water has done harm. It is not the water, but the application, which plays its part badly; it is the careless and inaccurate people who are the culprits. But, as is usually the case, the innocent water must bear the guilt.

The person who is about to take the cold whole-bath, undresses quickly and lies down in the prepared bath for one minute. Should he be perspiring, he sits down in the bath, i. e. he goes into the water only up to the stomach and washes the upper part of his body quickly and vigorously. Then he dips under up to the neck for a moment, goes out of the water immediately, and redresses without drying, as quickly as possible. A labourer may take up his work again; others must (at least for a quarter of an hour) take exercise, until the body is thoroughly dry and properly warmed. It is quite a matter of indifference whether that be done in a room, or in the open air; for my part I always prefer the open air, even in autumn and winter.

Whatever you do, my dear reader, do it rationally, and never transgress the right measure! Moreover the number of applications of a whole-bath should not, as a rule, surpass that of three a week.

When should I best begin with these whole-baths?

The important work of hardening the body, or which is the same thing, of protecting it against diseases, of making it able to resist them, can never begin too early. Begin at once — to-day; — but begin with easier practices (see means of hardening). Otherwise you would probably lose courage! You may begin with our cold whole-bath, as soon as you are strong enough, perhaps after a short preparation; if you are weak, after a longer preparation, according to circumstances.

This is a very important chapter. Be careful not to try to force anything, immediately, suddenly, with the strongest remedies; this would be, at least, an act of imprudence.

A man, ill with typhus, was advised by his doctor to go into cold water for a quarter of an hour. He did so, but got such a chill afterwards that he naturally would have nothing to do with such a bath in future. He cursed such a remedy. The decision of the competent judge was simply, that after such an experience, applications of water could not be used by that patient any more; besides the patient was already lost. With this sentence of death they came to me. I advised them to try the water again, but instead of a quarter of an hour, to let the patient remain in it for 10 seconds only (in and out); the effect must be different. No sooner said than done, and in a few days the patient was well again.

On such occurrences, I have always to struggle with the temptation, that the water is purposely applied in such a rugged, incomprehensibly violent way, in order to make people frightened at this wet were-wolf, instead of inspiring them with confidence in the water. I am a strange man, I know; therefore such fancies will, I trust, be pardonable in me.

Those who are in earnest, may after the application of means of hardening, begin with the ablutions of the whole body (see ablutions), and take them, provided the washing does not agitate them, at night before going to sleep, or in the morning when rising. At night no time is lost, and also in the morning all is done in a minute. Those who cannot take some exercise either by working or walking directly after the application, ought to lie down again for a quarter of an hour to get dry and warm again. This practice undertaken from 2 to 4 times a week, which is sufficient, or daily, is the best preparation for our cold whole-bath. Only try it! The first unpleasantness will soon be followed by a feeling of comfort and ease, and that of which you were afraid before, will soon become almost a necessity to you.

A gentleman of my acquaintance took his whole-bath every night for 18 years. I had not ordered him to do so, but he would by no means give up this practice. During these 18 years he did not have an hour's illness. Others who went into the bath 2 or 3 times a night, had to be detained from it; I had to forbid it to them. If the practice had been hard or insupportable, as people often cry out, they would surely have omitted it.

Those who are in earnest about hardening themselves, about preserving and increasing their strength, should fix their attention on the cold whole-bath;* but they must not let it rest simply with the resolution.

Vigorous nations, generations, families, have always been true friends of the cold water; and precisely of our whole-bath. The more the present age gets the character and name of effeminate, the higher time is it to turn back to the sound, natural views and principles of old.

There are still many families, especially such of high rank, distinguished men, who keep our water-cures as a family tradition, as it were, and a means of education, exceedingly important in the care of health, and who wish to secure it to their race, to their posterity. We need not therefore be ashamed of our business.

b. The cold whole-bath for the sick.

It is carefully mentioned in the third part with the special diseases, when and how often this bath is to be used. A few remarks of a more general character may find place here.

---

* For detailed effects see third part on „perspiration".

A strong nature, a healthy organism, is able of itself to evacuate the morbid matters which try to settle in the body. But the diseased body, weakened by illness, must be helped, in order to enable it to do its work by itself again.

This assistance is often given by the cold whole-bath, which in such a case serves as an excellent crutch or staff, as a means of strengthening.

Its chief application, however, is found with the so called „hot diseases", i. e. with all those diseases which have violent fevers as their forerunners and companions. The most dangerous ones are those of 39 to 40° and above; they take away all strength, burn down, as it were, the cottage of the human body. Many a patient, whom the illness has spared, becomes a victim to weakness. To look on, to wait for what may come of this terrible fire, seems to me to be dangerous and of grave consequences. Of what good are „a spoonful every hour", or the expensive quinine, the cheap antipyrin, or the poisonous mixture of digitalis, the consequences of which, for the stomach, all of us know? With such fires all medicaments are, and always will be, very insignificant remedies and febrifuges. Of what use lastly are all those artificial intoxicating physics which are administered to, or injected into, the patient, which really intoxicate him, so that he no longer knows, feels or perceives anything?

Apart from moral and religious views, it is indeed a miserable sight to see a patient lying half asleep, or rather half tipsy, with disfigured features, with distorted eyes! Can that do any good? Against such fever-fires nothing can help but extinguishing. Fire is extinguished by water, and so also the fire in the whole body where, as it were, everything is in flames, is best extinguished by the whole-bath. If it is repeated at every blazing up, i. e. as often as the heat, the agitation increases (in the beginning of the fever, perhaps every half hour), it will, with early application, soon master the fire (see inflammations, scarlet fever, typhus etc.)

I was told some time ago that in large public hospitals the bath was often applied to poor patients who could not afford the expensive quinine; I was glad to see in the news-papers lately that, especially in large military hospitals, in Austria, people had begun again to treat certain diseases like typhus with water. But why only typhus? I should like to ask. Why not, with logical necessity, all those diseases, which grow up like poisonous fruits, out of the mushrooms of fever?

Many are in great expectation to see this going on, among them also professional men.

One remark which perhaps belongs more to the ablutions, may find place here. All patients are not able to use the whole-bath; many of them are, perhaps, already so much weakened, that they can neither move nor turn themselves, nor be lifted out of bed; but must they on this account resign the application of cold water? By no means. Our applications are so manifold, and every kind of application has so many degrees or steps, that those who are most healthy, as well as those grievously ill, can easily find what is suitable for them. The only thing is to make a good selection.

Those who are afflicted with serious illness, who, on account of excessive weakness are unable to use the cold whole-bath, may take the whole-ablution as a substitute; and this can easily be done in bed by every patient, even the weakest. How to make it, is explained where the ablutions are spoken of. Like the whole-bath they are to be repeated as often as the heat or agitation reaches a high degree.

It is precisely with such grievously affected patients, who are, as it were, chained to the bed, that doubly great care must be taken not to make the great mistake of a too rugged application; it would always increase the evil. I could name a person who was bed-ridden for eleven years, and who during the whole time, was attended by a physician. Water-cures too, had been tried, but all in vain. The physician, when he found that this person had been cured by me in six weeks, declared that it seemed to him like a miracle. He came to see me and wished

to know what had been done. The whole proceeding
was the more incomprehensible to him, as in his opinion
there was not the least activity in the body, and all his
applications of water had remained unsuccessful. I told
the gentleman how simple the proceeding was, and how
still more simple the water-applications were. We both
acknowledged that a glimmering pine-torch was not to
be extinguished by a fire-engine; his water-cure had been
too rugged, mine was mild, slow and according to the
capability of endurance of the wretched body.

It has often excited my pity to hear, or to read,
how in many institutions and homes, people are fastened
to their beds for ten, or twenty and more years. They
are indeed worthy of pity!

But I cannot understand it and never could, except
in some few very rare cases. The bible, too, has its patient
of 38 years. I am quite sure that very many of the
bed-keepers, could be helped out of it by the simplest
water-applications, if only continued with perseverance
and punctuality.

2. The warm whole-bath

like the cold one is useful both for the healthy and the sick.

The manner of taking it is twofold.

The one bath (a) is sufficiently filled with warm water
to cover the whole of the body, and in this the person
remains for 25 to 30 minutes. At the end of that time
the other bath (b), filled with cold water, is quickly
entered, the person dipping in up to the head, but not
with the head. If no second bath is there, the whole
body is washed as quickly as possible with cold water.
This cold bath, or cold washing, must be finished in one
minute. The clothes are then put on, quickly, without
drying, and exercise taken for at least half an hour, either
in the room or in the open air, until one feels quite dry
and warm. Country people may immediately return to
their work. The water for this first bath must have a
temperature of 26 to 28°, for aged persons 28 to 30° R.
It is advisable to measure carefully and accurately with
a thermometer, which is easily obtained. But it is not

sufficient to put the quicksilver-tube into the warm water,
and take it out again at once; it must remain in the
water for a while. It is only by the standing still of the
quicksilver that it can be decided, whether a sufficient
length of time has been taken for the measurement, and
if the latter is correct. Those who prepare a bath, should
do it earnestly, being aware of their responsibility. Indifference and carelessness are nowhere less pardonable
than in such important services of charity.

The second way to take this bath, is the following.

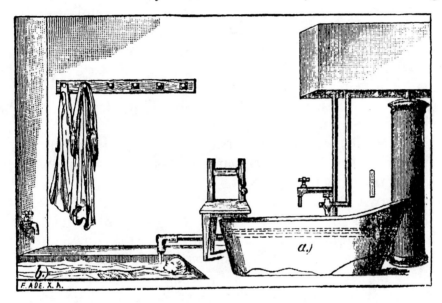

Fig. 5.

The bath is filled as mentioned before; but the
water has the temperature of 30 to 35°. With these
baths 35° should never be exceeded, (when, and in which
cases, they are to be applied, must always be said expressly,) but also no lower temperature taken than 28°;
on the average I advise and prepare them myself with
31 to 33° R.

Those who take this bath go into the warm water
not once, but three times, and also into the cold water
three times. This is the so-called warm whole-bath with
threefold change. The whole bath takes precisely 33
minutes; the different changing is done as follows:

10 minutes in the warm bath,
1 minute   „   „   cold   „
10 minutes „   „   warm   „
1 minute   „   „   cold   „
10 minutes „   „   warm   „
1 minute   „   „   cold   „

Without exception the proceeding must always be
concluded by the cold bath. Healthy, strong people sit
down in the cold-water-bath, and dip in slowly up to the
head. Sensitive persons sit down and quickly wash chest
and back* without dipping under. A whole ablution
answers the same purpose for those who are too much
afraid of the cold bath. The head is never wetted; if it
has become wet, it must be dried. Likewise after the
last cold bath no other part of the body is to be dried
except the hands, and these in order not to wet the
clothes when redressing.

For the rest, especially as regards the necessary exercise after the bath, the same rules are to be observed
as regarding the first baths.

I owe a few remarks here.

Warm baths alone, i. e. without subsequent cold
baths or ablutions, are never prescribed by me. The
higher degree of warmth, especially if it lasts and operates
for a longer time, does not strenghten, but it weakens
and relaxes the whole organism; it does not harden, but
makes the skin still more sensitive to the cold; it does
not protect, but it endangers.

The warm water opens the pores, and lets the cold
air in, the consequences of which are to be seen even
in the following hours. The cold baths or cold ablutions
following the warm ones, act as a remedy to the latter;
(I do not allow any application of warm water without
the following cold one,) the fresh water strengthens, by
lowering the higher temperature of the body; it refreshes
by washing off, as it were, the superfluous heat; it protects by closing the pores, and making the skin more firm.

----

* They throw as much water over their shoulders as is
sufficient to wash the back.

The same prejudice against the sudden cold following the warmth, meets us again here. It is precisely on account of the cold baths following, that the warm ones can, and must, be given at a higher temperature than is usual, or than I myself would agree to generally. The body is filled with so much warmth, armed as it were, that it is able to stand well the shock of the penetrating cold.

Those who are too much afraid of the cold bath at first, may take a whole ablution; they will thereby get courage. It depends entirely upon the first trial. Those who have once tried it, will never take a warm bath again without the following cold one, if only on account of the comfort it gives. To many who at first trembled with fear, but later on became used to the strange changing and liked it, I was obliged to trace strict limits to prevent the excess of good from turning to evil.

The prickling and crawling sensation on the skin, which is strongly felt upon going back to the warm bath, after the cold one, especially on the feet, need not frighten any one; later on it will seem like an agreeable rubbing.

For these two kinds of whole baths there is no necessity of preparations, e. g. to bring the body to the right temperature.

Here, as for all the warm baths, I never, or at least very seldom use warm water alone; decoctions of different herbs are always mixed with them.

a. The warm whole-bath for the healthy.

If I order warm whole-baths for healthy persons, i. e. comparatively healthy, (healthy, but weak persons,) I do so only in case where such weakened people cannot make up their minds to take cold baths, and solely for the purpose of preparing and ripening them by this warm whole-bath, with the cold one following, for the fresh cold bath.

My principles, and my practice, with reference to this are as follows:

I seldom, or almost never, order warm baths for quite healthy and strong natures, whose fresh, rosy complexion sparkles, as it were, with warmth and vital fire.

Nor do they desire them either, for they long for the cold water like a fish.

But I recommend them for younger people who are weak, poor of blood, and nervous, especially those who are inclined to cramps, rheumatism and such like complaints; and before all others to the mothers of families, who are worn out so early by every possible hardship. Such a bath with 28° R. and subsequent cold ablution, taken for 25 to 30 minutes, every month, would be sufficient for them.

For those who are inclined to articular disease, gout, podagra, two such baths a month would be better than one.

Younger persons should try the cold whole-bath in summer time.

To aged, weak people I recommend at least one warm whole-bath every month of 28 to 30° R., taken for the space of 25 minutes and concluding with a cold ablution, for cleanliness of the skin, for refreshment and for strengthening. They will feel quite renewed after each bath on account of the greater perspiration (activity of the skin) and the more vivid circulation of the blood.

b. The warm whole-bath for the sick.

In which cases of illness the warm whole-bath is to be taken, is said where the various diseases are spoken of.

Both kinds are in use, and with due precaution and exactness there is nothing whatever to be feared. These baths aim at a twofold purpose: In the one case they increase the bodily warmth by a new supply of warmth; in the other they operate the evacuating and dissolving of materials which cannot be removed by the diseased body itself.

The warm whole-baths are prepared as:

         Hay-flower baths,
         Oat-straw   „
         Pine-sprig   „
         Mixed   „

The manner of preparing as well as the effect of the two first kinds of baths, have already been mentioned in the description of the warm sitting-bath.

I only wish to repeat a few points for precaution's sake:

aa. The hay-flower bath.

A small bag filled with hay-flowers is put in a kettle full of hot water and boiled with it for at least a quarter of an hour. Afterwards the whole decoction is poured into the prepared warm bath, which is then filled up with warm or cold water until it has reached the prescribed temperature. This bath, the easiest to prepare and the most frequently used, is indeed the most harmless, the normal bath for the warming of the body. Healthy people, too, may take it, whenever they like. In my country there are many such water-men going about, surrounded by the odour of such hay-flowers. The coffee-brown water thoroughly opens the pores, and dissolves materials shut up in the body.

bb. The oat-straw bath.

A good bunch of oat-straw is boiled in a kettle of water for half an hour, then the decoction is used as above-said.*

cc. The pine-sprig bath.

It is prepared as follows: The sprigs (the fresher the better), small branches, even very resinous pine-cones, all cut in pieces, are thrown into hot water and boiled for half an hour, the rest as above-said. This bath, too, is of good effect against diseases of the kidneys and bladder, but not so strong as the bath of oat-straw. Its chief effect is on the skin, which is brought to activity by it, and on the interior vessels which it strengthens. This fragrant and strengthening bath, is the proper bath for more aged people, as mentioned under a.)

dd. Mixed baths.

Mixed baths, I call those, which are made with decoctions of several herbs, when the due quantity of any

---

* This bath has stronger effects than the hay-flower bath and is excellent for complaints of the kidneys and bladder; also for stone and gravel diseases and for rheumatism.

of them cannot be had. I have mixed them mostly with decoctions of hay - flowers and oat - straw, having them boiled together. The oat-straw bath becomes the more fragrant for it. I know it will be said: The baths would be good, but the whole affair is too expensive and too troublesome. This objection of one of my readers, would be a just one, if I were to send him to Reichenhall, Carlsbad or any other bathing-place, or if I were to order him to buy the expensive black little bottles with extract of pine sprigs, and to pour out the half or third of the contents into every bath. But, as it is, nobody has the least reason to complain, to make an excuse, or even to object. Even the very poorest can easily prepare all the baths, and in every case he will have the purest extract, which is nowhere to be had more genuine and unadulterated.

It was just for the good of poorer, and not wealthy people, that I have been looking out for these baths, in order that they should not be deprived of the benefit of a bath which is of so great influence on health in many cases. There is no necessity for journeys, but only a walk to the hay-rick, or barn, or at the utmost, to the neighbouring wood. Nor, are there, for the baths, other expenses to be made than a few steps or a good word. Every farmer willingly gives hay-flowers and a bunch of oat-straw to the poor; no fir-tree refuses to give him its cones and twigs; a wooden tub is among the household furniture of every one, or in case of need, a neighbour would lend it willingly. This will be sufficient as regards the expense.

With regard to the trouble, I simply ask: Is it less troublesome to yourself and your relations, if, you are thrown on your sick-bed for weeks, or if your neglected, excessively weakened, and never refreshed body slowly faints away? There can be no question about trouble and labour. If any one thinks it too much to fulfil the least of my prescriptions, I can only call him indolent and lazy. People of this kind would not, indeed, deserve such a bath.

3. The mineral-baths.

Here I must say a word about mineral-baths, as I have been asked to do so very often. My humble opinion on that point is this:

According to all the principles of my water-cure, I cannot agree with them, because I do not approve of anything forced and violent, whether effected from outward to inward, or directly to the inward. My verdict is, and always will be: The gentlest application is the best, let it relate to the water-cures, or to medicines, etc., and if I can obtain my purpose by one application only, I ought not to make use of a second one. We must help nature, help the diseased, or weakened organism gently, not rigidly and impetuously; we must, as it were, lead the sick body softly and gently by the hand, sometimes assist and support it more firmly, but not urge it too much, not drag and push it; we must not insist absolutely upon obtaining a certain thing by our remedies, but only co-operate with the body in accomplishing its work, and then give up this gentle, and gentlest co-operation, as soon as ever the body is able to help itself to proceed alone.

To give an instance of my system: no doubt it has not escaped any one's notice, that the everywhere known root and wire brushes, the rubbing cloth, etc., have no place in my water-cure. In former times, I used these things, though only in single cases, but I have since learnt that the water, by itself, without these more or less violent manipulations, (with them, the poor body has, besides all its work, also the trouble of bringing the kneaded, and brushed muscles, and the likewise worked skin, to order again) brings on the best effect, provided that it is applied rightly. According to my system the rubbing is done the whole day, and the whole night, by the rough linen or hemp shirt, which, once more, I heartily recommend.

The name „mineral bath“ already indicates a rigid effect. All these waters, whatever they are called, or wherever they are running, contain more or less, softer or sharper, salts. Such salt-waters, used interiorly, appear to me — please pardon the expression — like using a rough brush and granulous sand to cleanse or to polish silver or still

5*

nobler metal. Silver and gold are delicate and tender. But is it not the same with the interior organs? One breath darkens the silver; rough means of cleansing hurt, injure it. Under such treatment it may become shining, for the brush and sand take away dust and dirt. Yes, only too thoroughly, and the silver vessels will not stand such treatment, or to speak more correctly such misuse, for a long time. I need not explain further, nor say on what sensitive, soft, exceedingly noble metal such waters undertake their cleansing work.

And what does experience say to my assertion?

In large bathing-places the deceased are, for the most part, brought to the cemetery, to their last resting-place not at day time but at night; not with singing and music, but quite silently in order not to alarm, or to hurt the feelings of the other poor sufferers. But there are many, very many, carried there. Every year a considerable number of persons die in most of the different bathing-places. „He or she, came here for the first time in such and such a year; it did him much good.“ But the old complaint came, and she or he went there again. „In that year he was there for the second time,“ his relations say, „but it did him less good. The complaint came back in a higher degree, and nevertheless he could not be dissuaded from going there for a third time. He came back visibly stronger; he seemed to be quite cured. But he only came back to die at home.“ To many the expenses of travelling are spared by an early death at home. This story, and other similar ones, I have been told innumerable times. He who only goes to such places for entertainment's, and for pleasure's sake, need not be afraid about the above said, he only needs to consult his purse, which is subjected to a merciless cure, and most thoroughly pumped out.

Even common people, country people whose head no longer stands on the right place, i. e. on the humble one, who try to imitate, the better, the learned, the educated and advanced men, if they do not go to a bathing-place (fortunately, they are prevented from doing so by the lightness of theire purse) attempt many stupid things. Once a peasant came to me saying: „Well now, I have found out the best means of purifying the body; it is a kind of medicinal water, and I take it often." — „But what is it?" I asked him. With some hesitation he owned, that he dissolved a spoonful of salt in water and took this salt-water before breakfast. It did him good, he said, and he liked it better than the best mineral-water. (Of course, he was an enlightened man with a consumptive purse!) I admonished him; but he would not part with his self-invented cure. He continued to drink the salt-water for a while; but then he got disorder of the stomach and indigestion, poverty of blood, and at last he died, worn out and exhausted, in the best years of manhood.

So then, be always contented and reasonable, and never envy the rich and noble man, who seems to be in a better state and to have everything he wishes for. That would be foolish and not christian like.

Neither ought you to be jealous, if you see weak or consumptive people etc. go for a so-called change of climate to certain places, to Meran, South of France, Italy, or even to Africa; I always think that the best place for a fish is the water, the most splendid home for a bird is the open air, and the fresh nature. To me the most advantageous, the most favourable climate is the place and the country where God's creative power has formed me. Should the air become too sharp for me, well, then I will try to harden myself; if I fall ill, the water at home will serve me just as well as that of foreign countries. Is it God's will that I shall die, well, sooner or later it must come for all of us; and, as people say, the earth of the native country is less heavy, and in it the repose is better and more peaceful than elsewhere.

What, then, does experience tell us, concerning such mild and highly situated, airy places, experience which is every year proved anew? I simply put two questions: How many of those who, being really ill, fled there, have come back quite cured? How many have remained in the warmer climates, and have been buried there?

Therefore remain in your own country, support yourself honestly, and wash yourself daily!

V. Part-baths.

To the following baths I give the common name of part-baths, because they relate to single parts of the body, but chiefly in order not to be obliged to make still more divisions.

1. The hand- and arm-bath.

The name itself explains sufficiently, and with the complaints concerning them, it will be said when and in which cases these baths are to be applied, if cold or warm, for how long a time, if 2 or 3 minutes or a quarter of an hour; how often they are to be repeated, with which decoction of herbs etc.

One remark about the application will suffice. — Some one has, for example, a bad finger. I do not operate on the finger only, but also on the hand, the arm, the whole body. The bad finger is only a bad fruit of a bad sprig, a bad branch, a bad trunk. If the trunk is in good order, it will supply sufficient and good sap, and consequently the fruit must be good.

The applications, or the improvements of the sprigs and branches, i. e. of hand and arm, are to be accomplished by the hand and arm baths, together with the bandages.

2. The head-bath.*

The head-bath belongs to the most important part-baths. It is best taken, cold or warm, in the following way:

Fig. 6.

A vessel with water is put on a chair, and the upper part of the head (see fig. 6), the proper soil of the hair, is put into the cold water for about one minute, but if it is taken in warm water, for 5 to 7 minutes. Where the water does not reach the hair, it may be supplied with the hand, in order to wet all the hair.

* It has repeatedly been said in different places, that the head ought not to be wetted. The reason is that country

After the bath, the hair must be very carefully dried. And this should never be omitted whether the hair has become wet through the shower or through the vapour. Great care and exactness should be observed; otherwise serious complaints of the head, such as rheumatism, would likely ensue. After the drying one remains in the room, or puts on a cap or bonnet large enough to cover the whole of the wet hair, until the skin of the head and the hair are perfectly dry.

Many, especially young country people, do it in a shorter way. They simply dip their head several times into the trough of a pump, like a duck on a pond, or they hold their head under the water-pipe. It does them good. Quite right! Only do not go to any excess (too long or too often) and keep to the rules of thorough drying!

This bath is very good for those with short hair. With long hair* the water cannot penetrate to the skin so easily, which is the real purpose of the bath, and the drying takes more time. To such persons I advise the warm head-bath on account of its longer duration.

Sometimes I order the head-baths against complaints of the head, — but then always cold and short ones, — yet mostly to such people with whom the roots of the hair are the wrestling-place of all possible smaller or larger ulcers, tetters and dry pimples, a real mine of scurf and dust, if not of worse things, which, indeed, ought better to be concealed under the cloak of night, but by no means under the hair.

---

people in particular are not careful enough about the drying, and are therefore likely to injure themselves. As for the rest, it is just the head that is one of the most hardened parts of the body, particularly with men on account of its being exposed to every weather.

   * Short hair is a great advantage to health, e. g. with a disposition to complaints of the head, also for the care of the skin. Long hair is a nice ornament, a nice gift of the Creator; but it should always be well cared for, kept clean; brush and comb ought not to be spared. Every mother knows what, otherwise, would ensue.

To such I also give warm head-baths occasionally of longer duration, concluded by cold ablutions.

I wish to draw special attention to these head-baths. If in the country, in a small house and in a still smaller room, the little holes for light and air called windows, are never opened the whole winter long, the air must become at last so thick that it could be cut through, and every stranger coming into the room starts back with horror.

And if a room is never cleaned, never scoured, what an appearance must the floor have at last?

Can it be otherwise with the soil of the hair, if the long hair or the two or threefold wrappers on the head for half a year or more, never allow a breeze or a sun-beam to penetrate to the skin of the head, which apart from this, is naturally concealed?

And if water or soap never do their work there thoroughly, very thoroughly, what must it become like at last? There also can arise a morass of crusts etc., a rottenness, and many a mother could relate the consequences of it.

It is only too true, alas! that the care of the head is often much neglected. The face is washed every morning the whole year long, and many people think that nothing else is required. But it is by no means all. I particularly recommend the care of the head, both to young and old, but more especially to mothers, for the sake of cleanliness and health.

3. The eye-bath.

This may be taken either warm or cold. In both cases it is applied as follows:

The face is dipped into the water, the eyes opened, as it were, bathed for a quarter of a minute. After a pause of $1/4$ to $1/2$ minute, forehead and eyes are dipped in again. This may be repeated 4 or 5 times. The warm eye-bath (24 to 26° R.) should always be concluded with cold, either by taking the last bath with cold water, or by washing the eyes with fresh water. The bathing water ought not to be warm water alone, but mixed with herbs;

half a spoonful of ground fennel or a decoction of eye-bright has always served me well.

a. The cold eye-bath has an excellent effect on healthy, but weak eyes; it strengthens and refreshes the whole seeing-apparatus in its interior and exterior parts.

b. The warm (lukewarm) eye-bath is applied to moisten tumours on the exterior eye, and to dissolve and draw out all kinds of thick, purulent fluids of the interior eye.

C. Vapours.

The vapours like all our water-applications, operate in the gentlest manner and therefore entirely without harm and danger. Nevertheless the application of vapours requires great precaution. That which cures a sick person, if applied rightly and according to the prescription, may make a healthy person ill, if done with negligence and indifference. For example, if a person immediately after a vapour-bath, goes out into the open air without having taken the preceding cooling, he may not only become ill, but mortally ill: The application itself has not done any harm in such a case. I mention this first, not to make people anxious, but careful, and repeat that rightly used, there is never the least danger in the vapours.

Are vapours in general necessary for cure?

A woman when cleansing her linen, uses warm and cold water. The warm water is intended to dissolve what is to be removed, the cold water to float away the dissolved stuff. A similar process is going on in the cure. In diseases, too, several things, such as accumulations of blood, corrupted juices etc. must be dissolved and evacuated; this is done by warmth. Then the body must be strengthened and enabled to offer resistance; this is done by cold.

Every body must, therefore, possess a certain quantity, a certain measure of warmth, if its work is to be done rightly.

The healthy body possesses natural warmth in itself, and does not want any supplement.

Every sickly body very soon feels the want of the natural interior warmth; therefore a compensation of some kind must be given. With many patients the bandages are sufficient; with others the vapours, these artificial importations of warmth, as I like to call them, are of better service.

In what does the right application of vapours consist?

This question is not easy to answer; I will merely give my experience and acknowledge at the same time that I have changed my method very often.

At first I favoured the general practice which gave preference to the whole vapour-baths, and this I followed for 13 years. As, however, during the course of these years, I did not see the expected effects I changed my proceedings. Within 3 years this occurred even three times, until at last I recognised the present method as the most excellent and most advantageous; and for many years I have practised it with the best results. It is an extremely mild method, very carefully avoiding all ruggedness, by which the vapour is made to operate not simultaneously upon the whole body, but only upon parts of it.

But here I must go back a little.

About 30 years ago the Russian vapour-baths began to be put in practice in the South of Germany; but as many families were not able to use these medicinal baths, at that time only known in large towns, a substitute was invented for them, (so I think it was) in the form of the well known sweating-closets, which were to serve in a similar way as sudorifics.

I, too, had such a box made, with a closing door and an opening at the top, through which I could easily put my head. The supply of vapour was given from without; the patient or sweat-wanter sat or stood inside the closet, looking with silent resignation upon the thermometer placed before him.

A dry cloth was wrapped round his neck, to prevent the vapour escaping; wet compresses covered the head in order to keep it cool, while the whole body was in the highest degree of sweating, which took place even after 10 to 15 minutes. The vapour-bath was concluded by a whole shower-bath (a watering can of water) or a whole-bath. As often as greater perspiration was desired, I ordered the patient to go into the closet twice, for 15 minutes each time, and to conclude each time with a quick ablution of half a minute's duration.

The manner of preparing these whole vapour-baths seemed to me incomparable; but I could not understand how it was that the results were not equally excellent. In winter-time especially there were great difficulties. Within a few minutes the whole body, being completely enveloped by the hottest vapour, and attacked on all sides with the same violence, was put to the greatest sweating, and thereby acquired a great sensitiveness to cold. To me, at least, is was always very difficult after such a bath, so to protect the whole surface of the skin against the fresh, cold winter-air, that some spot of it did not suffer and so bring on complaints, and sometimes even sharp pains for a longer time.

I tried hard to remedy this defect, and I reflected upon it a great deal.

Just about that time I had reason to go to Munich. It was winter, and I was suffering from a rather bad catarrh. By chance I found a paper in which the almost marvellous effects of the Russian vapour-baths were exceedingly praised. It was there said: „Only try; one single vapour-bath is able to cure the worst catarrh." — I resolved to make the trial, so went to the institution, took such a bath, and really, having done so, I no longer felt any trace of my catarrh. But wait! Scarcely 5 or 6 hours had elapsed, when a fresh catarrh, doubly as bad as the old one which I had left in the Russian bath, took hold of my whole body.

„Why," I thought and whispered in my own ear, „this way of taking vapour-baths surely cannot be the right one." „Not to speak of myself, how could a weak, sick person, perhaps one dangerously ill, make use of such a thing which makes a strong, healthy man shudder? No, for such people there must be another kind of treatment."

All my further investigations and experiments led me to the conviction that the same principle adopted for all my water-applications, is also to be followed with the vapours; namely, that the gentlest application is always the best. The gentlest application I call that which is the most simple and the most indulgent towards the body. I should never use any vapour (to increase the natural warmth for example,) where a small water-application, a shower-bath or a half-bath is sufficient. I should never torment and enervate the whole body by a whole vapour-bath in cases where part-vapour-baths may suffice. Ne quid nimis, i. e. I remain even with the application of vapour in the golden mean, do not force nature to anything, but help her, support her kindly, and invite her by small remedies to do her work herself, alone and freely.

All my vapours are in truth, only part-vapours, i. e. they operate directly on parts of the body only; nevertheless, none of them are without influence on the whole body. It is precisely this, which seems to me, the great advantage. The vapours touch, or weaken the suffering part only, and leave the whole body untouched and unimpaired. The latter remains in its whole vigour, and while the suffering part, attacked by vapour, is in full labour, the body is at rest for a while, in order after a short time to impart some of its vigour to its weakened companion.

Many of my vapour-applications are taken simply as a preparation for the water-applications, to make them practicable and perhaps more effective, or to co-operate in the interior of the body (e. g. by dissolving in the wind-pipe and the lungs) with the exterior application of water. It is very seldom indeed that one of the vapours is used by itself as a separate whole application.

The necessary precautions with regard to cooling, dressing, and movement, are given with the description of the single vapours.

I must here caution against an illusion.

It very often happens that one of the different vapours, especially that for head or feet, operates in a most favourable way. These vapours, because they are strongly dissolving and evacuating, make the patient feel easy, comfortable, and most cheerful and happy; consequently there arises a danger of misusing that which is good in itself, of repeating the vapours too frequently, and by this, of doing great harm to the health by imprudence.

Modus est in rebus! Only make it a rule and a duty to keep to the right measure!

For good advice I will mention some particular cases.

A person recovering from typhus, or some other serious illness, has still on, or in his head or elsewhere great accumulations. Vapours would be of great service, of course, but only very few, and these lighter hand or foot-vapours; for we have to do with an individual poor of blood and juices. To extinguish a match, I do not require a smith's bellows; a soft breath is sufficient.

It is the same with all persons who are poor of blood. The warm vapours give them comfort; but too many of them would be as so many blood-, warmth- and life-suckers.

But stout, corpulent persons can certainly support a great many vapours and much sweating?

It is very often just this kind of people who can endure them least of all, for the reason that they are poor of blood. With such individuals I am most sparing with vapours, and prepare the bandages to operate for good transpiration of the skin. Where the skin is in good order, there is no want of much sweating.

A patient complaints of violent pain in his feet. He wishes to apply foot-vapours to his emaciated, spindle-like legs. How foolish it would be to grant his request! Such a poor skinny creature has nothing to spend in perspiring. Give him instead of vapours, half-baths and frequent shower-baths on his knees.

The vapours I apply are the following.

1. The vapour for the head.

The application of head-vapours requires some little preparations. There must be a small wooden tub (see fig. 7), more deep than wide, with handles on which the hands can lean, and a well closing cover; moreover,

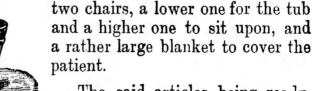

two chairs, a lower one for the tub and a higher one to sit upon, and a rather large blanket to cover the patient.

The said articles being ready, the tub is placed on the lower chair and three parts filled with boiling

Fig. 7.

water, then well closed with the cover and a damp cloth, in order to keep the vapour inside until it is to be used. The patient has the whole upper part of his body bare and a dry cloth round his waist to prevent the garments from becoming wet by the perspiration as it flows down. He sits on the higher chair, and leans the palms of his hands on the handles of the tub, the upper body bent

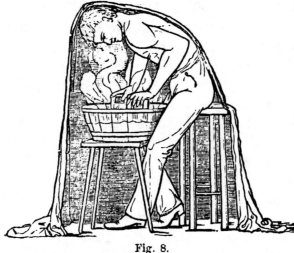

over the tub (see fig. 8); then both he and the tub are enveloped with a large blanket, lightly, but on every side, and in such a way that there is not the least opening left through which the vapour may escape. When this is done, the attendant stands

Fig. 8.

opposite the patient, and lifting the blanket from below, takes away the closing cover and the wet cloth; then the vapour comes forth like a glowing stream and penetrating to head, chest, back, and to the whole upper body, begins its dissolving work.

The attendant must be careful that weaker patients who are subject to pain in their back, are seated comfortably, have good support for their back etc. On the other hand he should not take any notice of complaints and manifold exclamations, such as: I cannot bear it any longer! I shall get a stroke! etc.

In the first moment one may be frightened by the unusual glowing temperature; but one soon gets used to the tropical climate, and quickly finds some little advantage. At the first shock of the hot clouds it is well to take a more upright position, to raise the head, to turn to different directions, etc. When the patient is more accustomed to it, and the heat is diminishing, the body returns to its prescribed, bent position.

There is absolutely nothing to be feared. Not one case has come to my knowledge, in which the head-vapour, applied exactly as prescribed, has done the least harm. I have applied it to the most different persons, with the most different complaints, but always with a good result. The vapours have never hurt anyone, but those self-wise people have hurt themselves, who without any precaution or rule, did what they liked, not what was prescribed. An application lasts from 20 to 24 minutes. During the whole of this time the patient ought not only to hold his head over the vapour, but also to open his eyes, nose and mouth as much as possible, and let the vapour stream in as much as he can bear.

After the elapse of 20 to 24 minutes, the blanket is taken away and the whole upper body quickly washed with fresh water. In winter time the patient takes exercise in his room, in summer in the open air, until the skin is properly dried and in a normal temperature of warmth.

Here I am obliged to give some important remarks, which should not, by any means, be overlooked.

The vapour of pure water is not quite favourable to the eyes of some persons, or to the stomach by inhaling it. Therefore I always mix herbs with the water.

First of all I recommend fennel, which has proved of excellent effect.

One spoonful of ground fennel is sufficient for an application. Also herbs of sage, common yarrow, mint, elder, ribwort, and linden-blossom, are of very good service. Should you not be able to get any of these, take a handful of nettles or hay-flowers and mix them with the water; these herbs may be despised, but nevertheless they are of good use.

In general the vapour works its effect quickly; with most persons the drops of sweat begin rolling down the forehead even after the first 5 minutes; but after 8 or 10 minutes they come forth from all the pores.

But there are patients, generally those who are poor of blood, with little vital heat, with whom the vapour has not such an easy task. Here assistance may be given by taking about the sixth part of a brick, made red-hot, and putting it into the water about 10 minutes after the beginning of the application It gives a violent roar, and the clouds of vapour arise anew more thickly and lively.

Directly after a vapour-bath (which, as well as the following cooling, is always to be taken, in winter, in a heated room), the patient should not venture to go into the open air, without a previous cold ablution, by which the pores opened by the vapour are closed again.

In winter it is well to walk up and down in aheat-ed room for about half an hour, before going out into the open air. Without this precaution not only a catarrh, but, according to circumstances, even a serious, mortal illness could be caused. The said cold ablution may be made in different ways. The simplest way, which I especially recommend to weaker persons who depend on the assistance of others, is to wash the patient quickly with a towel and fresh water. With tumours and pustules on the head, eruptions of the head, running ears, in general with complaints which require much evacuation from the head, this kind of ablution is to be applied with the first and second head-vapours. Has this been neglected, the consequences, such as a violent humming in the ears etc. will be disagreeable, though not exactly dangerous. With the following applications, when the evacuation has been effec-ted in a greater measure, the second kind of ablution, the real upper shower-bath, may be used. The upper shower is given by slowly pouring 1 or 2 watering-cans of cold water over the vapoured parts, with the exception of the head, i. e. the hair; the chest is to be well washed. The further rules are the same as for the showers, i. e. after having dried face and hair carefully, the clothes are put on quickly without drying the other parts of the body; then exercise is to be taken either by walking or working, until the body is entirely dry and in normal warmth.

If after the head-vapour bath an opportunity presents itself of taking a cold whole-bath for one minute at the utmost, it will be well to make use of it.

The effects of this application are very important; they extend to the whole surface of the skin of the upper body, the pores of which are opened by them; then they act upon the internal organs by the dissolving and evacuating of matters in the nose, the wind-pipe, the lungs etc. Against colds caused by getting wet, or by a sudden change of temperature, against complaints of the head, humming in the ears, rheumatic and spasmodic complaints in the nape and the shoulders, against asthma, against mucous fever not yet advanced, all these being companions of the different catarrhs, the head-vapour is of excellent service. Two applications within three days are generally sufficient for a complete cure. If the catarrh is only beginning, one single vapour will remove it, no matter where it may reside.

Whoever has an inflated head, a disproportionately thick neck, or swollen jugular glands, may take two or three of such vapours a week. In cases of inflammation of the eyes, caused by colds etc. or of blear eyes, do the same. The latter patient may expect a still greater success, if in the evening of the day on which the head-vapour has been used, a warm foot-bath with wood-ashes and salt is taken for a quarter of an hour.

I have applied the head-vapour with the best result in cases of congestions or even after strokes. In such undoubtedly critical cases, people are apt to be deceived and to get frightened by assuming that such a vapour will draw every drop of blood to the head. This fear is entirely groundless. Nevertheless I myself keep to the practice — which in the two above named cases I recommend to every one — of always reducing the time of application to 15 or 20 minutes, and of ordering a vapour foot-bath to follow the head-vapour as soon as possible.

As a head-vapour bath has a strongly dissolving effect, and as too copious perspiration would likely bring on great weakness, this application ought not to be used too frequently. As a rule the number of two a week should not be exceeded. In rare cases where special dissolving and evacuating are necessary, the head-vapour may be used for one week every second day, but with reduced duration, the minimum 15 minutes, the maximum 20 minutes.

2. The vapour foot-bath.

The same service which the head-vapour bath renders to the upper part of the body, is rendered to the lower part by the vapour foot-bath. The application is made as follows:

A rather wide and thick blanket is placed lengthwise on a chair, upon which the patient sits down with bare feet and legs. A wooden foot-bath (fig. 9a) is a little more than half filled with boiling water and put before him. On the upper edge of the bath at the handles, two small pieces of wood are fastened, on which the patient can easily put his feet, or instead of these one piece (fig. 10b) may be put from handle to handle. Great care must be taken however about secure fastening, in order to prevent the danger of their giving way and scalding the patient's feet. The most simple contrivance would be perhaps to put in the bath a small foot-stool reaching to the edge. When the patient is ready with his feet over the steaming water, the thick blanket is laid round his feet and the tub in such a way as to entirely prevent the steam from escaping, and by this proceeding the warm element as-

Fig. 9.

Fig 10.

cends, to the feet, to the bowels, and higher. (See fig. 10.)

For these vapours I usually take lighter, boiling decoctions of hay-flowers. The effect of this application. as well as that of the head-vapour, can be increased by putting a hot piece of brick slowly and carefully into the water every 5 or 10 minutes. I say slowly and carefully; for it must never be allowed to fall into the water; the latter would splash and scald the feet. The number of hot bricks as well as the duration of the vapour-bath, depends on the higher or lesser degree of the intended effect. Often it is only the soles of the feet which are to be brought into perspiration, e. g. in the case of sweating feet; but in some cases the vapour is used to bring the whole of the legs, the thighs included, some-times the abdomen, and sometimes the whole body into perspiration.

Fig. 11.

I have seen many who by this very simple and primitive application were bathed in sweat, as when subjected to the most violent sweating apparatus with 2 or 3 feather-beds. The mildest application is with one red-hot brick and a duration of from 15 to 20 minutes; but to produce the highest effects of a real vapour-bath. it will be necessary to renew the glowing brick every 5 to 10 minutes, and to extend the time of the application to 25 or 30 minutes.

The vapour-bath is always followed by a cooling application which depends on the extension of the parts bathed in perspiration: If only the feet and legs as far as the knees are sweating, a quick cold ablution with a

6*

towel will suffice; stronger persons may take a knee-gush. If the thighs and abdomen are in perspiration, a half-bath is sufficient: but if the whole body too, is seized with perspiration, then the whole body must also be cooled, either by a half-bath with washing of the upper body, or by a whole-bath, or a whole ablution. The rules regarding these applications, are to be found in the passages concerning them (baths and ablutions); the rules concerning the proceeding after the vapour foot-bath are the same as those for the head-vapour.

The vapour foot-bath is mostly applied for the manifold sufferings of the feet, e. g. in cases of great, badly smelling perspiration where a dissolving of foul juices is required; of swollen feet, probably caused by accumulations of juices and blood; in cases of cold feet, whose temperature of warmth is at zero, and to which the blood can no longer find its way, as it were. By these vapours new activity is awakened and new life inspired; sometimes, however, they only serve against the different complaints, as necessary preparations for other applications and as means for their success.

Persons suffering from whitlows, nails growing in etc. who are in danger of blood poisoning, on account of wrong treatment of corns, tearing out of nailroots, for example, should quickly apply this vapour.

More increased applications, which are intended to operate more or less on the whole body, are undertaken in cases of spasmodic complaints of the bowels, especially when caused by colds, and against head-ache originating in determination of blood to the head.

To individuals poor of blood, who need more warmth pumped into them, before any cold-water-application is undertaken, slight foot-vapours have very often been of good service.

As a rule regarding the repetition of this application, the same must be observed as respecting the head-vapour, i. e. it must be given very sparingly. Once or twice a week it is often prescribed, but three times only seldom, for various special cases.

Only one more remark! Many times people have complained of the great trouble of preparing and taking these vapours prescribed by me. But let me ask every well-meaning person: which is the more simple, my foot-vapour or a sweating bath after having taken so many cups of hot tea, a torture of so many hours duration, under so many feather-beds? — a sweating-bath, which is seldom or never taken without the most violent head-ache and other pains!

3. The close-stool vapour bath.

This vapour bath is of excellent service, on account of its easy preparation, convenient application and ex-ceedingly dangerless effects. Even those, who are seriously ill, and whom, on account of their weakness, it is very difficult, to bring to the desired perspiration, may be brought to it very easily by this vapour.

The boiling mixture is poured into the pan of the close-stool and the patient sits down on the latter; the attendant taking care that the beneficial steam does not escape. The hot steam ascends quickly to the body and soon produces more or less profuse perspiration, which often increases to a real sweating-bath, i. e. to a general sweating of the whole body. The application is made for 15 to 20 minutes. If it seems desirable to keep the patient perspiring for a longer time, he is laid down in bed (because sitting could be trouble-some, and the effect of the vapour would perhaps not last long enough); the sweating will continue without any special covering. After the vapour a whole ablution, a half-bath with washing of the upper body or a whole-bath according to the condition of the patient, must conclude this application.

For persons, who are seriously ill, the easiest and least dangerous will be a whole-ablution.

The effect of this vapour-bath is of course to dissolve and to evacuate. The evacuations are accomplished in the form of perspiration. I never use water alone for this vapour; the well known herbs of hay-flower, oat-straw, but first of all shave-grass (horse tail) are always mixed with it.

Against diseases of the kidneys or stone I use vapours of oat-straw; against spasmodic or rheumatic conditions of the bowels, against ulcers on the bladder, in the first stages of dropsy, such of hay-flower decoction.

The manner in which the vapour is to be used alternately with the cold-water application is explained in the III. part, where the different diseases are spoken of.

I have used the vapour with shave-grass decoction with the most striking and astonishing results in all those most painful cases where the urine could not be discharged, and consequently the poor patient was tormented and almost driven to madness and despair by the most dreadful pain. The morbid conditions of the bladder, mostly caused by colds and inflammation, were removed by the hot shave-grass vapour in a proportionally short time, and the organ did its purifying work as before.

4. Special vapour applications on particular diseased parts.

In many cases the vapours, alternately with other water-applications, are of very good service against complaints of the eyes, the ears, the mouth, the fingers, the hands, the arms, the toes, the feet etc. Some instances may explain this.

A poisonous insect stings a hand, an arm; the limb begins to swell and to cause violent pain, the inflammation threatens to spread about, etc. Bandages on hand and arm together with vapour on the suffering part will soon sooth the pain and bring help. For this purpose the hand or the arm is held over the vessel containing the boiling water.

A wound has been polluted by poisonous matter, and blood-poisoning threatens to set in; no time is to be lost. Quickly prepare a hand or foot-vapour for dissolving and evacuating.

Someone has been bitten by a dog suspected to be mad. Before a physician and other help is at hand, a vapour will bring at least a provisory help to the endangered person.

Violent cramps are tormenting a patient on certain spots on arms or feet. Do not delay treating them with vapour.

For exterior applications of the above named kinds I usually take decoctions of hay-flowers.

For eye-vapours a decoction of ground fennel, eye-bright, or shave-grass, does very well; for vapours for the ears, decoctions of blind-nettles, stinging-nettles, or common yarrow; for phlegm in the throat, a decoction of yarrow, ribwort, or nettles.

As regards the time of duration, an application should never exceed 20 minutes; the shortest duration is 10 minutes.

Those vapours which are taken by inhaling, and which are calculated for interior operation, or which concern the eyes or ears, ought to be taken carefully, never excessively warm, and least of all, hot.

D. Shower-baths.

The shower-baths I apply are the following:

1. The knee shower.

The legs being uncovered to the knees and the clothes kept back as far as possible to prevent their getting wet, the patient sits down on a chair, both his feet standing in a prepared vessel as if to take a foot-bath.

The shower is given by means of a small watering-can (such as is used in a green-house, which can easily be managed with one hand). The first can

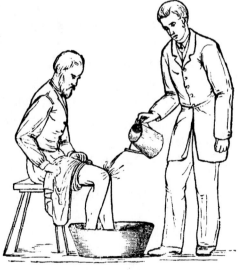

Fig. 12.

is to be poured out more fully and abundantly, and applied
to both feet from the toes up to the knees. The following
cans are directed in a less strong jet, now higher, then
lower, to particular parts of the feet and legs, especially
to the knee-pans (in the middle, and on the right and
left of them) and the calfs of the legs in such a way that
the water runs down rather proportionately. The contents
of the last can are emptied over the feet like a washing off, not being poured out from the small opening,
but from the large one. The number of cans used for a
knee-shower differs from 2 to 10, each containing from
13 to 15 quarts.

Weak and invalid people experience great difficulty
in bearing this shower at first. It is not quite easy to
any beginner. I have seen men who, at first thinking
one was making fun about this trifle, began to tremble
like aspen-leaves and in vain tried to disguise the penetrating pain caused by this water gush, which came on
them like electric shocks. This is the best proof of the
electrifying, refreshing and strenghtening power of this
shower-bath.

For those recovering from illness, for persons poor
of blood, all those whose feet-bones do not wear solid muscles, but only thin, miserable flesh-wrappers, I never
prescribe more than 2 or 3 watering-cans for the commencement; also for every beginner the first application
should not exceed 2 cans. On the following day they may
increase them from 4 to 6, by and by from 8 to 10. The
painful feeling will disappear after 8 to 10 showers; the
next jet is expected with pleasure, with a kind of longing, for the patient feels what a remarkably strengthening effect it has on the effeminate feet.

The knee-shower is given, as a rule, in connection
with the upper shower-bath. This will be explained where
the upper shower-bath is spoken of. It is not meant,
however, that the knee-gush must always be taken immediately after the upper shower.

2. The shower for the thighs

forms a continuation of the knee-shower towards the abdomen, but as thigh-gush proper it excludes the watering of the abdomen. With this shower the thigh is well as the lower parts of the body, are brought under treatment. The first can of water is poured rather quickly over the whole of the legs from the toes to the upper thighs; the following ones may flow over them in

Fig. 13.

Fig 14.

a nearly equal manner. Patients who still possess the power, would do better by taking this shower (as well as every other) in a standing position; they have thereby the advantage of the calves and shins being watered in an equal and simultaneous manner by the water flowing down on them; for an equal and simultaneous watering is by me always looked upon as one of the good qualities of a shower.

The effect of the thigh-gush is the heightened effect of the knee-gush; it could, therefore, always supply the place of the latter. But as substitute it fares as the reservemen do in public offices; it is seldom applied in my water department. It forms the most natural bridge the natural transition from the knee-gush to the lower-shower, the heightened, increased thigh-gush, thigh-gush in the widest sense of the word. As often as the name thigh-gush appears in the following pages, it is to be understood (I should like to say always) as the increased thigh-gush.

3. The lower-shower bath

(heightened, increased thigh-gush) is taken by pouring the first can of water on the lower part of the back, beginning at the feet and continuing to above the hips, the follow-

ing 3, 4 or even 6 cans being poured in an equal manner over the whole of the lower part of the body (from the front as well), but especially about the loins and hips. As it extends to the whole of the lower part of the body, it has received the name of „lower shower". Like the thigh-gush it is more advantageously taken standing. (See fig. 15.) This gush must regularly follow the foot-vapour, unless the half-bath or standing in the water is preferred. The more water is used, and the higher the jet is allowed to fall, the greater are the effects of this shower. As a rule the jet should not fall from a greater height than 8 or 9 inches.

Fig. 15.

4. The shower for the back

forms a continuation of the lower shower. It is given in such a man-ner that the whole back, from the neck to the heels, of the person taking the shower, is wetted with the first can of water; the contents of the following 3 to 5 cans are poured out in an equal stream be-ginning at the neck and continuing down to the coccyx, and then from the left to the right shoulder-blade. The jet may fall higher or lower, stronger or weaker. The whole of the spine is rather plentifully co-vered, but it may be remarked that

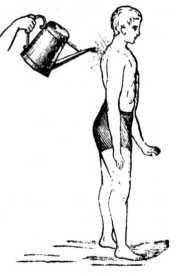

Fig. 16.

with very sensitive and excitable persons the spine should be spared as much as possible, particularly in the beginning. A quick ablution of the chest, abdomen and arms should always accompany or conclude the shower for the back. I say accompany or conclude as the former may be effected by using the water which, when poured out on the back, flows off to the front.

When this is not done, the ablution is taken immediately after the shower. The washing may be spared to the legs by standing during the application, in which case the water flowing downwards serves as an ablution.

The shower for the back works with special strengthening effect on the spine, and aids the circulation of the blood more favourably and powerfully than the preceding showers.

5. The whole shower-bath.

It extends, as the name indicates, to the whole body from the neck to the feet both sides.

It is to be applied as follows:

The patient sits in the bath, or in a wide wooden, or tin vessel, on a small board, dressed in bathing-trousers or a bathing-shirt. The shower is given partly on the back, partly on the front, with about 4 cans of water. The first must wet the whole body. The following three or more cans are given in such a way, that the jet is directed to all parts of the body, especially to the spinal marrow and the chief sympathetics, i. e. to the nape

Fig. 17.

and both sides of it, then to the pit of the stomach.

This shower may be recommended to healthy, especially corpulent persons.

It hardens, increases the circulation of the blood, strengthens and raises these individuals poor of blood and shy of water, from their excessive sensitiveness

A person feeling cold and shivering, should not take any shower, until the proper natural warmth has been restored, either by exercise or by artificial assistance, e. g. by the foot or head-vapour. It may be taken in summer and winter time; in winter, of course, in a heated room.

For sickly and weakly people the water not only may, but must be tempered, at least to the temperature which the water in bathing places has in summer time (15 to 18°).

Along with the statements of the different diseases it will be explained in which cases, and how often, the whole shower is to be applied. I often prefer it to the whole bath and order it in those cases where I advise to operate in a more effective way, e. g. to persons who suffer from rheumatics, by showering on some specially afflicted part.

To patients who require a particularly strong dissolving and evacuating process, I give the following application after the whole shower. The shirt which has become wet by the shower, is wrung out quickly and well, and then put on as a bandage (see bandages) in which the patient remains for an hour or an hour and a half.

In other cases it is, of course, taken off and fresh linen put on. The patient takes exercise until he feels quite dry and warm.

Only one slight remark more. I neither apply nor approve of the showers coming from a height, and therefore falling with force, which are used in many places, or the violent douches. I absolutely cannot understand what may be intended by such vigorous blows with healthy, much less with sick people. To wash the body, we do not use a fire-engine; who should think of such a thing?

For showering these real water-storms are not necessary; because a disease is either curable, and then gentler application will bring on the desired effect, or it is incurable, in which case this rugged treatment would not only bring no help, but very likely harm.

6. The upper shower-bath.

The patient takes off all the clothing of the upper body, and, to prevent the remainder getting wet, puts

a cloth round his waist. The tub into which the water
is to run off, may stand on a low chair or foot-stool,
instead of on the floor, in order to make the bending

down easier; it serves
also to spare the head,
i. e. to diminish by a more
upright position, the
determination of blood
to it. The patient leans
both his hands on the
bottom of the tub in
such a way that the
upper body takes a hori-
zontal position, and the
water poured on it can
flow down into the
tub. (See fig. 18.)

Fig. 18.

The first can extends
to the whole back, beginning on the right arm and right
shoulder, and continuing to the left shoulder, and left
upper arm. (a.) It serves principally to wet the whole
part where the shower is to be given. The second can (b.)
as well as the third (c.) are poured chiefly over the great
sympathetic on both sides of the 7th cervical vertebra,
then over the whole back and the spine, always concluding one part of one of the upper arms. The whole part
under treatment must be showered proportionately 3 or
4 times, the patient receiving, as it were,
3 or 4 editions of water, which flow over
the upper body and the chest down to
the tub. I advise those who are un-
experienced in this, to simply pour the
water in an equal manner upon the back
of the patient so that it forms, as it
were, a covering for the back and the
latter appears as if covered with a cloth.
The head is to be spared as much as
possible; but the neck must get a strong

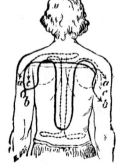

Fig. 19.

shower. If a person has long hair, the head is not to be

touched at all; if the hair is short, a gentle and sparing shower on the head is given. With nervous people care must be taken that the spine is not watered too strongly or for too long a time. The gush would be felt like a piercing knife, and the patient would not be able to bear it, although there is no danger whatever. The attendant gives the jet of water more or less fully, higher or lower, i. e. stronger or weaker, according to want or purpose. At the same time he must give heed, if the patient complains of special pains at some single spot, and he must see, if, perhaps, there are symptoms of pimples anywhere, of ulcers, accumulations of blood (blue stains), tumours etc.

The more proportionately the water flows over the watered parts, the easier it is to stand the gush, and the quicker an equal warmth on all spots will be produced.

There are people (especially those who are already corpulent or inclined to stoutness) with whom the reaction does not take place for a long time. This is to be perceived by the skin remaining without colour, just as it was before the shower, not reddened by the returning blood streaming to the watered parts. In such cases it will be good to wash the wetted back slightly with the hand after the first can, by this little rubbing the skin is incited to activity. As a rule at the third or fourth gush the entire reaction takes place.

For weakly persons one can is sufficient. To beginners 1 or 2 may be given, to those more advanced 2 or 3, to healthy and strong persons 5 or 6 cans. But the feeling of comfort must by no means lead to excess.

After the shower the chest is quickly washed, face and hands dried, the clothes put on without drying, and exercise taken either by walking or working.

The upper shower-bath (if an ablution is not given) must invariably succeed the head vapour-bath. Besides this it is regularly taken in connection with the knee-shower in which cases it is taken first, the knee-shower following after the entire re-dressing of the upper body. But again I distinctly say that the knee-shower is not bound to follow the upper shower.

Both shower-baths take a most prominent place amongst the means of hardening; and may be applied to persons of both sexes without the least fear of harm.

I know people who apply both showers to themselves every morning when rising.

First they take the upper-shower by pouring water down their back by means of a clever handling of a small can, or better still, by turning on the water-tap in a wash-house or bath-room and letting the moderate jet of water play upon their back. They move under the flowing water just as they please and as it

Fig. 20.

best suits their purpose. Afterwards they direct the stream of water to their knees in the same way. In 5 minutes time it is done and a great benefit bestowed upon the whole body.

Those who object to have the shower-bath given by another person, and yet cannot well do it themselves, may wash the upper part of the body with very cold water, then putting feet and legs into a vessel partly filled with water, they may take some water and let it slowly run down the knees and feet. Even with this primitive self-application of both showers the good effect will be obtained.

7. The arm-gush.

As the legs receive special treatment by the knee and thigh gushes, so likewise it can often be of very good service to give the arms a special watering, too.

The gush begins at the hands and is directed upwards to the shoulders; it is always given from both sides, and generally one can of water suffices for one arm. Sometimes this gush is ordered and taken simply as a hardening means for the arms, sometimes it is useful for dissolving accumulations of matter in the arms, sometimes to allay inflammations and to ease the pain caused by them, and sometimes to banish rheumatism from the arms. It is a great benefit for those who are poor of blood, and for chlorotic people. Those who have a running spring at their command may hold both arms under it for one minute, and they will surely not be reproached by me with not having chosen a proper arm-gush.

8. The head-gush.

If I were to pass by this gush in silence I should not be doing justice to an application which has been of great service to me in cases of complaints of the eyes and ears. This gush is taken by pouring the water over the head and letting the jet play about the ears, on the cheeks and even for two seconds on the closed eyes. At first one can of water is used, afterwards two. It will not be unnecessary to insist again on the thorough drying of the hair after the head-gush.

E. Ablutions.

The ablutions are divided into whole and part ablutions. We shall here speak of both kinds. The principles regarding the rubbing and not-drying are admitted here also. The chief thing with every ablution is that the water should uniformly and as much as possible equally be applied to the body or to the particular part to be treated. Rubbing or kneading are entirely out of the question. If sometimes a vigorous washing is prescribed, a quick performance of the act only is meant. Those whole or part ablutions are the best which are done the most proportionately and the quickest; none should last more than one or, at the utmost, two minutes.

This, I think, sufficiently demonstrates, how greatly my system differs from that of similar institutions, in which patients are often subjected to a treatment with cold water for an excessive length of time.

Let me once more repeat the fundamental and universal rule to be strictly observed without exception in every one of my water-departments. No one whose body is not sufficiently warm, who is shivering with cold, should take any cold water application. A transgression of this rule must have fever, catarrh and other complaints in its train.

1. The whole-ablution.

a. The whole-ablution for the healthy.

The whole-ablution extends, as the name indicates, to the whole body (except the head) which is to be washed instantaneously.

It is done in the easiest way as follows:

Take a coarse, rough towel, (with the small bathing sponge it cannot be done quickly enough), dip it in cold water and begin by washing chest and abdomen. Then the back is washed which is more difficult to reach; but every one will soon find out the easiest and quickest way of doing so. The ablution is concluded by the washing of arms and legs.

The whole application must be finished in one, or at the most in two minutes. Every ablution of longer duration can be of bad effect. Moreover, care must be taken not to make this application in a draughty place.

Without drying, the clothes are put on as quickly as possible, and exercise taken either by working or walking until the skin is perfectly warm and dry again.

When and how often may healthy people take the whole ablution?

When rising, in the morning, every one washes his face and hands, and at this time the whole ablution would be exceedingly suitable. The temperature of the body is then highest, because the lying in bed has increased it; the washing would be an agreeable cooling, would be refreshing, would drive away sleepiness and make one vigourous, lively and fresh for the day's work from the first beginning. There is no question of loss of time; for the whole ablution takes but one minute, and then work may be taken up without delay.

How many people living in town take a morning walk in spring and in summer! Let them once try the whole-ablution before doing so. I am quite sure, they will not need a second recommendation.

It would not be wise, if those who cannot go for a walk, or to work immediately after the whole-ablution, would on that account omit it; for if they were do lie down again for a quarter of an hour, after having taken the application, this would answer exactly the same purpose.

If you can make up your mind to undertake this little exertion every day, or at least every second or third day for some time, you will soon experience, what great benefit you have thereby rendered to your body.

If you have no spare time early in the morning, any hour of the day will be suitable for the ablution. Go to your bedroom, to the wash-house etc. for 2 or 3 minutes, and the beneficial work is done. If only we were not so comfort-loving and shy of water!

The black-smith, having finished his work, washes his face to cleanse it from soot and coal-dust; the peasant coming home from the field, washes his hands, and in the hot summer-time before every other refreshment, he takes a mouthful of water, to rinse his mouth and palate. How wisely both of them would act if, after their fatiguing day's work, they were to wash away the last drop of perspiration in a whole ablution! Would that this refreshing and strengthening practice were better known!

But not every one will derive the aforesaid benefit from this ablution at night, for with many it causes a rather unduly excitement of the nervous system. Therefore, try a few times to find out, if you are able to bear it, in which case bedtime will be found the most convenient for such applications.

I have recommended the whole-ablution, which is a milder application, instead of the whole-bath against sleeplessness with the best result.

In winter time I always advise people first to lie in bed for about 10 minutes, and only then when the whole body has become thoroughly warm to undertake the ablution.

b. The whole-ablution for the sick.

It is precisely with sick people that I have learnt not only how little profit is derived from rubbing, brushing, etc.. but moreover, how much harm is done through it by disproportionate warming, excitation, etc.

Regarding the whole-ablution for sick people the main point to be well observed is, that no part of the body, even including the soles of the feet, be neglected, but that the entire surface of the body be very quickly and as equally as possible touched by the water.

For sick people I always order the ablution to be taken as follows:

The patient sits up in bed, or, in case of great weakness, is supported by someone.

The back is quickly washed, along the whole of the spine; this is done in half a minute, and the patient can lie down again. Then chest and abdomen are washed; those who are not excessively weak, generally do this themselves. In one minute or less, this also is accomplished; in the same manner the arms, and lastly the legs. In 3 or 4 minutes, all is over, and the patient feels as if beginning a new life. With good will and kind care this benefit may be afforded to one who is seriously ill as easily as the washing of hands and face.

7*

After a few applications, the person administering it will find the proceeding an easy one.

Should the whole-ablution really be too much for a person who is seriously ill, 2 or 3 part-ablutions may be applied instead. In the morning chest, abdomen and arms are washed, in the afternoon, back and feet. Or chest and abdomen may be washed in the morning, the back in the middle of the day, and the arms and legs in the afternoon.

A careful, quick ablution can never do any harm, even if it is done with the freshest water, which is always the best.

When, and how often, the whole-ablution is to be taken by patients, is said where the different diseases are spoken of.

I only wish to observe here, that especially in violent fever, and also in cases of diseases accompanied by such fever, e. g. typhus and small-pox, the whole-ablutions play a chief part and are always taken instead of the cold whole-baths, when the latter for some reason or other cannot be taken.

The time for the repetition of the ablution is indicated by the increasing heat and the agitation connected with it; according to circumstances it may be repeated every half hour.

I have cured many diseases like catarrh, mucous fever, small-pox, typhus etc. solely by the use of the whole-ablution.

For weak natures I very often use vinegar diluted with water instead of water for the ablution· not to speak of its more thoroughly cleansing the skin, and opening the pores, it has also a strengthening effect.

It is very often said that the ablutions with wine, spirit, etc. (I except the vinegar) are of extraordinary good effect. I have tried such ablutions very often, and scrutinised them; but the effect was always but the ordinary one, sometimes less than that.

Years ago the French brandy was considered as the „Non plus ultra" of all means of washing; thousands of bottles were sold and bought; but then for some years it was no longer spoken of, and it is only lately that this spirit is again making a tour round the world.

Such remedies have appeared at different times like the comets. Oftentimes they drag a big tail after them; but then they disappear for ever. They are no regular, ordinary stars, shining quietly night after night without interruption and without ceasing. I should like to compare the water with the latter. It operates, and its application will remain, when such „extraordinary" streams have long ceased flowing, partly because they did not stand the test.

My most sincere wish is that the water may open its path everywhere, but especially into those circles which could do so much to make its beneficial effects known to, and appreciated by, all others.

2. The part-ablution

does not relate to the whole body, but to certain parts of it. It is performed with the hand, or with a coarse towel, dipped in water. For the rest the rules are the same as above.

If a finger or a toe, a foot or a hand, or any other part of the body be inflamed — then use the water to extinguish whenever and wherever there is fire.

Detailed particulars regarding the time when such part-ablutions may be necessary, are given with the special cases of diseases.

F. Bandages.

In the first place we name

1. The head-bandage.

This can be applied in a twofold way.

The whole head, face and hair is entirely wetted, so that the water penetrates to the skin; but the hair must not drip with water; that would be too much of a good thing. A dry cloth is put closely round the head, so as to prevent the air from entering, leaving only half the forehead and the eyes visible. In less than one hour, even in half an hour the hair will be dry.

This ablution and covering of the head, may be repeated once, twice or even three times. Only be careful that the cloth covering the wet head is quite dry when put on. The second and third application should each last half an hour; but before every fresh application the hair must be thoroughly dry.

At the end of the last application accustom yourself to the practice of washing neck and head quickly with cold water, and of drying them as after the morning washing.

A still better way of application is the following, especially in cases where strong secretion of unhealthy matter is intended.

The head is washed as above said. This time the bandaging is done with two cloths, first with the hermetically closing one, as in the first application, and then with a lighter woollen cloth likewise closely fitting. Should the heat in the head be very intense, the under cloth as well as the hair might be wetted.

If the application is to be made for a longer time, the renewing of the wet cloth must not be delayed, at the utmost for no longer than 25 to 30 minutes.

The application is concluded as above said.

Complaints of the head, especially rheumatic ones, originating in colds or sudden change of temperature; scurfs, dry eruptions, small ulcers on the skin of the head may be treated successfully with the head-bandage.

2. The neck-bandage.

The milder form of the neck-bandage consists in wetting the whole neck with the hand or a towel, and then bandaging it carefully, but not too tightly, with a dry coarse linen cloth, going 3 or 4 times round the neck, to prevent thereby the entrance of the fresh air to the wetted spot.

The second way of applying the bandage is by dipping a soft towel in fresh water and putting it round the neck. The wet towel is covered with a dry one, and both of them with a woollen or flannel bandage, or any dry woollen material; but always be careful about the hermetical closing.

My entire experience compels me to disapprove in general of applications of long duration; they very often bring about the contrary of what was intended: impairment instead of improvement, which very often is the only reason why the applications lose their credit, the confidence of the public. A patient who is thus frightened and disappointed will scarcely ever be reconciled to the water-applications; all the powers of persuasion and conviction will be useless.

I wish to extend this general remark to all the bandages.

The bandages all together are especially intended to prevent excessive and irregular streaming of the blood to any particular spot, to draw away the blood from a particular spot, and take away excessive heat, but if the bandages are allowed to remain too long, the whole night for instance on the diseased spot, this spot will become warmer and warmer; more blood will flow towards it; at last the heat will become exceedingly great, and by this the inflammation must get worse.

I entirely disapprove of applications of many hours' duration, more particularly of whole nights'. According to my system a complete application lasts for one hour, at the most one hour and a half; and every half hour, according to circumstances every 20 minutes, the wet bandage is to be renewed, i. e. re-dipped in water and put round the neck again. This re-dipping may take place from 2 to 4 times during an application. It is not the same with every patient, but depends on the more or less intense heat which is felt. The feeling of a certain uneasiness and agitation may be the guide as to when the time for changing is come.

Against inflammations of the throat, against difficulty in swallowing, against many complaints of the head, the neck-bandage is prescribed; at the same time it is well to assist its effects by applications on other parts of the body e. g. on the feet (wet socks) or on the whole body.

3. The shawl.

The shawl is a special application for the chest and the upper part of the back. For this a piece of coarse linen, one, or one and a half yard square, is used. The linen is folded in a triangular form, dipped in water, wrung out, and put on next to the skin as an ordinary shawl. (See fig. 23 and 24.) It is then covered hermetically with a dry wrapper of linen or woollen material. The patient soon perceives an agreeable warmth, the shawl becomes warm, and by and by even hot.

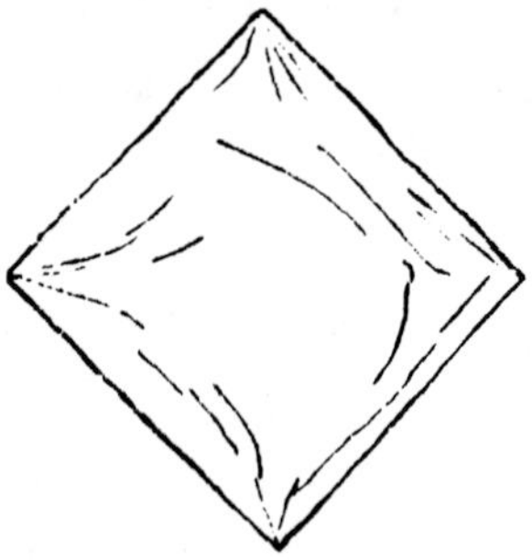

Fig. 21.

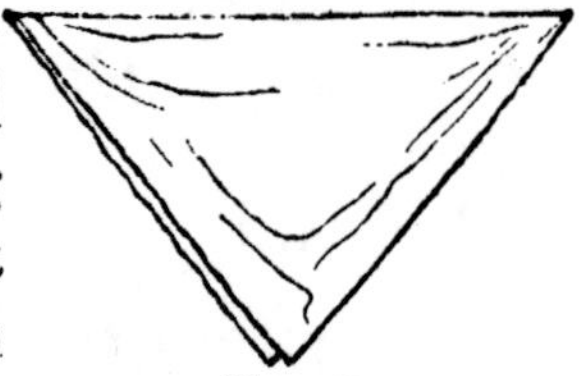

Fig. 22.

The duration of this application may be from half an hour to one hour and a half, in rare cases for two hours, the latter when a stronger effect is wished for.

In cases of longer duration the renewing, i. e. the dipping of the bandage, ought not to be overlooked. It should be done after half, or three quarters of an hour, usually then when the heat is great, and the bandage becomes warm or hot.

Fig. 23.

Fig. 24.

This perfectly harmless bandage operates in a dissolving and evacuating manner, and is prescribed against congestions, in the first stages of inflammations on, or in the head, feverish catarrhs, phlegm in the throat, in the wind-pipe, or on the chest.

It has always been of the greatest service to females who were suffering from melancholy, or whose mind was disturbed. In connection with another equally slight application the shawl was quite sufficient to draw the blood away from the overfilled head.

This second application was generally wet socks, foot-bandages, or a warm foot-bath with ashes and salt.

4. The foot-bandage.

This bandage is always an important auxiliary application, i. e. it is used to assist other applications. We have two kinds of foot-bandages, namely:

a. The foot-bandage proper.

Country people whose time and means are limited, take this bandage in the simplest way, by putting on at night a pair of wet socks, and over them dry woollen stockings, and during the time of application they may lie in bed under a good covering.

If you object to this, you may dip coarse pieces of linen, or a linen-bandage into a mixture of half water and half vinegar, swathe the feet with them to above the ankles, put a dry covering around (a flannel bandage is the best,) and then wrap yourself well up in bed.

The application lasts for one hour, one and a half or two hours, and this time must be spent in bed.

In case of great heat (the application is chiefly intended for the removing of heat, as for instance in case of inflammation of the lungs, or pectoral fever, or inflammation of the bowels) the bandage must be renewed, at every increase of heat.

In all cases where morbid juices are to be extracted from the feet, where the heat is to be taken away, where the blood is to be drawn down from the upper part of the body, this foot-bandage is of excellent service.

Do not confound it, however, with the foot-bath and its effects! The duration of the foot-bath is much shorter, and therefore its effect is more limited. It indeed leads the warmth, the blood, to the feet; but a purification, an evacuation of morbid juices cannot be effected by either a cold or a warm foot-bath.

I must not forget one application of this foot-bandage. If you are able to bear the water-applications at night, put on wet socks before going to sleep; of course dry ones over them. By so doing you will lose no time; you will sleep exceedingly well, and need not trouble about the time of duration. But remember that when awakening in the night, or early in the morning, the wet socks must be taken off at once.

To country people, who are very tired at night, this foot-bandage gives great relief, even more thoroughly than the cold foot-bath.

If you are suffering from cold feet, only try this foot-bandage at night.

I also have often recommended it with success to people with sweating feet, but only after they had taken several foot-vapours.

b. The knee-bandage.

This bandage reaching above the knees operates in the same way as the one described under **a,** but more strongly than the foot-bandage proper.

The wet linen bandage which, when used as foot-bandage, reaches above the ankles, here extends to above the knees, and is well covered with dry, if possible, woollen wrappers.

The time of duration, as well as the other rules, are the same as for the foot-bandage a.

I strongly recommend this bandage, for drawing off heat from the upper body, for removing great weariness, and especially for the loosening of tormenting gases.

It is not to be confounded with the „standing in water to above the knees", which is spoken of with the half baths. That application is only of a strengthening nature, but is powerless to secrete or draw out unhealthy matter.

5. The lower bandage

is thus called, because it is principally employed against complaints of the legs and the lower part of the body. It begins under the arms and reaches down over the feet. Shoulders and arms are not touched and must, when the patient lies in bed, be well covered with the shirt or better still with warmer clothing, in order to keep them warm.

The lower bandage is prepared and applied as follows:

A woollen blanket, as wide as possible, is extended lengthwise on the sheet which covers the mattress or the straw-bed. The linen prepared for the bandage must be. large enough to go round the body twice, in many cases 3 to 4 times, and to reach down over the feet. It is doubled, then dipped in cold water, well wrung out so as no longer to drip, and laid in the form of a rectangle in the bed upon the prepared blanket. The

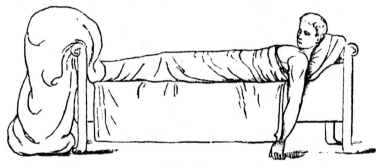

Fig 25

patient lies down on the wet sheet, tucks it in on the right and left side, but in such a way that wet comes on wet, and no part of the body remains uncovered. The blanket, which was laid under the wet linen is then drawn together over this as a protecting and hermetical wrapper; the whole is carefully covered with a feather-quilt. In most cases, an extra covering will be required for the feet. (See fig. 25.)

The matter is not as complicated as it may appear when reading. The whole can be facilitated in this way:

The patient being still out of bed, dressed perhaps with bathing trousers, wraps himself up in the wet bandage according to the prescription, and then lies down on the extended blanket. In order to accomplish all as quickly as possible and to prevent him from being unduly exposed to the air, some one else may easily help him to smoothe the wet bandage, to put it right, to fasten the edges, and lastly to cover the patient carefully.

I know many persons who can, without trouble and in the shortest time (that is the main point), prepare and apply all the larger bandages without any assistance.

One remark may find place here, to take away the horror which may have seized many when reading this.

If you cannot overcome your aversion to the cold water, if you have little natural warmth, tender nerves, etc., you may simply dip the bandage in hot water.

For weakly people, for those who are poor of blood, and especially for the aged, I do not exactly order the dipping into hot water, but I always prefer it.

The application of the lower bandage lasts one, one and a half, sometimes two hours. The feeling of cold which is experienced at first, will soon give way to an agreeable warmth.

Poor country people make a much shorter proceeding of it. They take an old, rather worn out, and therefore less stiff flour-sack, dip it into the water, wring it out thoroughly, and then slip into it to under the arms. In this comical attire they lie down on the extended blanket in the bed, and wrap themselves well up with this and the feather-quilt. Hundreds have tried this kind of „sacking". Don't be ashamed of it; the sack will agree very well with you!

The effects of the lower bandage which is always taken in connection with other applications are various: Warming, dissolving, and evacuating. It produces these effects, as has already been said, particularly on the bowels. Against swollen feet, rheumatics and gout, against complaints of the kidneys, flatulence, cramps etc. it is always used as a valuable auxiliary.

Instead of simple cold or warm water, I very often use decoctions of hay flowers, sour hay, oat-straw, pine-twigs, for wetting the bandages. The sour hay is a substitute for hay-flowers; both of them are good against urinary diseases, and, in a subordinate way, against gravel and stone complaints.

A decoction of oat-straw has always proved of good effect against gout and gravel; decoctions of pine-twigs, for weakly constitutions, for leading out gases and for removing spasms of the bowels.

6. The short bandage

is the one most universally applied. It forms a separate application of itself, i. e. it operates on the whole body without any connection with other water-applications. It raises the natural warmth, and on the other hand takes away the too great heat, according as its application lasts for a longer or shorter time.

„This bandage is worth everything,“ some one used to say; „it is among the bandages what the thiller is among the other horses.“

The advantage that every one can apply it to himself, easily and conveniently, has much contributed to its being liked as a general favourite. The short bandage begins its wrappings like the lower bandage, under the arms, and ends above the knees. A course piece of linen of such a breadth is wetted, wrung out and put round the body closely. A blanket closes the wrapper hermetically, and the feather-quilt brings on the necessary warmth. (See fig.)

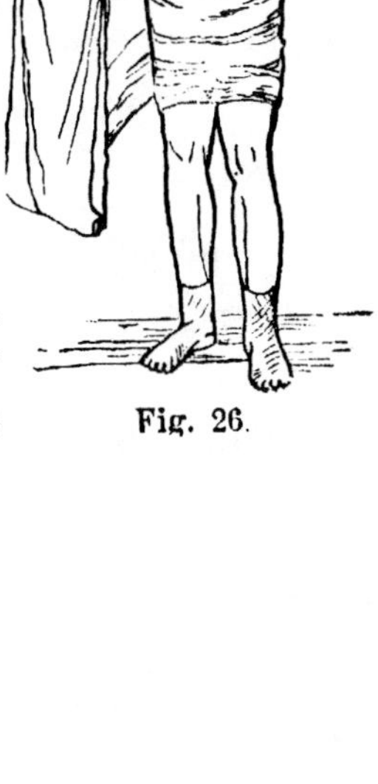

Weak and aged persons and in general all those of poor blood, not only may, but ought to apply the bandage warm.

Fig. 26.

The whole application lasts according to prescription, one, one and a half, sometimes two hours.

If healthy people would take a short bandage every week, or at least every fortnight, they would entirely prevent a great number of diseases. It also operates favorably and in a purifying manner, on the kidneys, the liver, and especially on the bowels, which it purifies from shut up winds, troublesome gases, retained matters, and superfluous water. Dropsy, complaints of the heart and stomach, very often originating in a pressure of gases upwards, and ceasing as soon as the latter are removed, are unknown guests to the friends of the short bandage. I know a number of such true friends, who sleep many a night enveloped in it, and enjoy thereby an excellent rest until morning.

Against phlegm of the stomach, diseases of the heart and lungs, against various complaints of the head and throat, the short bandage finds its manifold applications. Further particulars are to be found in the third part.

Whenever I am in doubt about a complaint, or if I want to ascertain the exact seat of a disease, the short bandage is always my truest and best adviser.

Patients whose bowels are weakened, no matter by what cause, I advice to rub the abdomen either immediately before or after the short bandage, with lard or camphor-oil.

Against cramps, I sometimes order a single piece of linen to be dipped in vinegar and put under the bandage, next to the skin. For cramps accompanied by a feeling of cold, warm bandages are more suitable.

7. The wet shirt

is an often used and much liked application which by its very name sufficiently indicates what is meant by it.

An ordinary linen shirt is dipped in water, wrung out thoroughly, and put on as usual. The patient lies down in bed upon an extended blanket, wraps himself up well, or is wrapped up by some one else, and then covered with a feather-quilt.

I know a gentleman who found even this too com plicated. He stood in a bath, covered with his shirt and had a can of water poured over his whole body. Then he was wrapped in the woollen covers. He could not praise highly enough this „first and best application," and spoke in glorious terms of how it brought on good sleep, and a happy cheerfulness, made the mind brisk, and refreshed the body.

The patient remains in the wet shirt for one, one and a half, or at the utmost two hours. With regard to its effects, I have made the experience that it opens the pores and extracts, like a not too strong vesicatory: that it appeases, removes congestions and spasms, brings on proportionate natural warmth, and highly improves the general health, by its distinguished effects on the skin. I have applied it, with very great success, against dis- temper of the mind, to children suffering from St. Vitus's- dance, and such like cases, and especially against diseases of the skin. If, in the latter cases, strong evacuations were wished for, eruptions such as in scarlet fever etc. to be brought out, I ordered the shirt to be dipped in saltwater, or in water mixed with vinegar.

8. The Spanish mantle.

This strange appellation is not of my invention but, being now universally in use amongst the water-friends of mine, I have no reason to look for another name.

The Spanish mantle, called also the large bandage, is a whole application of itself, like the whole-bath and the short-bandage, because its effects extend to the whole organism. Nevertheless in serious and dangerous illnesses it is always used only alternately with other water- applications.

In what does this greatest bandage consist?

A kind of mantle is made of coarse linen. It resembles a wide shirt, open in front, and reaching down over the toes; it could also be called a wide, long, linen night-gown. (See fig.) This mantle is dipped into cold water, wrung out and put on like a shirt, one part folding well over the other in front. For weaker people, for the aged, for those poor of blood, or afraid of water, the mantle may be dipped into hot water. The bed must be prepared beforehand, so that the woollen covers are ready to receive the cloaked patient. The best way is to spread a very wide blanket, or two smaller ones, broadwise on the mattress or straw-bed. The patient lies down on them, and is then closely wrapped in the blankets and covered with a feather-quilt. (See fig.) It is important that the putting on of the wet mantle and the wrapping up in wool, are done as quickly as possible, in order that the exposure to the fresh air be limited to the shortest space of time possible.

Fig. 27.

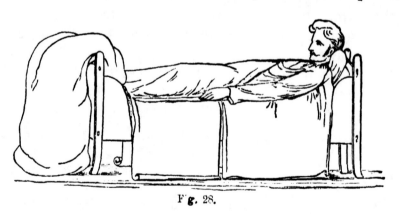

Fig. 28.

Once a patient came to me who was suffering from every possible infirmity. Congestions, hemorrhoids, tormented him, and a fattiness of the heart caused him great anguish. He made it a rule to put on the Spanish mantle once, or twice, a week; and after having done so for some time, all the above named complaints, together with others were, as he called it, blown away. From that time up to this day the gentleman uses the Spanish mantle as a universal remedy; and as he has not much spare time, he puts it on when he goes to bed, and only takes it off when awakening during night, or early in the morning. He had a second Spanish mantle made, of strong woollen material, which served him instead of the blankets, and which made the help of others, for the application, unnecessary.

The time of duration of an application is one, one and a half, or at the most, two hours. It depends on the strength of the individual, but especially on the corpulence. For a weakly country-man one hour, or one hour and a half, will be sufficient; for a brewer, two hours may be prescribed without hesitation.

If you wish to know in what manner, and how strongly the Spanish mantle operates, simply inspect the water in which the bandage, after the application, must always be washed most carefully. You will find it quite thick; you will be astonished, and think it almost incredible, that this bandage is able to extract such dirt. I remember cases where the white linen of the mantle seemed to be dyed yellow, and no lather, but only the bleaching on the grass, could give it back its former colour.

The Spanish mantle thoroughly opens the chief pores of the whole body in the mildest (by no means rugged) manner; it evacuates all dirt, phlegm etc. I need not say how beneficially it must, therefore, operate on the normal temperature of the body, and on the general health.

I especially apply this great bandage in cases of rather general catarrhs, affecting, more or less, the whole body, mucous fever, gout, artic la: disease, small-pox, typhus, to prevent strokes etc. You will find it very often mentioned in the third part, where the various diseases are spoken of.

If the mantle is dipped in decoctions of hay-flowers, oat-straw, or pine-twigs, it operates exceedingly well against complaints (gout, gravel etc.) the healing of which is particular to these plants.

G. Drinking of water.

Regarding this I can be very brief. I caution against two extremes, i. e. against two views, transgressing the right measure. Some decennaries ago, there were water-drinking tournaments. He who could master the highest number of pints ("Masserl"), was the greatest hero. A quantity of 4, 6, 8, 10 pints daily was not at all a rarity. Up to this day the thought is haunting about in many a mind, that much water-drinking must make healthy. Yet this idea is to be preferred to the other, which whispers to the glowing brain that 3, 4, 5 pints of brown barley-water (beer) would not be too much fluid for the quantity of solid food which a person consumes daily!

To people of the second kind it seems that just the contrary of the above said is right; they do not drink any water for weeks, even for months; for in their opinion the drinking of water does no good; they shun the beer: still less would they take wine, which seems to them but a poisonous spirit. I will try to show that here too the golden way lies in the middle between the two extremes.

Some minutes before the clock strikes, it gives a warning. Has then the great Workmaster, our Creator, made something which is only half complete. something which is only a blunder? Or has man brought disorder into His wonderful order? Yes, the latter is the case. The infinitely wise Creator, God, makes the hunger announce itself, when it is time to eat, and the thirst knock, when it is time to drink. The human body, this living watch with the best work, would go without fault, if foolish man would not throw dirt and sand and other filth, between the wheels, and thereby disturb, perhaps even destroy, their regular movement.

Tame and wild animals look out for food as often as they feel hungry; they run to the fresh spring to drink as often as they are thirsty. As soon as they have satisfied their hunger and thirst, they take no more.

Man does just the same by a regular mode of life, whether he be healthy or sick.

Therefore our special and highest principle on this point, a golden principle, which ought to be observed by every one, is this:

Drink as often as you are thirsty, and never drink much!

I know people who, the whole week long, perhaps, do not drink one drop of water; others who, at breakfast, take the usual glass and are satisfied for the whole day. They never feel thirst; the reason is that by our manner of preparing food, a good quantity of water is conveyed to the body daily. Except when caused by great heat in summer, or by such heat as is generally the forerunner of an illness, the real thirst is a rare guest with many people; and to me, at least, it is always a puzzle, how, nevertheless, so many people occasion such real inundations to their poor stomach without any necessity. Such doings cannot, of course, remain unrevenged.*

---

* Here I must say a word about drinking at table, chiefly during dinner. By country people it is scarcely done, at least, not in any great measure. The matter rather concerns town people and those of higher standing. To drink between eating, is not good, people say. I know many physicians, especially such of the ancient school, who advise healthy people against it, and strictly forbid it to their patients. Whosoever has an observing eye and some experience, knows that all those who like much drinking, always complain of bad digestion.

That cannot be otherwise. But why?

While the food is being masticated, it is, or should be, mixed, quite penetrated with saliva, which is prepared for this purpose by special organs, the salivary glands.

It would not be wise to swallow anything solid, 1. e. to bring it to the stomach, before the important preparatory work of crushing and softening is well done. After that, the so prepared food is, in the stomach, soaked with the gastric juice. The purer, the better, the more primitive, i. e. unmixed, this essential juice is, the better the digestion and its results, i. e. the better also the juices and the nourishment which are prepared by digestion and offered to nature for completing and perfecting the different parts of the body.

If, then, some one takes food and pours a strange fluid, be it water, wine or beer, upon it, this food is no longer penetrated by the pure gastric juice; it is, at least, partly, soaked with the supplied water, beer or wine.

Drink as often as you are thirsty, and never drink much!

Country people do not like the heavy shower of rain; they assert that it is not fertilizing, and does more harm than good to the fields. On the other hand, they assure us that those great morning fogs which wet the peasant's hat until it drips, are their dear friends, because they bring and promote the "best fertility".

The body, especially the stomach, requires fluids, in order to dilute its gastric juice, from time to time to augment it, and to become master over all the solid inhabitants. It announces itself every time it is in need; sometimes it knocks gently by a mild desire for water, sometimes it calls, and shouts loudly, by a violent thirst. Then you should always listen to it, let the shouting come from a healthy, or from a sick stomach; but never give it more than is wholesome for it; small quantities at regular intervals; in diseases especially, in the heat of fever, rather take oftener, e. g. every 5 to 10 minutes, one spoonful than a glassful at once. The latter would not appease the thirst, but add a new complaint to the existing one.

If a person applies this overpouring to his stomach 6 or 8 times during one meal, he, first of all, dilutes the gastric juice in such a way that it is no longer fit to serve as a digestive essence; and he further causes his stomach to be filled, or rather tormented, with a 6 or 8 fold food-mixture. How then can he complain if his stomach cries out with pain, if his digestion is bad, which is so often the case!

In what way is the drinking to be regulated?

If you are thirsty before meals, well, then drink! The thirst announces a want of juices. Moreover, the gastric juices are thick and want a dilution.

At table do not drink at all, or very little, in order that the purest gastric juice may soak and penetrate all, even the last mouthful of food.

If, a good time after meals, the food-mixture again wants some fluid to help the stomach to digestion, in other words, if after 1, 2 or 3 hours you are thirsty, you may drink, but moderately.

It is precisely on this point that I have consulted many able physicians; they all perfectly agreed with me, and attributed the multitude of complaints of the stomach, in a great measure, to the transgressions relating to the quantity of drink.

One example of my proceeding may conclude this passage. A person is suffering from costiveness; the bowels are tormented with great heat, and the poor patient with a violent thirst. He thinks he could drink 2, 3 or 4 glasses of water, one after the other; it seems to him as if it were poured into a burning furnace. That I believe; the mass of water goes to the stomach, and then, without touching the suffering part, or influencing it favorably, makes a quick travel through the body, until it comes out entire, and even floats away with it a good quantity of the indispensable gastric juice. Instead of the many glasses of water, let the patient take only one spoonful every half hour during one day. He will experience quite another effect an effect which must necessarily be the result of a rational treatment.

The small quantity of water is soon taken up by the gastric juice, and easily mixed with it. The repetition following every half hour, gives more copious juices, which, flowing through the body and the bowels, in a normal way, cooling, softening and dissolving, soon put an end to all stagnation and constipation. Numberless persons have followed my advice in this point, and they quickly found help. Probatum est!

Much has been said and written lately about the effects of drinking hot water (30 to 35⁰ R. as coffee or tea), especially on chronical diseases. I myself have, years ago, obtained good results when prescribing it to my patients. Who would blame, or condemn a person for preferring the warm water to the cold fresh element! That is simply a matter of taste. I have, however, found by experience that cold, living water, does the same, or even better service. For myself I prefer it to all lukewarm or hot water. Let everyone choose what he likes best!

Part the second.

Apotheca.

———◆◆———

„Benedicite universa germinantia in terra Domino!"
„Let every herb of the earth praise the Lord!"

General remarks and division.

Among all the things which I abhor and hate, the proprietary drugs, the trading with remedies which are kept as a secret by their inventors, hold a prominent place.

No one shall ever reproach me with such a thing. Therefore in this second part, I open all the drawers and cases of my apotheca, and let every one look into them, even to the last little tea-box and the smallest oil-bottle.*

Every chemist's shop contains a great many expensive things; but in mine, there is not much of the extra-ordinary to be found. This I own quite willingly, and instead of a defect, I consider it a great recommendation for my apotheca.

Nearly all my teas, extracts, oils, and powders are prepared from medicinal herbs, which were formerly esteemed, but are now very often despised; herbs which are to be had for a trifle, and which our dear Lord has planted in our own garden, in the fields, many of them

---

* The receipt alone of the secretive oil which is used externally in special cases (never internally) has been reserved to prevent misuse. Even if I were to make it known, people would not derive any benefit from it, because the chemist is not allowed to give it unless the receipt is shown each time, and I myself cannot and dare not forward it, as I am neither a physician nor a chemist.

round our houses, many on remote, unfrequented spots, so that we can gather them free of cost.

I have written my little book first of all for poor sick people, for whose benefit, keeping before my eyes the heavenly reward, I also carry on this troublesome business, or, if you like to put it so, to spoil other people's trade. It was for them that I purposely inquired after the likewise poor old acquaintances, setting aside many other things. For long years, I have examined and experimented, dried and cut up, boiled and tasted. There is not one little herb, or powder, which I have not myself tried and found good. My only wish is that my old acquaintances may be respected again, at least by one class of people.

I have long deliberated before I resolved to add this apotheca to the applications of water, which in themselves are sufficient, lest these remedies which assist the water by operating inwardly, could be looked upon as a vote of mistrust in the water.

But there are patients who, from unconquerable fear of water, would have great difficulty in resolving to make a course of water-applications, often necessary for some considerable time. I wished to facilitate the cure for them, in other words, to reduce the water-applications, to simplify them, and shorten their duration. This can and will be done by giving assistance to the exterior cure (with water) by an interior cure (with remedies).

Those who inspect all the articles of my apotheca, will see at once that they, like the water-applications themselves, have a threefold aim, i. e. to dissolve morbid matters in the interior, to evacuate them, and then to strengthen the organism. Regarding this, I believe I may justly affirm, that both cures, the interior and the exterior, harmonize and work together with perfect unity. I caution people against an illusion.

Whoever thinks that the water-applications are to be used very rigidly and harshly, is mistaken.

Whoever is of the opinion that he ought to use interior remedies often and in great quantities, is likewise mistaken. Always and in all cases, keep to the golden principle: the gentlest application, be it exterior or interior, is the best.*

Plants with doubtful effect, like althea, liquorice wood etc.; with the least unfavourable effects, e. g. on the stomach, like senna-leaves, hops, etc., above all, poisonous plants, I have put aside on principle.**

How good is God! — I cannot help saying it from my inmost heart. He not only makes the earth bring forth all that is necessary for the support of life, for our daily bread, He who in His infinite wisdom has created everything according to measure, number and weight, makes in His paternal love numberless little herbs spring up from the earth in order to bring comfort to man in days of sickness, mitigation and healing to his body convulsed with pain.

How good is God! Oh, that we could recognize it! Let us search for the little herbs which announce themselves by the smelling bottles attached to them by the Creator, the aromatic wholesome scent; and let us, when gathering them, glorify with filial gratitude our infinitely loving Father, who is in Heaven!

---

* There are many patients who think that a great number of medicines, pills etc. must cure them. I remember well a very able physician who ordered as little medicines as possible, and often complained of the foolishness of persons who, against the verdict of the physician, are always crying out for medicines. "If such intolerable fools came and tormented me," he once said, „I gave them pills made of bread with a small, indifferent mixture, simply to give them the smell of chemistry. They took the pills, and when I saw them again, I was sure to learn that these pills, the best they had taken in all their life, had cured them."

** One word about sweets and dainties. When I hear of men tending to such childish things, it makes me feel quite annoyed; if I hear the same of children, I pity the poor creatures, and deplore the shortsightedness or want of watchfulness of the parents. To offer such things to a sick person, would be an inexcusable offence. I absolutely and decidedly condemn all these dainties, whatever their name or reputation may be! The stomach and other parts can be entirely ruined by them.

Our house-apotheca must consist of four chief divisions, and some smaller compartments.

In the chief divisions we put

    In the 1st   the tinctures,

    ,, ,, 2nd (the largest): the different teas,

    ,, ,, 3rd : the powders,

    ,, ,, 4th : the oils.

In the smaller compartments everything not belonging to one of the said four divisions, is to be arranged in good order.

Also the linen pieces for bandages (always clean and fresh), the cotton wool, etc. may be put in one of the smaller compartments.

The tinctures and oils must be kept in bottles; the different teas and powders either in strong paper bags or, which is better, in boxes. (If you order new ones, let them be oval and proportionate, though of different sizes, and put them in ranks like soldiers. This makes the apotheca a pleasure to look at, and gives it a good appearance, and that is due to it too. Keep all in a cool, but not damp place (to prevent mouldering), and not in a too remote part of the house.

Every bottle, every box, or paper bag must have the name of its contents written very legibly on it. The best way is to put the different medicines of every division in an alphabetic order.

Above all great order is to be kept in the apotheca. Any one going to it for the first time, must be able to find in a moment every bottle, every tea, etc. Moreover great cleanliness is required. There must never be found, I will not say a layer of dust, but not even an atom of it on any box; there must not be any stain of dirt or oil hanging down like carelessly combed hair, on any bottle. not even on the oil-bottle.

Nothing is more dishonorable to a house than uncleanness; mark well as a rule: The estimation of a house rests on the condition of two things. If those things are in good order, the conclusion is that everything else is in order too. If the contrary is the case, a less favourable judgement on the inhabitants of the house must be given.

Will you know what things I mean?

They are: Apotheca and closet.

The best way to keep the apotheca in good order will be for the mother or a diligent son, or the most cleanly and orderly daughter to take the care and responsibility of it.

They will look upon it as a matter of honour to keep the strictest and most conscientious cleanliness, and will always have a duster close at hand. If they hold this office well, which will be a benefit to the whole house, to all its members, they may joyfully remember the words of our Saviour: "Inasmuch as you have done it unto one of the least of my brethren, you have done it unto Me."

At the end of this second part, I have mentioned what should generally be found in such a small apotheca.* Do not keep unnecessary things; by and by one or the other remedy may be added.

Here I wish to say a word about the preparation of tinctures, teas, and powders.

Tinctures or extracts.

The interior virtue, the healing juices of a plant can be drawn out in various ways. We get the best and strongest in the real so-called extract.

It is prepared as follows:

Choose from the herbs, berries, etc. of which you wish to get an extract, the very best, the ripest, the most perfect ones, and dry them on a wooden board in the open air, but (remember this well) always in the shade, never in the sun. The drying will show you which are not quite perfect for use.

After having well dried the herbs, berries, etc., cut them in pieces, if necessary, and put them in a bottle (wine-bottle). This is to be filled with real corn-brandy — which I prefer to everything else — or if you cannot

* With every medicine it is precisely said in which form it may be used, whether as extract, powder, tea, oil, etc.

get it, with pure spirit or other brandy, closed hermetically, and kept for some time on a moderately warm spot.*

I have sometimes kept such bottles standing for a year and longer still, and only then poured off the juice of the herbs soaked with the spirit as extract. In case of necessity, you may use it even if it has only been mixed a few days before.

The tinctures are taken by drops, in some cases (it is always expressly said) a tea-spoonful is given as the smaller dose, and a table-spoonful as the greater one.

Teas.

The weather being dry, you may perhaps on your way home from the fields, or when going out to look at your standing crops, take a ramble to gather here one medicinal herb, and there another. Those growing on dry ground, or on the sunny hill-side, are to be preferred; the plants gathered in their best blossom, will bring you the most excellent, and in your sufferings the most beneficial fruit. Many of the herbs are growing in your meadow or kitchen-garden, near your house or your barn. You need only show your ten years old boy or your little girl what to do, then you will not lose any time by gathering the herbs, and will give pleasure to your children.

The garden and field herbs are to be renewed every year, i. e. fresh ones gathered and the old ones thrown away.

Every mother knows how to prepare tea. For one cup she takes as much of the dried herbs as she can hold with three fingers, pours boiling water into the little pan upon the tea-leaves or blossoms, and lets it boil for some minutes, then she pours out the prepared tea.

Prepared in this way tea has the finest taste with the best aroma peculiar to every plant; but it is not the strongest tea.

---

* All the herbs, berries, etc. used for extracts, may also be put in wine, as is said at the place relating to them. This wine, however, is only fit for immediate use, not for long keeping.

In my own apotheca, the herbs are really decocted for a longer time, thoroughly stewed so that not a particle of the healing power is lost, but all is caught in the water.

How it is to be taken, either by cupfuls or spoonfuls, is said with every disease.

Powders.

The powders are prepared by grinding, or by crushing in a mortar the dry roots, leaves, grains, or berries of the medicinal herbs.

Many patients find it easier to take the powders than the teas. The prescribed powder is strewn like a spice (pepper, cinnamon,) on the food, or mixed with a drink, so that the patient does not perceive it.

The vessels in which the different powders are preserved, must be very carefully closed in order to prevent the dust from getting in.

Oils.

The preparation of oils which are not bought at the chemist's, is specially given with every disease for which they are to be used.

It is precisely by the clean appearance of the oil-bottles that the sense for order, cleanliness etc. makes itself known.

Medicines.

The medicines* of which I make use arranged in alphabetical order, are the following:

1. Almond-oil.

The sweet almond-oil deserves one of the first places among the oils in the apotheca. It operates on various infirmities and complaints, interior as well as exterior ones, in a softening, cooling and dissolving manner.

It dissolves phlegm in the wind-pipe, or in the stomach, and in the latter case it restores appetite and digestion.

In inflammations, especially in the dreaded inflammation of the lungs, it cools. Such patients ought to take one teaspoonful of almond-oil, three or four times

Almond tree.

(Amygdalus communis L.)

---

* Illustrations of all plants mentioned in this part are to be found in two enlarged editions, published in English language by the Editor (Kösel, Kempten), and entitled:

An **Atlas of Plants** for Seb. Kneipp's "Water-Cure".

  A-edition with phototypies.
  B-edition with coloured phototypies;

and sold by all booksellers. Apply for a prospect to be sent post-free.

a day. When applied externally, this oil is of especial service to those who suffer from various diseases. The almond oil is to my knowledge the best anodyne and dissolving remedy for such complaints as humming in the ears, sharp pains in the ears, cramps in the ears, obdurate ear-wax. Pour six or eight drops into the suffering ear and stop it with cotton-wool.

If your hearing is becoming difficult through cold, draught, or rheumatism, pour seven or eight drops into one ear, and on the next day pour the same quantity into the other ear each time stopping the ear with cotton-wool. After a few days you may wash the interior of the ear with luke-warm water, and you will see the result. It would be better to let a competent man syringe the ear with an ear-syringe.

Tumours with great heat (inflammation) should be rubbed softly with almond-oil; it will ease the piercing pain and cool the burning heat.

The so-called, often so painful "chinks" of country people, wounds oiginating from sitting, lying or riding, etc., no matter on what part of the body, may be exceedingly well treated by a soft rubbing with sweet almond-oil.

If you cannot get this oil, take salad-oil instead (see page 76).

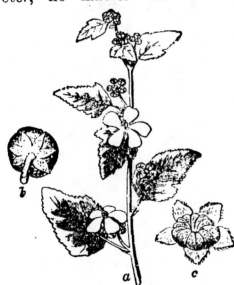

2. Althea.
(Althea officinalis.)

It is much used as tea for colds I do not like it very much, because it has proved deficient to my expectations. Already when boiling it, you get a clammy mass which in a comparatively short time becomes slimy and thereby — which often occurs — must de-

Althea. (Althea officinalis L.).
a. Top of the branch (three eights of its natural growth).
b. fruit seen from the back,
c. fruit seen from the front.

prive the patient of all appetite. I never recommend such medicaments. To speak mildly, herb and root of this althea are somewhat suspicious to me. Therefore I always choose herbs which do the same services without any doubt.

3. Alum.

Alum is corrosive; therefore it is suitable for foul and bad wounds. I have seen how it even prevented a not too far advanced cancer from spreading.

Suppurated, grown-in nails ought to be treated with alum.

The application is as follows:

Alum is either pulverized, i. e. pounded to a fine dust and directly strewn on the wound, or it is dissolved in water, and this solution used in the form of ablutions, or linen wetted with it, is laid on the wound.

When the wounds are quite cleansed from matter and putrid flesh, the alum operates in a contracting, drying, and speedily healing, manner.

Diluted alum water is a proved remedy for teeth on which putrid flesh with stagnant blood has grown.

It is also already known and used for washing mouth and teeth, or as a gargarism.

Anis.
(Pimpinella Anisum L).
a. Plant (the fourth part of its natural growth),
b. top of the blossom,
c. fruit,
d. cross-section of the fruit (six times magnified).

4. Anise. (Pimpinella anisum.)

Anise like fennel is to be recommended highly. Its operation on gases (winds) is far superior to that of fennel. In most cases both remedies are mixed together.

The oils of anise and fennel can best be obtained at a chemist's shop. Against the above named complaint it is sufficient to take four to seven drops on sugar once or twice a day.

5. Barbadoes Aloes. (Aloë vulgaris.)

Barbadoes aloes (the powder is bought at the chemist's) is of good effect both for interior and exterior use.

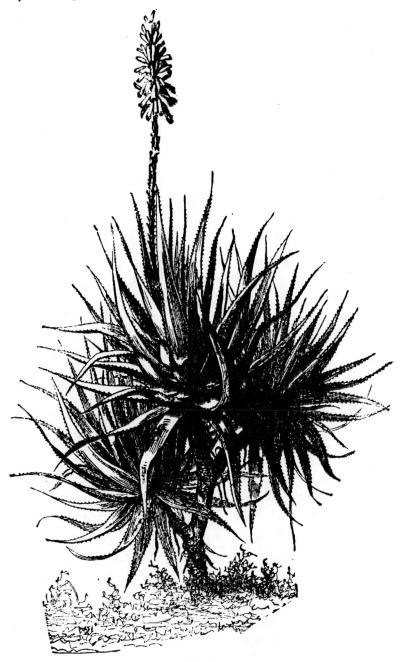

Aloë
(Aloë vulgaris Lam.)

9*

One to two pinches of aloe-powder, boiled with a teaspoonful of honey, thoroughly purify the stomach without the least trouble. If the aloe-powder is mixed with that of other herbs and prepared as tea, its effects are still more lasting. The mixture is generally prepared as follows: One pinch of aloe, sufficient elder-flowers, for two cups of tea; a small tea-spoonful of Foenum graecum, one teaspoonful of fennel. These two cups of tea are to be taken within two days. The effects, which do not consist in violent purging, but only in a copious evacuation of the bowels, appear only after twelve to thirty hours.

An application of aloe with St John's wort and common yarrow, will be mentioned later on.

Aloe shows the same cleansing power for exterior application, as it does when used interiorly. An excellent eye-water may also be prepared from it for diseased, dim, red-edged, blear eyes, which discharge matter and other dirt. A good pinch of this powder is put into a medicine-glass, hot water poured upon it, then shaken, and the eye-water is ready for use. Three or four times a day the eyes are washed with it, both within and without. The irritation and burning which is felt at first is of no consequence. Old wounds, putrified flesh, are exceedingly well cleansed and healed by such water. A piece of linen is for this purpose dipped in the aloe-water and put on the suffering part.

If ulcers, or rather the sharp fluids running from them, prevent the formation of new skin on any part of the body, aloe powder is strewn on the place of the ulcer, thick enough to cover the whole open wound, which is then tied up with dry linen. This is repeated daily. The powder by absorbing the morbid matters forms a solid crust, under which the new skin will soon appear.

Fresh wounds, as well as old ones, are very quickly closed by aloe. Moreover this clean and cleansing remedy can never bring any harm wherever it may be applied, either in an eye or a wound.

6. Bark of oak.

Are we then to use even the bark of oak as a medicine? Certainly, be it fresh from the tree, or dried.

Young bark of oak, boiled for about half an hour, gives a sanative decoction. A small towel is dipped into it and tied as a bandage round the neck; such bandages give great help to people afflicted with thick throats, and even with a goitre, if it has not yet grown too large and firm, this decoction operates as a most effective and harmless remedy. Complaints of the glands are removed just as thoroughly by these bandages.

Whoever is troubled with prolapses of the rectum, may often take sitting-baths with a decoction of oak-bark, and also from time to time an enema of a diluted decoction.

Oak.

(Quercus pedunculata L.)

a Branch with male blossoms,
a. fruit-bearing branch,
c. cross-section of the germ,
d. germ cut lengthwise.

The troublesome and often dangerous fistules on the rectum are dissolved and healed by the decoction.

Also hard tumours, if they are not inflamed, may be treated and dissolved in the same way.

Tea made of oak-bark operates like resin in a strengthening way on the inner vessels.

7. Bilberry. (Vaccinium myrtillus.)

About the end of July it is the children's delight to go to the woods; for then the bilberries are ripe, a favourite fruit with little people. Old children, too, are fond of these berries. In large towns, in the fruit markets, this black fruit is to be found in basketfuls. Many a student's thoughts wander back to the happy years when he used to gather bilberries with his little sister.

No house should be without a good supply of bilberries, dried and put by for the year. They are of manifold use.

Two or three handfuls of bilberries are put into a bottle, and good, real brandy poured upon them. The longer they stand (even for years) i. e. the better they are extracted, the more powerful a medicine will this berry-spirit be. If you are suffering from slight diarrhœa take from time to time some dried, raw berries, chew and swallow them. Very often this mild remedy is sufficient. In large bathing places I have seen patients, who, to prevent disagreeable surprises on their walk, were provided by the experienced and thoughtful landlady with such little diarrhoea-stopping pills.

Bilberry.
(Vaccinium myrtillus.)

a. Flowering plant,
b. branch bearing fruit (both one third of their natural growth),
c. receptacle with stamen, the corolla being removed (twice the natural growth),
d. cross-section of the seed (4 times the natural growth).

Violent, continuous diarrhœa, accompanied by great pains, sometimes with loss of blood, is stopped by taking a spoonful of bilberry brandy in a quarter of a pint of warm water. The same medicine may be repeated after 8 or 10 hours. Another repetition will scarcely be needed. Show me a more harmless, and at the same time more effective remedy in a chemist's shop.

The same bilberry spirit, when taken in cases of dangerous dysentery, assists in a most effective manner the exterior application of water (warm compresses of water and vinegar on the abdomen).

The tincture of bilberries is the first and most indispensible among the tinctures of our apotheca. It is of good effect in all the above named cases, and is always the best helper of the bowels.

The dose depends upon the degree of the disease; the smallest is 10 to 12 drops on sugar, the greater about 30 drops, the greatest a tea-spoonful, taken in warm water or in wine.

8. Bitter Aloe.   (Agave Americana L.)

This plant's home is far away in America. Thence it has been brought to us; and it is not seldom to be seen in the windows of the friends of flowers, standing prominent among all the other plants. It is conspicuous and easily recognized by its very thick, pulpous, and rather long, sea-green and thorny leaves. Blossoms are seldom to be seen on it; but if the effects of the fleshy leaves were known, no flourist would certainly let this exotic plant be wanting among his flowers.

The effects are these:

One of these leaves boiled in water and a cupful of the decoction taken, purges stomach and bowels. This plant is also a remedy for liver complaints and for jaundice, if it is pulverized and a pinch of it taken twice a day.

A leaf boiled with a teaspoonful of honey in half a pint of water and taken in small quantities, will take away interior heat, and will prove especially serviceably in cases, where there are blisters on the palate, or a whooping-cough has arisen from the interior heat. A smal particle of the leaf, boiled with an eggspoonful of honey, takes away the heat from the eyes, if they are

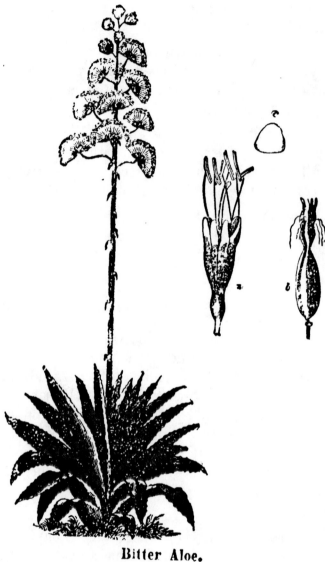

Bitter Aloe.
(Agave Americana L.)

a. Flower, *b.* receptacle after the time of flowering, *c.* cross-section (less than its natural growth).

thoroughly washed with it. If you have hurt yourself, or have got an ulcer on any part of your body, the application of this leaf will relieve you, for it is an excellent remedy.

Worm-wood, boiled with aloe, drives out the bad watery matters, from which dropsy is likely to originate; moreover it improves the stomach.

On account of its many good qualities I advice every lover of flowers to give this plant a place among his flower-pots.

9. Black-thorn-blossoms. (Prunus spinosa.)

Black-thorn-blossoms are the most harmless purgative, and should be found in every apotheca in the first and most easily accessible row.

How often one feels in the stomach, the bowels, the whole body, that a speedy purgative would be good, even necessary; one looks and sighs for an easy remedy, and it could be so easily found.

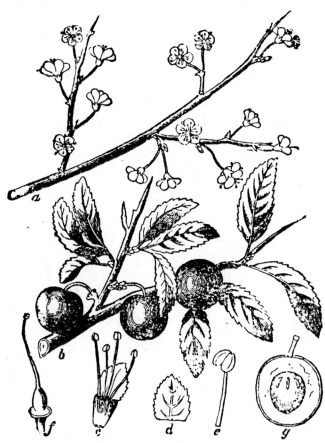

Black-thorn-blossoms.
(Prunus spinosa L.)

a. Flowering branch, b. fruit-bearing branch ($\frac{2}{3}$ of its natural growth). c. part of the calyx, d. sepal of the same, e. stamen; f. pistil, g. stone fruit cut lengthwise in its natural growth.

Take some black-thorn-blossoms, boil them for one minute, and take one cupful of this tea daily, for 3 or 4 days together. It operates gently, without any disagreeableness and trouble, but nevertheless thoroughly. I can strongly recommend this tea as a purifying and strengthening remedy for the stomach.

10. Bog-bean (Menyanthes trifoliata)

is a plant growing on marshy soil and generally near flowing water. Where the water cannot find an outlet and forms smaller or larger puddles, this marsh-plant grows

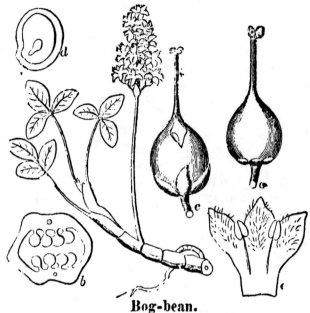

Bog-bean.

(Menyanthes trifoliata L.)

a. Ripe fruit, b. cross-section of the same, c the same bursting (everything twice to 6 times of its natural growth), d. cross-section of the seed (6 times its natural growth), e. part of the flower (twice its natural growth).

among other sour grasses. It has three leaves and a very bitter taste; therefore it is called in German: Bitterklee or bitter-clover. This herb gives an excellent tea for the stomach; it operates well on the digestion and prepares good gastric juices.

Bog - bean, distilled with brandy, produces the so-called bitter-spirit, which has the same good effects.

11. Bone-dust. (See chalk dust.)

I always prepare three kinds of powder from this bone-dust. The first is the so-called:

a. Black powder.

I take the sound bones of healthy killed cattle, and expose them to red heat until they are burnt to coals. These black bone-coals are finely pounded, and the exceedingly simple and harmless black powder is ready. The second kind I keep, is the so-called

b. White powder.

I burn the bones to chalk, i. e. so long until they have the appearance of fresh burnt chalk. It is indeed chiefly chalk that I get then; for the admixed salts or other stuffs are by far the smallest part. The calcined bones are pulverized, and thereby I obtain a powder resembling chalk-dust; it is the so-called white powder. The third kind I call

c. Grey powder.

One part of white, one of black powder, one part of triturated white incense-grains mixed together make a powder of a greyish colour, hence the name.

If you read my remarks about chalk-dust, you will understand why the powder of bone-coals plays a part, and a very important one, in my apotheca.

Its effects are most striking if it is used after serious illnesses or by patients who are much weakened, whose strength is in a very low state. In many cases I myself have been astonished at the results.

Perhaps you may wonder why I prepare three different kinds of powder from the same bones. These three kinds of powder correspond to the different degrees of weakness from which the patients are suffering.

Convalescent people whose whole organism needs strengthening, even children who, like crippled little forest-trees live a miserable existence, and whose strength, no one knows why, is not increasing according to their age (to this class belong especially those children who are suffering from the so-called rickets,) take the black powder every day, either in water or in their food, one or two pinches of it.

I give the white powder to patients with whom it is evident that the machine works but slowly or lazily, that the digestion and the formation of blood are out of order, that many parts of the body get but sparingly and irregularly what is necessary to them for growth and development, that particularly the skeleton is shaking like a decayed brickwork and threatening to tumble down. Like a mother who gives the baby such food as is suitable to its mouth and stomach', I serve, so to speak, the poor hungry bones with bone-dust, in order to keep them together. The grey powder, as the admixture of incense shows, is especially to be given to such patients or convalescent people, whose interior vessels are in a state of great weakness.

Now, my dear reader, you know the secret of the black, white and grey powders, of which many, very many patients could tell you, and about which there has been so much guessing and disputing.

Believe me, by these powders alone I could have become a rich man! I abhor and condemn by principle the secrecy with remedies, and I fully agree with those who brand and condemn it as a sham and quackery.

My remedies have no need to shun the brightest daylight. Let every one examine and choose the best!

12. Bran.

How incomprehensibly we act in many points, is to be seen clearly by our treatment of the bran. Every servant girl gives the bran to the pigs, the bran, which, I should like to say, is more wholesome and nourishing than the flour itself. A housewife would act much more reasonably, if she would keep in her own custody the nourishing and wholesome bran, and impart this precious, nutritious and healthy remedy to her weak children.

Weak, convalescent people and children, like best the food which is easily digested. The weakest nature will be able to digest a decoction of bran, the extract, as it were, of the fruit itself.

Take bran from wheat or rye and boil it for three quarters of an hour in water. Then squeeze out the bran, mix honey with the decoction and boil this mixture again for a quarter of an hour. The patient takes half a pint of this drink twice a day. White bread, dipped into this sweet juice, will be found very enjoyable.

I scarcely know a better drink for children and old people; they will always be thankful for the refreshment.

Would that all of us tried to become more simple, more natural and more easily satisfied! May God grant it; for much depends upon it!

13. Brier.

A mother who takes care of her apotheca, not only picks the pretty roses from the wild rose tree (Rosa canina), but she also carefully gathers the so-called hips, and this not only for making sauces, but also for sanative purposes. She will search with still greater zeal in her own garden or elsewhere, if there is any one in the family suffering from gravel or stone in the kidneys or bladder, these dreadful and painful diseases. She knows that brier-tea will ease the pain and purify the affected parts. .

I know a very old gentleman who in former years had suffered much from gravel and stone, and often did not know what to do, or where to seek for help. This tea was recommended to him, and he got so accustomed to it and so fond of it, that for years past, the usual cup is never allowed to fail at night before going to bed; he likes it better than a glass of the best wine.

Brier.
(Rosa canina L.)

„These are my spiritous liquors," he said; „this is the oil which keeps the almost stopping machine of my old body working from day to day."

The husks are taken from the hips; then dried and the tea prepared from them.

14. Camomile. (Matricaria chamomilla.)

Camomile tea is used for colds, especially if they are attended by fever, for gripes, cramps, strong congestions, etc.

The little bags with camomiles, which are so useful for warming in various cases, are so well known and liked in every house, that it seems quite unnecessary to say anything further about them.

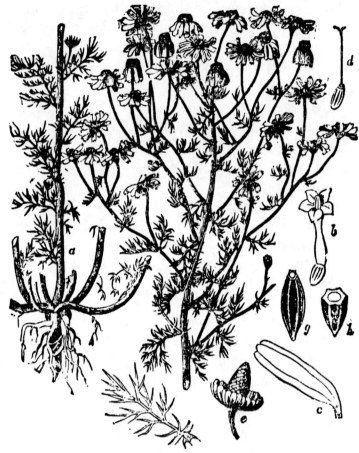

Camomile.

(Matricaria Chamomilla L.)

a upper and lower part of the plant (half its natural growth), b. central yellow flower, c. outer white flower, d. pistil magnified, e. calyx and bottom of the flower, f. leaf (natural growth), g. fruit, h. cross-section of the same (magnified).

15. Camphor. (Laurus Camphora.)

The application of camphor is generally known and used. It operates in a softening, alleviating and lenitive manner.

It is used as camphor-spirit and camphor-oil.

Camphor-spirit is prepared by dissolving a piece of camphor, as large as a hazelnut, in half a pint of spirit, and is only used externally as embrocation for contusions, sprains, rheumatics, and spasms.

Many people use it as a strengthening remedy for the limbs, they are quite right in doing so.

Camphor, pounded with olive-oil, salad-oil or almond-oil until it is dissolved, is called camphor-oil. It is an excellent remedy for rheumatism and pains in the back; it also soothes the violent pains, caused by the various kinds of rheumatism and similar tumours and cartilages.

Camphor.
(Laurus Camphora L.)

a. Stem (one third of its natural growth). b. corolla (3 times its natural growth, c. corolla extended (3 times its natural growth), d. stamen (6 times the natural size).

Caraway (Carum carvi) see Fennel. Page 155.

16. Centaury. (Erythraea centaurium.)*

What remarkable names were given by our forefathers to many herbs! And this was because they well knew their value. Our herb therefore, must have been highly valued by them. Its use is already indicated by its very bitter taste.

Tea from centaury evacuates the gases retained in the stomach, drives away useless and unhealthy acids, assists and improves the gastric juices, and operates advantageously on the kidneys and liver. It is the best remedy against heart-burn.

* In German it is called „Tausendguldenkraut" that means a herb of a thousand florins worth.

Whosoever is suffering from disturbances in the blood, especially from poverty of blood, or too strong circulation, etc., will obtain relief from the centaury.

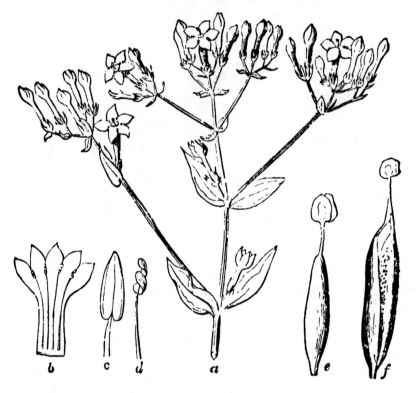

Centaury.

(Erythraea Centaurium L.)

a. Flowers, b. cut and unrolled flower, c. young stamen, d. old stamen, e. pistil,
f. ripe fruit.

17. Chalk-dust.   (See bone-dust.)

Who has not noticed how fowls and domestic animals swallow grains of chalk or mortar?

And who has not heard how it is necessary to hide the chalk in school, as many a child would take it away and eat it like sugar, with a passionate delight.

Should not the chalk indeed be useful to man in many cases? The above mentioned occurrences lead to mature reflections. I have used great quantities of chalk myself and advised others to use it; and the results were remarkable, i. e. extremely favourable.

The chalk contains lime, sulphur, and other substances, or rather let us say building materials, which are necessary to the human body especially for building up the skeleton, this splendid and wondrous building of the most able architect.

With weak people the building might perhaps be a failure or be wanting in solidity; there is, as it were, no good lime to join sand, stones, and everything else together.

To such persons, even to very weak children, I give a pinch of chalk-dust once a day, in water, or in their food. The dust having neither taste nor smell, can be taken without difficulty.

Whoever is suffering from a weak digestion, who in general cannot grow and thrive properly in spite of every care bestowed upon him, may try every day the indicated pinch of chalk-dust.

"Here gypsum has been strewn," was written by Franklin in large letters on his splendidly flourishing cloverfield with such or at least similar chalk-dust. Such or such a person has been chalked, I could say of many patients who fell into my hands.

But before all other patients I recommend this white dust to chloroties; they ought to take daily not only one, but two pinches of dust, one early in the morning, the other at night. By this white powder their own white colour will soon be transformed into a healthy, bright red.

Still more effective than chalk-dust is bone-dust.

18. Cloves.

Clove-oil operates in a similar manner as almond and salad-oil, with which it is also frequently mixed.

It has proved of especial service to me against foul gases, and bad, foul juices in the stomach.

As a rule four to six drops of clove-oil are taken on sugar once or twice a day. (See page 146.)

19. Coal-dust.

Coal-dust is always made of charcoal. The finest and best is that obtained from linden-wood, which is prepared even by many chemists. If linden-wood cannot be had, any other charcoal will do. The coal just taken out of the fire, is the most effective. To obtain the above-named coal-dust, it must be thoroughly pounded.

After diseases which have strongly affected the digestive organs, this coal facilitates the work of convalescence a great deal. It may sound strange, but it is true! The easiest way to take it in such cases, is with milk and a little sugar. The quantity may be a small tablespoonful daily; it can be taken all at once or in two portions.

Cloves.
(Eugenia caryophyllata Thunb.)

Consumptive persons may take daily at different times, two pints of milk, with a tablespoonful of coal-dust mixed with each pint.

It is of special effect against diseases of the liver. The powder is then also taken with milk.

This powder strewn on suppurating, discharging ulcers, once or twice a day, dries them up, and thus assists and hastens the formation of a new skin.

20. Cod-liver oil.

An able physician of the army once expressed himself to me thus: "With cod-liver oil great mischief is done, and the use of bad cod-liver oil has often been followed by very grievous consequences. There are islands where it is of use as a remedy for scrofulous complaints, but on the whole I reject it."

Of course, no one is bound by this opinion. For my own part I never make use of cod-liver oil; for I do not consider it a remedy, and as I am afraid of bad cod-liver oil as food, I replace it by other kinds of nourishment, which are far more effective.

21. Colt's-foot. (Tussilago Farfara.)

The creator has made many plants, which are so little esteemed or even despised by man, that every one seems to find pleasure in treading them under foot. This is the fate of the colt's-foot, because it is generally looked upon simply as a weed. But those who know this plant, esteem it highly, and take care of it as an excellent remedy.

Colt's foot.
(Tussilago Farfara L.)

a. Flowering plant (half of its natural growth), b. plant with leaves (one third of its natural growth), c. calyx and receptacle, d. female floret as in the ray (magnified), e. hermaphrodite floret as in the disk (magnified).

To purify the chest and the lungs, it is advisable to drink tea from colt's-foot. Asthma and coughs can be removed very easily by the remedy, especially if an inclination to consumption exists. You may put these leaves on the chest, either in a piece of linen or without it. They extract the heat, stop feebleness, and remove fevers. They have an especially good effect on open wounds; they remove the heat, the redness, and draw out the injurious matters.

The leaves are most effective against sore feet, when the spots look black and blue, and are srongly inflamed; they take away the heat and the pains; if laid on the sores repeatedly, they are an excellent remedy. Therefore the colt's foot is a superior remedy for inflamed wounds, erysipelas, and similar complaints. These leaves can also be used interiorly, if dried in the shade, pulverized and taken two or three times a day. A small salt-spoonful is a dose; it may also be taken with the food.

22. Common Elder.

In the good old times the elder-bush stood nearest to the house, but now it is in many ways displaced and rooted up. It ought to stand near every house as part of the household, as it were; or if cast aside it should be brought back to its post of honour, for every part of the elder-tree, leaves, blossoms, berries, bark and roots are all efficacious remedies. In spring time, vigorous nature strives to throw off matters that have gathered together in the body during winter. Who does not know these states, the so-called "spring diseases", such as eruptions, diarrhœa, colic, and such like?

Whoever wishes to purify juices and blood by a spring course of medicine, and to get rid of injurious matters in the easiest and most natural way, let him take six or eight leaves of the elder-tree, cut them up small, like one cuts tobacco, and let the tea boil for about ten minutes. Then take daily during the whole course, one cup of this tea, fasting, an hour before breakfast.

This most simple blood-purifying tea cleanses the machine of the human body in an excellent manner, and with poor people it takes the place of the pills and Alpine herbs, and such like which now-a-days are found in fine medicine chests, and which have often very strange effects.

This course may also be undertaken at any other time of the year. Even the withered leaves make a good purifying tea.

Common Elder.
(Sambucus nigra L.)

Who has not eaten cakes made with elder-flowers, the Suabian so-called "little cakes"? Many people bake them just at the time when the tree is shining in its white spring-adornments, and they say these flower-cakes are a protection against fever. I know a place which is often visited with the ague, and there in spring you will see these elder-flower or fever-cakes on every table. I have never examined this minutely and critically; let those people remain in their faith, for such fare is good and wholesome.

Elder-flowers also purify, and it would be good if in every home-dispensary a box of dried flowers were kept. Winter is long, and cases can occur in which such a dissolving and sudorific little remedy may prove of excellent service. Harm can never be done by it.

From organisms in which dropsy has commenced, elder-root prepared as tea, drives out the water so powerfully, that it is scarcely excelled by any other medicament.

The berries which in autumn are often boiled and eaten as porridge or marmalade, were highly esteemed by our forefathers as a blood-purifying remedy. My departed mother undertook such an elder-flower course every year for a fortnight to three weeks. This was the chief reason why our ancestors forty or fifty years ago, had at least two elder-trees planted before their houses. As the higher classes now-a-days travel, and often to distant lands, to make use of the expensive grape cure, so our parents and grand-parents used to go to the elder-tree which was close at hand, and which served them so cheaply and often much better than the expensive grapes. Some years ago, I was among the Austrian Alps, and saw there to my great joy how the elder-tree was still honoured. "Of that," said on old peasant to me, "we do not let a single berry go to waste." How simple, how sensible! Even the birds before they commence their autumnal travels seek out everywhere the elder-trees in order to purify their blood and strengthen their nature for their long journey. What a pity that man, on account of art and affectation no longer feels or takes notice of all these natural instincts, "the sound mind!"

If the berries are boiled down with sugar, or better still with honey, they will prove especially good in winter time for people who have but little exercise and are condemned to a sedentary mode of life. A spoonful of the above preserve stirred in a glass of water, makes the most splendid cooling and refreshing drink, operates on the secretion of the urine, and has a good effect on the kidneys.

Many country people dry the berries. But whether these dried berries are boiled as porridge, or stewed to eat, or eaten dry, in all forms they are an excellent remedy against violent diarrhœa.

Because the exceedingly good services rendered by the elder-tree, are no longer remembered; this faithful and formerly so highly esteemed house-hold friend is in many ways rejected. May the old friend be brought once more to honour!

23. Common Nettle. (Urtica doica L.)

The common nettle is the most despised among the plants. Many delicately nerved souls are stung and burnt on hearing the mere name of it. Are they right? I heard lately that a herbalist, I believe in Bohemia, wrote a whole pamphlet on nettles and their importance. He starts on the right path again, I perfectly agree with him! Nettles are indeed for the connoisseur of the greatest value.

Common Nettle.
(Urtica dioica L.)

a. male plant, b. female plant (half its natural growth), c. male flower, d. female flower, e. the latter open (magnified).

Fresh nettles just gathered, dried and made into tea loosen the phlegm in the chest and lungs, cleanse the stomach from matters gathered there, which they expel chiefly by means of the kidneys.

The roots of the nettle operate even more powerfully than the leaves, whether they are used freshly dug up in summer or dried in winter. Dropsy in its first stages can be cured by tea made from nettle roots.

Those who have bad blood, should in summer eat frequently nettles boiled like spinach. In Italy the people are especially fond of herb soups. Herb dumplings made with nettles are nourishing and wholesome. Let those who are suffering from rheumatism and who can no longer find any remedy for it, rub or strike the suffering part with fresh nettles for a few minutes daily. The fear of the unaccustomed rod will soon give way to joy at its remarkable healing efficacy.

Cowslips.
(Primula officinalis L.)
a. Complete plant, b. calyx, c. and d. corolla, e pistil, f. fruit (magnified).

24. Cowslips. (Primula officinalis L.)

Only the dark yellow cowslips are valuable for the house apotheca. Their perfume already betrays that a special healing fluid must be hidden in each tiny chalice. If you chew two or three of these little funnels you will soon feel what medicinal contents they hide. Whoever has an inclination to articular diseases or is already afflicted with this infirmity should drink daily, for some considerable time, one cupful of cowslip tea. The violent pains will give way, and gradually disappear altogether.

25. Dwarf Elder.   (Sambucus ebulus L.)

On the borders of woods, especially in parts which have been thinned, the dwarf elder may be seen standing above three feet high, bearing in July the great white umbellar blossoms, and in autumn the splendid, heavy, and bright umbellar grapes.

Tea prepared from such roots, expels the water, and purifies the kidneys, it is therefore of extraordinary effect in cases of dropsy. I know several cases in which the rather advanced disease has been entirely cured by such tea.

Also against other complaints in the abdomen, springing from bad juices, it operates well: it removes the juices through the urine.

Dwarf-elder tea prepared from the powder has the same effect.

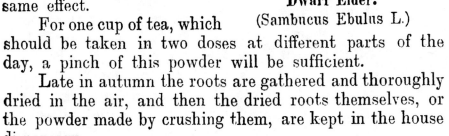

Dwarf Elder.
(Sambucus Ebulus L.)

For one cup of tea, which should be taken in two doses at different parts of the day, a pinch of this powder will be sufficient.

Late in autumn the roots are gathered and thoroughly dried in the air, and then the dried roots themselves, or the powder made by crushing them, are kept in the house dispensary.

26. Eyebright.   (Euphrasia officinalis L.)

As a reward, and out of gratitude for its faithful services, our forefathers gave this little herb the pretty name of "Eyebright" (in German, "Augentrost" = Eyes' comfort). Often when no other remedy would help, this little flower gave to the eyes the last comfort. I have very often recommended it, and with good results.

When the aftermath harvest is half-ripe about **August**, you will find this salubrious little herb on almost every meadow. It is often disliked by the farmers on account of its crowding out the forage plants with its plentiful growth. Both the dried and the pulverized leaves are used as tea and as powder. The eyes are well washed with the tea two or three times daily, or little pieces of linen are dipped into it, and fastened over the eyes by means of a bandage during the night. It will cleanse the eyes, make them clear, and strengthen the sight.

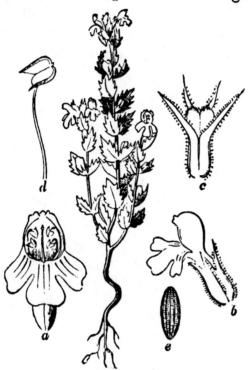

Eyebright.

(Euphrasia officinalis L.)

a. Flower seen from the front,
b. flower seen from one side,
c. fruit in the calyx (three times their natural growth.)
d. a stamen, } six times their natural growth.
e. a seed,

According to my practice, I let the patient make interior use of the powder at the same time, by taking daily a pinch of it in a spoonful of soup or water. But this does not exhaust the healing power of the little herb. It might also be called the stomach comfort. On account of its innate bitterness, its tea is good as stomachic bitters for regulating the digestion and improving the juices of the stomach. Just give it a trial, dear reader; the little herb will not be niggardly with its comfort to you.

27. Fennel. (Fœniculum officinale All.)

The fennel corns must not be wanting in any home-dispensary as the complaint for which they bring help so frequently occurs; I mean the colic with its attendants, the spasms. The mother quickly boils a spoonful of fennel in a cup of milk from five to ten minutes, and gives the potion to the patient as warm as possible (never too hot that the inside may not be burnt).

Its effects are mostly very good and very quick. The quickly spreading warmth eases the spasms, the colic abates, and disappears.

Exteriorly there should be, as is given in other places, a warm compress of water and vinegar (in equal quantities) laid on the abdomen.

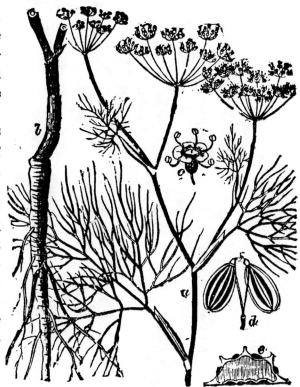

Fennel-powder, sprinkled as spice on the food, removes the gases from the stomach and the lower regions.

The powder is made by roasting (drying) the corns, and then grinding them in an ordinary coffee mill. Fennel oil is obtained at the chemist's. Fennel, used as eye-water, does not appear as anything new to many a reader who has been cured by it.

Half a table-spoonful of fennel-powder is boiled with water, and the

Fennel.
(Foeniculum officinale All.)

a. Stem, top, b. stem and root, c. flower, d. fruit burst open, e. cross-section of one half of it.

eyes are washed with the decoction about three times a day.

The eye-vapours operate in a still more cleansing and strengthening manner.

I always add one or at least one half spoonful of fennel-powder to the water used for the head-vapour; in this manner every head-vapour serves as an eye-vapour at the same time.

Similar effects as from fennel are obtained from anise and caraway. Oftentimes two or even all of these three medicinal corns are mixed, ground together and used.

28. Fenugreek. (Fœnum græcum.)

Of the seed of this plant a powder is prepared with which many of those who use my water-applications are well acquainted. They appreciate, and make use of it. The powder is quite harmless, and may be used without the least fear.

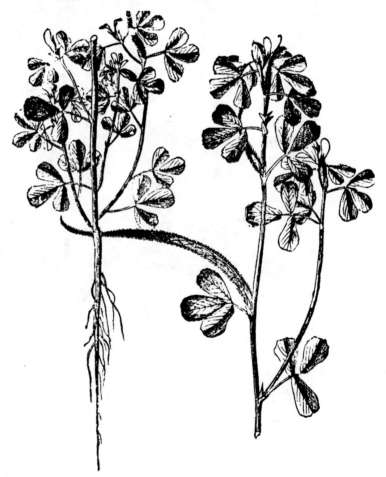

Fenugreek. (Fœnum græcum.)

On the inside it works as a cooling remedy in fever. In throat complaints with great heat in the throat, the tea affords a good gargle. A teaspoonful of the powder is sufficient for a middle-sized cup of tea, which is either drunk or used as gargle during the day (every hour or oftener, one tablespoonful.)

As to exterior application, Fenugreek is the best of all remedies for dissolving tumours that I know of. It works slowly, painlessly, but lastingly and thoroughly. It is applied in a manner similar to linseed; the powder mixed with water is boiled to a paste, and put on the suffering part in linen rags.

In cases of wounds on feet these poultices heal the inflamed margin of the wound, and prevent the formation of putrid flesh as well as blood-poisoning.

Fœnum graecum can be bought at every chemist's.

29. Gentian. (Gentiana lutea L.)

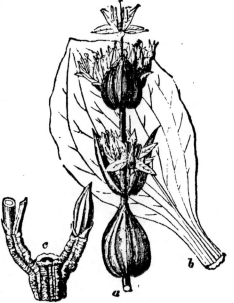

Gentian.
(Gentiana lutea L.)

a. Top of the stem with flowers (half its natural growth), b. leaf, c. part of an underground stem (very much smaller than its natural growth).

The yellow gentian is found particularly on the montains, but you can easily and with very little cost get trustworthy people to gather it for you. Before all, I advise you to prepare extract of gentian. The gentian roots are for this purpose well dried, cut small, and then put into bottles with brandy or spirit.

This extract is one of the best stomachics. Put six to eight table-spoonfuls of water into a glass, and pour in twenty to thirty drops of extract; take this mixture daily for some time. The good digestion will soon be indicated by a no less good appetite. If the food is felt to lie heavy in the stomach, and is troublesome, a little cordial made with a teaspoonful of extract in half a glass of water, will soon stop the disorder.

Gentian is likewise very good for cramp in the stomach. When, after a long journey, during which for days together eating fares badly and drinking still worse, people arrive at their destination dead tired and almost ill, a tiny bottle of gentian tincture taken by drops on sugar, will render excellent services.

Nausea and attacks of faintness are removed by taking a teaspoonful of tincture in water; it warms, enlivens, and brings body and mind to peace again.

Gentian utilized as tea renders similar services. Either the cut up roots or the gentian powder itself, are boiled and the decoction taken as tea.

30. German Leopard's-bane.

(Arnica montana L.)

Arnica is renowned throughout the world as a superior medicinal plant. It is beyond my comprehension why this fact is disputed by so many who could testify its truth, or ought to do so.

As tincture of arnica is so well known, and in such general use for the washing of wounds, for compresses, etc. it does not seem necessary for me to say anything further about it. The tincture is not expensive, but any one can easily prepare it himself. The blossoms are gathered at the end of June or the beginning of July, and put in brandy or spirit. In about three days, the tincture may be used.

German Leopard's-bane.
(Arnica montana L.)

31. Grains of resin or incense.

As the drops fall from a burning candle, so resin often drips from the bark of the fir or the pine tree. Any one going into the woods in summer or autumn, can see these drops, looking like suspended tears, white as wax, clear as honey, and fresh as spring water.

Resin is the blood of the fir and pine, and when such powerful trees are wounded, they often bleed profusely.

This resin which adheres so firmly, and to all appearance contains precious granulous matter, must surely have a special healing power. Five to six of such resin globules or resin-tears about the size of a pea, taken daily for some time as pills, strengthen the chest and operate in a remarkably strengthening manner on the interior vessels. I knew a very weak priest who used to take a good quantity of this resin fluid every day. "I owe the strength of my chest," he often said, "to this strong syrup."

Those who do not live where these resin pills can be obtained, may take instead of them grains of incense of the white kind. Incense is only a superior resin. Six to eight of such grains are a good cure for the chest. The fear of not being able to digest these little resin stones, as a high imagination might call them, must not alarm you; nature can work such goods very well indeed.

32. Honey.

The former generations maintained that young people should by no means take much honey, it being too strong for them; on the contrary, old people were "helped on their legs again" by it.

I have made manifold use of honey, and have always found its effects excellent. It operates in a dissolving, purifying and strengthening manner.

It has long been used as an admixture with tea for catarrh and obstructions of phlegm.

Country people know well how to apply honey ointment for exterior sores or ulcers. I strongly advise those who are not skilful enough to treat such sores with water, to make use of this simple, harmless and effective remedy rather than of any other smearing stuff. The preparation is most simple. Take equal portions of honey and white flour, and stir them well together by means of a little water. Proper honey ointment should be solid, not liquid. Honey is also a good interior remedy for different lesser complaints. Smaller ulcers in the stomach are quickly contracted, broken, and healed by it. I would not advise honey to be taken by itself, but I strongly recommend it taken mixed with a suitable tea. Without admixture this superior extract operates too strongly; before it has passed the throat, it has made it already quite "rough".

If on account of catarrh, or any other similar complaint, swallowing becomes difficult, let a teaspoonful of honey be boiled in a cup of water; by so doing, every singer will obtain the best and sweetest gargle.

Even if a drop happens to go down, there is no need to be afraid of injuring the stomach, or of poisoning.

The purifying and strengthening honey-water for the eyes is well known. Boil a teaspoonful of honey in a cup of water for five minutes, and it is ready for dipping in the linen for the eyes.

I know an old gentleman above sixty years of age, who prepares his daily table-wine. He puts a tablespoonful of pure honey into boiling water and lets it boil for a while, and the drink is ready. It is said to be wholesome, strengthening, and relishing. "I owe my health and my vigorousness in my old age," said he, "to this honey-wine." May be! This much I know from my own experience (I have prepared a great deal of honey-wine, seen a great deal of it drunk, and sometimes drunk a glass of it myself): it is dissolving, purifying, nourishing, and strengthening; and it is good not only for the weak sex, but for the strong sex too. It always reminds me of the honey-mead of the ancient Germans.

To these unadulterated beers, as Tacitus relates, they attributed their health and their great age. Whoever as a true son of our ancient fathers feels so inclined, can find the recipe for this now unused drink on page 198.

33. Juniper. (Juniperus communis L.)

Who does not know the Juniper-berry?

Juniper, when used for fumigation, spreads an agreeable odour through the rooms and passages, and improves the air. I am no friend of the so-called "fumigation" with sugar, vinegar, etc. for I do not see how one can speak of fresh air there. But if it is a question of disinfecting a room in which a patient with an infectious disease, or a corpse has been lying, or at the time of infectious illnesses to purify the air by fumigating, then I always like such juniper-vapour. It thoroughly destroys all fungi, and whatever the volatile infection and disease-bringer may be called.

Juniper works with similar effects upon the interior of the human organism. The berries fumigate, as it were, the mouth and stomach, and ward off contagion.

Those who are nursing patients with serious illnesses, as scarlet fever, small-pox, typhus, cholera etc.

Juniper-berry.
(Juniperus communis L.)
Shrub or tree 3 to 28 feet high
Fruitbearing branch (smaller than natural growth):
a. male flowers, b. female flowers (almost natural
growth), c. seed capsule, d. the same cut lengthwise.

and are exposed to contagion by raising, carrying, or serving the patient, or by speaking with him, should always ch w a few juniper-berries (six to ten in a day). They give a pleasant taste in the mouth, and are of good service to the digestion. They burn up, as it were, the harmful miasms, exhalations, etc. when these seek to enter through the mouth or nostrils.

Those who are suffering from a weak stomach, may try the following little course with juniper-berries.

The first day they should begin with 4 berries, the second day take 5 berries, the third day 6, the fourth 7, and so increase by one berry every day until the twelfth, on which they will take 15 berries; then they may continue for five days longer taking each day one berry less. I hnow many whose stomach, filled with gases and thereby weakened, has been purified and strengthened by this simple berry-cure. Juniper berries have been noted since olden times as a remedy for stone and gravel, and for complaints of the kidneys and liver; also in all cases where foul gases, foul, watery and slimy matter are to be removed from the body. Not only the berries, but also the young shoots of the juniper bush are made use of for tea, in the first stages of dropsy, and also as purifying medicine.

The oil is best bought from the chemist. The tincture can be made at home with wine, brandy, or spirit.

I would not praise the father or mother of a family, who were certainly very careful and diligent in preserving their meat and vegetables with berries from the juniper bush, and were punctual and careful in fumigating their dwelling with the same, but who allowed their body, the dwelling of their soul, to lie in dust and dirt. They ought to apply such a fumigator for this much more important dwelling, at least a few times in the year.

34. Knot-grass. (Polygonum aviculare L.)

There grows a little plant quite unnoticed, generally near houses, but especially on farms, and also along the edges of lanes; it bears the name of knot-grass. It is so called, because on every joint there is a little knot.

This herb, the stem of which has many sprouts, reaching a length of twenty inches, or even more, works with great effect on stone-disease, if one or two small cupfuls are taken daily.

A gentleman had for years together, great pains in his kidneys, and from time to time sand and gravel came away. He drank this tea for several days, and related that hundreds of larger and smaller stones were discharged, and thereby the pain also disappeared. As this plant expels gravel from the kidneys and bladder, it also operates in a purifying manner on the liver, stomach, and chest. This little herb cannot be sufficiently recommended

Knot-grass.
(Polygonum aviculare L.)

35. Lavender-oil.

Lavender-oil is sold at any chemist's. It should not be wanting among the home-remedies.

Five drops taken on sugar assist the digestion, and give a good appetite:

Those who are troubled with wind, with headache caused by rising gases, or with nausea, take this oil as given above. I have often used it with the best results for those afflicted with mental derangement, and I maintain that, in very many cases, the cure depends upon the removal of the gases, which have especially bad effects on the brain. In my opinion much too little attention is generally paid to these gases in the treatment of such patients.

Those who have ever suffered from flatulency know what a dreadful part these raging winds play in the body.

11*

Lavender. (Lavandula vera DC.)

a. Plant in natural growth,
b. calyx seen from the back (three times its natural
   growth),
c. flower cut open,
d. flower seen from the front, opened.
e. stamen,
f. stamen,
g. ovary with style,
h. fruit (6 times its natural growth).

} 10 times their natural growth,

Against loss of appetite, congestions, giddiness, and all the many different sufferings of the head, the dose indicated in the beginning of this paragraph will afford great relief.

36. Limetree-blossoms.

(Tilia grandifolia and parvifolia Ehrh.)

It is almost solely the elderly people of the old school who still gather the once so well liked limetree-blossoms. They are quite right, and need only remain conservative with regard to their old custom.

Lime-blossom-tea together with elder-blossom-tea are the best known teas for producing perspiration. Concerning perspiring, as it is usually carried on, I have my own particular opinion, which is not at all in its favour. On the other hand, I willingly use the blossoms for the vapours which produce, and supply the place of perspiration.

Lime-blossom-tea has excellent effects on such complaints as old coughs, obstructions of the lungs and wind-pipes, troubles of the abdomen which have their origin in obstructions of phlegm in the kidneys.

Instead of the limetree-blossoms, I use the St. John's-wort with or without admixture of common yarrow; see St. John's-wort page 182.

Limetree-blossoms.
(Tilia grandifolia and parvifolia Ehrh.)

37. Linseed. (Linum usitatissimum L.)

Linseed poultices are everywhere known, and in general use. The effects obtained by it (cooling, softening, dissolving,) are the same as those of the Foenum graecum. I prefer the latter as it seizes the enemy with more vigour and energy. (See page 166.)

38. Mallow. (Althaea rosea L.)

Among the flowers in the garden, mallow must not be missing. When the good creator painted their blossoms, so pleasing to the eye, he poured a drop of medicinal sap into the paint for every little leaf.

Mallow-blossoms, especially those of the black mallow prepared as tea, cure throat infirmities, and loosen the phlegm on the chest. These blossoms are generally mixed with those of the mullein.

Mallow.
(Althæa rosea L.)

For vapours, whether it be for inhaling, or particularly for ear-vapours, the mallow proves of great service.

39. Mint.

(Mentha piperita L., and Mentha aquatica L.)

Peppermint and water - mint are both fit for use, and have very little difference in their effects. I prefer the water-mint whose effects are stronger. The mints are counted among the principal remedies

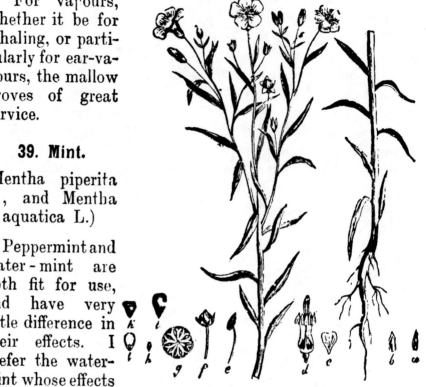

Flax. (Linum usitatissimum L)

a. and b. sepals, c. petal, d organs of reproduction, e. stamen. f. fruit, g. section of a capsule, h. seed, i. the same magnified, j. cross-section of the same, k. the same cut lengthwise.

for strengthening the stomach and assisting the digestion. Their spicy scent already indicates that this little herb must occupy an important place among medicinal plant.

If those who are suffering from violent headache. bind mint across their forehead, they will soon experience relief and ease.

A cupful of mint - tea taken every morning and evening, assists the digestion and gives a fresh and healthy appearance.

The powder renders the same service if one or two pinches are taken daily in the food or in water.

People weakened by illness, seized with palpitation at every trifle, suffering much from nausea and frequent vomiting, should frequently make use of mint-tea and mint-powder.

Mint-tea prepared with half water and half wine, and a cupful taken daily for several days, takes away a bad breath.

Peppermint.

(Mentha piperita L. et Mentha aquatica L)

Mint-decoction, prepared with vinegar, stops blood vomiting.

Mint, prepared in milk or tea, and drunk warm, removes abdominal pains.

Would that every house-wife would give this noble little plant, (together with the rue) a corner in the garden! They would reward the little trouble by the refreshing perfume which they so generously exhale at every touch.

40. Mistletoe.   (Viscum album L)

This parasite, which thrives particularly well on old trees, is nevertheless an excellent medicinal plant. I cannot impress it strongly enough upon mothers to make acquaintance with this plant.

It is of especially good effect on the blood. Flux of blood is stopped by the tea from mistletoe. I could give a list of cases in which a single cup has been sufficient for this purpose.

Also for other disturbances in the circulation of the blood, this plant and its perfectly harmless tea may be made use of.

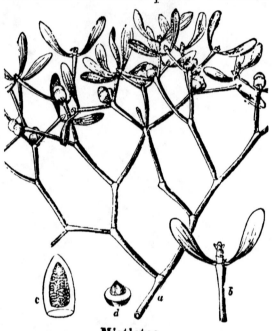

Mistletoe.
(Viscum album L.)
a. branch [half its natural size], b. flower [magnified], c. seed [magnified], d. section of berry, smaller than its natural growth.

Shave-grass may be mixed with mistletoe in equal quantities; also santala, a red powder, serves well for admixture; see "Santala" page 176.

41. Mullein.   (Verbascum Schraderi Meyer.)

The blossoms of the mullein, or wool flower are carefully gathered by country people. They know that they are very effective in winter-time as a gargle, and produce a still more effective tea for complaints of the throat, catarrhs, phlegm on the chest, and for difficult breathing.

I once again warmly recommend such tea.

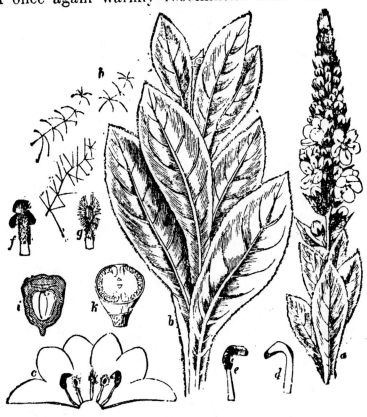

Mullein.
(Verbascum Schraderi Meyer.)

a. and b. Parts of the stem [one third of their natural growth], c. extended flower, d. stamen with declinate filament, e. the same seen from a side, f. stamen with regular, erect filament, g. the same seen from a side, h. hairs of the villous filament [20 times their natural growth], i. section of the seed [15 times its natural growth].

As a rule I mix the blossoms of the black mallow with the blossoms of this plant (in equal quantities); such tea works in a still more powerful and dissolving manner on the loosening of the phlegm.

42. Oats. (Avena sativa L.)

A thorough boiling extracts the strengthening substance of the oat-grain; barley may also be treated and used in the same manner. Such a drink, nourishing, easily digested, and cooling for interior heat, is an excellent nutrient, a real cordial for convalescent persons who have been excessively weakened and exhausted by small-pox, typhus, and other similar diseases. How often do I lament that just for such poor creatures, (who need before all new, healthy blood,) every possible kind of drink is prepared, except such drinks as these!

Oats.
(Avena sativa L.)

a. Panicle [one half to one third of its natural growth], b. pedicel [natural growth], c. glume [half again its natural growth], d. anther [4 times its natural growth], e. pistil [6 times its natural growth], f. fruit enclosed by the glume, g. inside of the fruit without glume, h. outside of the same, i. vertical section of the same, j. cross-section of the same.

The preparation is simple. A pint of oats are washed six to eight times with fresh water, then put into a quart of water, and boiled down to a pint. Two spoonfuls of honey are afterwards mixed with it, and the mixture is again boiled for two minutes.

43. Ribwort. (Plantago lanceolata L.)

When the country people have wounded themselves at their work, they seek quickly for ribwort leaves, and do not cease squeezing until they have forced a few drops out of the rather stubborn leaf. This sap they either put directly on the fresh wound, or else they moisten a little rag with it, and place it on the wounded part.

If the leaf refuses its medicinal sap, and only becomes soft and rather moist with rubbing, they place the soft leaf itself on the wound. Is there any danger of blood-poisoning in this proceeding? The ribwort knows nothing of that. Such a dressing is the first, but sometimes the best necessity-dressing; for the healing of such wounds progresses rapidly. The plant sews the gaping wound together as with a golden thread, and like rust never gathers on gold, so all putridness and proud flesh flies from the ribwort.

The effects of this plant on interior parts are not less advantageous. Would that hundreds of people would gather these medicinal leaves in spring or summer, crush them, press the sap out of them, and drink it! Numberless interior

Ribwort. (Plantago lanceolata L.)

complaints, which shoot up like poisonous mushrooms out of the impure blood and the impure juices, would not arise. Those are wounds which, truly, do not bleed, but which are in many ways more dangerous than bloody ones.

The dried leaves of ribwort yield likewise a splendid tea against interior phlegm-obstructions. The newspapers often bring us long praises about the excellent effects of ribwort, and still longer ones on the ribwort-juices prepared in this, or in that place.

Many buy such things at a dear price. My dear reader! be your own gatherer, preparer, and apothecary! You need have no fear. Of one thing you are certain: you will get genuine wares.

With the dried leaves of ribwort, lungwort (Pulmonaria officinalis L.) can be well used in equal quantities.

44. Rosemary. (Rosmarinus officinalis L.)

Would it not be a shame if this spicy herb escaped the attention of the gatherer for the household apotheca?

Rosemary is an excellent stomachic.

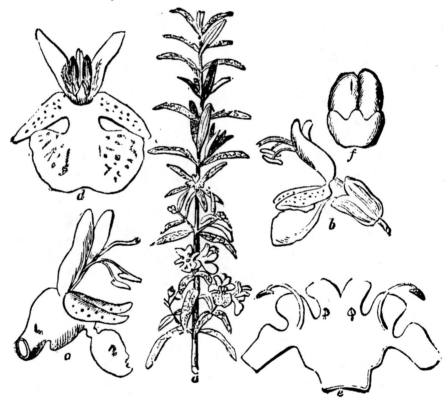

Rosemary.
(Rosmarinus officinalis L.)

a. Stem (one third of its natural growth), b. flower seen from a side, c. corolla seen from a side, d the same extended, e. the same seen from the front (one fourth of its natural growth), f. fruit.

Prepared as tea, it cleanses the stomach from phlegm, gives a good appetite and good digestion. Whoever likes to see the medicine glass, this comforter in illness, shining on his table, let him fill it with rosemary-tea, and take from two to four tablespoonfuls morning and evening. The stomach will soon become sensible, i. e. will not stick fast much longer in phlegm.

Rosemary-wine, taken in small doses, has also proved an excellent remedy against heart-infirmities. It operates in a sedative manner, and in cases of heart-dropsy it works strongly on removal through the urine. Such wine renders the same service in dropsy in general.

Against both complaints, three or four tablespoonfuls, or a small wine-glassful, of this pleasant drink are taken daily, morning and evening.

The preparation of this wine is exceedingly simple. A handful of rosemary is cut up as small as possible, put into a bottle, and good, well-kept wine poured upon it; white wine is preferable.

Even after half a day's standing, it may be used as rosemary-wine.

The same leaves may be used a second time.

45. Rue. (Ruta graveolens L.)

The excellent effects of this noble sanative plant is unfortunately by far too little known. The plants speak to us through their scent. How clearly and impressively does the rue announce its good will to man, for whom it was created in order to help, to ease different sufferings; just as if each little leaf were a little tongue.

Would that we always understood this speaking! The rue operates, no matter how and where applied, in a powerful and strengthening manner.

If only a little leaf is chewed, its effects are at once felt on the tongue. Its taste also refreshes the whole mouth; this effect of it is lasting like that of sweet-smelling incense filling a house. Against congestions of blood in the head, feelings of pressure on the head, and giddiness, tea made from rue acts in an excellent manner;

it is not less efficacious against difficulties of respiration,
palpitation, and all abdominal complaints (cramps etc.),
which have their origin in the weakness of the whole
body, or in particular organs of the body. I particularly
recommend this tea to all those who have an inclination
to the above named weaknesses, to cramps, hysteria etc.

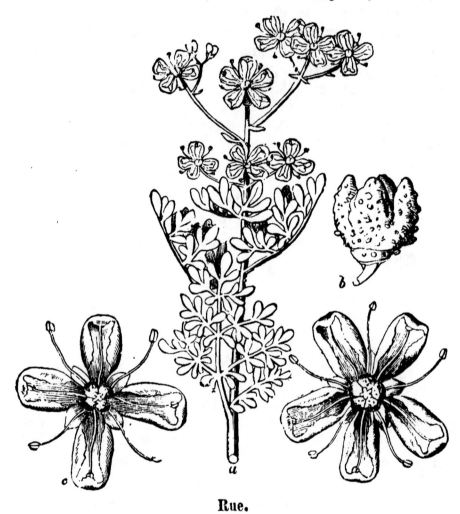

Rue.

(Ruta graveolens L.)

a. Stem (one third of its natural growth), b. fruit, c. fruit with 8 stamens, d. fruit
with 10 stamens.

Rue put in spirit, may be taken instead of the tea
for the complaints mentioned, ten to twelve drops on
sugar, twice (at the utmost) a day.

Rue-oil is likewise taken. The preparation of the latter is as follows: the dried leaves of the rue are crushed and put into a glass; then fine salad-oil is poured upon them, and the glass is put in a warm place for some time.

Afterwards the oil is poured off and taken in drops, the dose being the same as for the spirit.

46. Sage. (Salvia officinalis L.)

Those who have a garden near the house, will not forget when replanting it, the pretty ornamental sage

Sage.
(Salvia officinalis L.)

a. Stem, b. fructiferous stamen, c. extended flower, d. ovary with style, e. flower seen from a side.

plant. I have often seen the passers-by take a leaf and rub their black teeth with it. This proves that sage has a cleansing power.

Old, suppurating wounds, if washed with a decoction of sage, will quickly heal.

Sage-tea will remove phlegm from the palate, throat, or stomach.

Sage boiled as tea in wine and water, purifies the liver and kidneys.

The said effects are stronger when wormwood is mixed with sage (in equal quantities), and the mixture prepared as tea.

Powder from this medicinal plant, sprinkled on the food like pepper, sugar or cinnamon, operates against the given complaints in the same manner as the tea.

47. Salad-oil.

Salad-oil is that kind of oil which is used in the preparation of food, especially salad. It is generally called either sweet-oil or salad-oil. The pure, fine olive-oil is a superior kind of the same oil.

Read over what has been said about almond-oil; only when this cannot be had, salad-oil may be used instead. If there is only a small supply of almond-oil, salad-oil may be mixed with it.

The here named salad-oil ought to be pure Provence-oil, or at least pure rape-oil. The manner of using it (how and where) is the same as that for almond-oil.

48. Santala.

Santala or sandal is a red powder from the sandal-wood tree, serving for red dye; it can be bought from every chemist.

I always mix this perfectly harmless remedy with mistletoe-tea, by adding two pinches of sandal to a table-spoonful of mistletoe leaves, thus increasing the effects of the mistletoe-tea. See "Mistle-toe" page 168.

49. Sauerkraut.

Sauerkraut is well known to every German as pickled cabbage. It may also find its place here as a remedy.

In cases of hurts, burns, and such like accidents, against great heats, etc. a poultice of fresh sauerkraut (just taken from the tub) will be of excellent service.

Refer to the disease in question.

Sandal. (Pterocarpus santalinus L.)

a. Branch (one third of its natural size), b. corolla, extended, c. pistil.

The remedy is the more noteworthy, particularly for country people, the easier and quicker they have it at hand.

50. Secretive oil.

There are cases where so many morbid matters have gathered in the body that it is exceedingly difficult to dissolve them entirely and lead them out. The difficulty does not consist in the doubtful capabilities of the water or of the different applications, but rather in the question: would not the necessary practices to be prescribed, and the tediousness of such a course frighten away such patients, especially those of a weak nature, and thus frustrate all endeavours? This thought has occupied my mind very much, and my experience has constantly urged me on to new and earnest consideration.

It then occurred to me that many an interior complaint suddenly disappeared, as soon as an eruption showed itself on the exterior.

Could not, so I asked myself, such an eruption be brought about by artificial means? In other words, could it not be possible by some means or other to help the morbid matters, concealed in the interior of the body, to break through, to entice them out on the surface of the skin, and so relieve the water-cure of a good deal of its work?*

After long seeking, I found an oil which renders this service in an excellent manner, in many cases with remarkable results. It is not, as has been said, absolutely necessary for cure, it is no "conditio sine qua non"; the water can do the work alone. But the oil aids and furthers considerably the often very difficult work of the water. The oil is only used exteriorly, and solely in those cases in which by this means the morbid matters can be led out in the easiest and most advantageous manner. The effects are entirely harmless, but thorough, penetrating to the very interior.

The manner of application may be illustrated by a few examples.

Someone complain about his eyes; they are inflamed; they run a great deal, and cause acute pain. In this case, I gently rub the surface of the skin behind the ears, in order to warm it a little, and then softly put three or four drops of such oil on the warmed spots.

----

* Patients who have visited hydropathic institutions, assure us that the appearance of an eruption is regarded as a sign that the whole course will have the desired effect.

After half an hour the pa'ient already feels the effect, a slight stretching of the skin and burning; after about twenty-four hours innumerable little pustules filled with matter appear, which increase according to the quantity of morbid matter to be extracted. They afterwards dry up and fall off in crusts. If the first attempt fails, i. e. if the oil does not act within the space of thirty hours, the next day a few more drops are put on the red places. The effect will surely not fail, and the poisonous matter, which caused the inflammation in the eyes, will be secreted at once. To many persons afflicted with eye-infirmities, the said oil has brought relief within one to two hours, and within a short time the eyes were clear and healthy.

Violent tooth-ache torments another patient: the gums are swollen, the jaw pains as if it were broken, the most painful excitement tortures the whole head. As in the first case, a few drops of our oil are rubbed behind the ears, or on the back of the neck. The result must be a favourable one.

It is a peculiarity of the oil that in the first and more distinguished task of extracting, it wounds the oiled spots, but as soon as it has done its duty, it heals them quickly and well.

I do not in the least consider the oil a secret remedy; I have communicated its ingredients to many a trusty friend. But in order to prevent misuse or mistakes of different kinds, I have thought it better not to publish the receipt.

51. Shave-grass. (Equisetum arvense L.)

The manifold and excellent effects of this medicinal herb cannot be too highly estimated. It not only cleanses the house-utensils, for which it is considered a first class polisher by all house-wives, but it also heals the interior and exterior infirmities of the human body.

On old injuries, putrid wounds, on all, even gangrenous ulcers, or caries, shave-grass operates in an extraordinary manner. It washes away, dissolves, burns out, as it were, all that is injurious. The herb is used

12*

either as decoction for ablutions, bandages, vapours, and compresses, or it is wrapped up in wet cloths and laid on the suffering part.

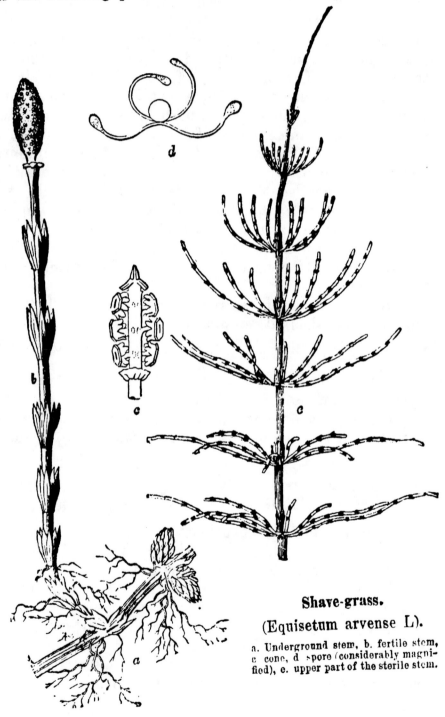

Shave-grass.

(Equisetum arvense L).

a. Underground stem, b. fertile stem, c. cone, d. spore (considerably magnified), e. upper part of the sterile stem.

Further particulars are given in Part III. The services rendered to the interior parts by the shave-grass, are still more manifold.

Its tea purifies the stomach. A cupful is taken from time to time (not daily). It eases the pains caused by gravel and stone-disease, and above all relieves the sufferers who have difficulty in discharging their urine. For this it stands alone, is not to be replaced, and is invaluable.

Shave-grass vapours, specially for this disease, are here only just hinted on. Exactly such diseases are frightfully painful — and so frequent! Take particular notice of the simple herb, which may be had without any trouble whatever! Such patients should take daily a cupful of shave-grass-tea, together with the required exterior application.

For bleedings, blood-vomiting, it counts among the first and best teas. Those who vomit blood should take it without delay. I know cases in which after four minutes even a perfect cessation took place.

In cases of violent bleeding at the nose, such tea is drawn up through the nostrils. It operates in a contracting manner, and its effect is soon felt. Such as are visited with hemorrhages, I recommend to drink daily one or two cupful of this tea.

There should be a sufficient supply of shave-grass kept in every home-dispensary, so that in times of need, which often occur suddenly, it may be quickly at hand.

52. Silver-weed. (Potentilla anserina L.)

The silver-weed grows best, as its German name (Gänsefingerkraut) implies, where the geese like best to be. It is found in the vicinity of houses, on commons, and along the roads.

People have named it, after its mode of operating, cramp-herb.

Tea made from silver-weed is an excellent remedy in attacks of cramp, in the stomach, abdomen, or elsewhere. Even in cases of tetanus — in so far as this can be worked upon — this little herb renders very good service. At the commencement of the attack, or better still, when symptoms of the cramp first appear, the patient should be given three times daily, very warm milk (as warm as possible) in which such herbs (as much as can be taken with three fingers) have been boiled as for tea.

A greater effect may be obtained if at the same time as the tea is taken, a poultice is made of the boiled herbs and laid upon the afflicted part.

No mother of a family should omit to gather and dry a sufficient supply of such herbs. She knows herself how painful such frequently occurring spasmodic attacks are, and how it gives still greater pain if she sees her dear ones suffering without being able to help them.

Silver-weed.
(Potentilla anserina L.)

53. St. John's-wort.   (Hypericum perforatum L.)

St. John's-wort, on account of its great effects, formerly bore the name of witch's-herb. Now-a-days both itself and its services are quite forgotten.

This medicinal herb has a particular influence on the liver; its tea is an excellent remedy for it. A small admixture of aloe-powder increases the effect, which ‘can be observed chiefly in the urine; whole flakes of morbid matters are sometimes washed away with it.

Head complaints arising from watery matters or obstructions of phlegm in the head, or from the gases rising to the head; stomach spasms, slight obstructions of phlegm on the chest and lungs are healed at once by tea made of St. John's-wort.

Mothers, who are caused a great deal of trouble and anxiety by their little bed-wetters, could tell us much about the strong effects of such tea.

If St. John's-wort is not to be had, common-yarrow (Achillea millefolium L.) may be used in all the given cases.

54. Strawberries. (Fragaria vesca L.)

What joy for children when they bring the first basket of straw-berries to their parents, their pastor, or their teacher! What enjoyment when the first dish of strawberries (with or without wine) is brought on the table as dessert!

Not only the fruit of this little plant, but the leaves also are gathered by many a mother returning from her hard work, full of care for her weak little ones; for tea from strawberry-leaves, that she knows well, is an exceedingly good and cheap nourishment.

How does she prepare this tea? She takes as many dried strawberry-leaves as she can pick up with three or four fingers, pours about half a pint of boiling water on them, and then covers the infusion closely. After fifteen minutes, she pours the tea off, and she has pure strawberryleaf-tea.

St. John's-wort.
(Hypericum perforatum L.)

Then she mixes with it hot milk, a little sugar, and the drink is ready.

If the mother were to take wood-roof (Asperula odorata L.) instead of the third or fourth part of strawberry leaves, the tea would gain in taste and value.

The strawberries themselves as a strengthening remedy are by no means to be dispised. To convalescent persons, who feel great weakness and enervation after serious diseases, they are given together with other nourishment.

Strawberries.

(Fragaria vesca L.)

Those who in summer take daily for some time, e. g. half a pint of milk mixed with a quarter of a pint of strawberries (as is often done in the South of Germany,) or a piece of good rye-bread with a quarter of a pint of strawberries, twice a day, will soon feel their exceedingly benificial effect. If the strawberries are preserved like cherries etc., the above course may be undertaken with the best results even in winter.

In cases of great interior heat, strawberries render great service even to invalids in summer. What a splendid refrigerant, can be prepared with them for the poor sufferer parched with thirst!

Similar portions of strawberries are often recommended to those afflicted with gravel and stone-disease; those suffering from liver complaints could even take as much as a pint daily at different times, and such as are affected with an eruption arising from morbid blood, half a pint both morning and afternoon.

It is remarkable how the earth offers to man just this fruit in such abundance. Would that our understanding and gratitude corresponded at all times to the loving bounty of our Creator!

55. Succory or Chicory. (Cichorium intybus L.)

The succory (Wegwart in German) waits on every path for him who desires to gather it for his dispensary It is also called "sun-whirl" as its leaves are always turned to the sun. When you look at it, the good succory, with its half-starved looking stalks and entangled leaves, it seems like a "rough-head" among all the other plants. Only the colour of its blossom, rather brighter than that of the corn-flower, brings it in some degree into reputation and respect again.

Appearances are often deceptive; and so it is with the succory, for its interor is golden.

Tea made from succory, removes phlegm from the stomach, takes away the superfluous gall, purifies liver, milt and kidneys, and leads out the morbid matters through the urine. For this end two cups of tea are taken daily, for three or four days, the one before breakfast, the other in the evening. The same may also be taken in order to restore the stomach when it has been upset by any kind of food etc., and to assist the digestion.

Succory or Chicory. (Cichorium Intybus L.)

a. Complete plant, b. underground stem, c. flower (natural growth), d. pistil, e. fruit (magnified).

For cramps in the stomach, also for painful inflammation on the body, a poultice made by boiling the herbs and flowers and then wrapping them up in a cloth, is laid on the stomach or painful places. This is renewed two or three times daily.

The herbs are very often put in spirit. Decaying limbs are restored by this spirit when rubbed well with it about twice a day.

The roots as well as the other parts of the plant are useful for the given medicinal purposes. They are rooted up most easily in rainy weather.

56. Tonic laxative I and II.

Forty or fifty years ago it was customary at an exactly given time to be bled, at another, a term carefully noted in the almanach (a certain quarter of the moon), to take the yearly or half-yearly purgative. How times, opinions, and people who form them, change!

Even in our days many people will not give up the idea that, from time to time, the stomach needs a thorough mustering and clearing away.

One could laugh if it were not, in all earnestness, most lamentable. In truth, if those of a regular, simple, and healthy mind reflect on the conduct of certain people, I feel almost tempted to say, of whole classes of society, and on the food and drink which they take, then indeed the above idea is not unfounded.

If the dreadfully tormented and sinfully overstrained (because over-loaded) stomach could give a sound, it would cry out and call for help against that kind of unreasonable malefactors! But as it is, it must "swallow" all, and thereby certainly be miserably ruined.

Therefore, first of all I recommend a reasonable mode of life, a worthy treatment of the labourer which lays the indispensable foundations for all further work. Thus only will and can this faithful and diligent worker, the stomach remain healthy.

Should unexpectedly — it may easily occur — a misfortune happen to it also, I advise most decidedly against drastic (too strong) purging; I reject all purgatives which operate violently, let them be called whatever.

By purging surely nothing else is understood, than striving to produce a more copious evacuation of the bowels, without injuring the health and bodily strength. But this can be done in so simple and harmless a manner! The herbal remedies do not, so to speak, seize the stomach as an enemy, but as true friends they walk arm in arm with it supporting it and raising it to proper activity. They only offer it their juices as means to assist its own means of digestion (juices of the stomach).

For a long time I have selected from among the different plants, those which having the most excellent particular effects, still only when their particular healing virtues act collectively "viribus unitis" (with united powers,) efficaciously assist the stomach, i. e. when weakening it by thoroughly dissolving and removing all morbid substances, they strengthen it at the same time that it not only does not suspend its work for a single hour, but does not even grumble and complain about it.

I think I have found the remedies and their mixture. Both kinds of tea shall be no secret; on the contrary, I wish that very many may use them, and prepare them for the relief of others.

The first receipt is this:

Take two tablespoonfuls of pounded fennel, two table spoonfuls of crushed juniper-berries, one tablespoonful of Foenum graecum, one tablespoonful of aloe-powder; mix them all well together, put them in a box, and keep them in a dry place. The remedy operates after twelve to thirty hours. The tea is taken generally at night before going to bed; a small cupful is a dose. One teaspoonful of the mixture is sufficient for a cupful; it is boiled for a quarter of an hour, then poured off and drunk either cold or warm, with or without sugar.

Strong persons may drink a cup of the tea on two succeeding days.

Weaker patients would do better to divide the cupful for two or three days, so that they take four to six tablespoonfuls like medicine every evening. Without any uncomfortable feeling, they will experience its effects.

With many who make use of this tea, it will be entirely without result, although they feel its active work in the interior. The police seek, but sometimes find no thief. The tea seeks; but where there is nothing to find and remove, it leaves all else in peace, and thereby does not cause that great and lamentable weakness, which otherwise always follows purging.

In the same manner as upon the evacuation of the bowels, this tea operates also on the urine. Even great obstructions of phlegm on the chest are removed by it.

Cases have often occurred to me in which after tedious diarrhœa, difficult to stop, this tea has removed the remainder of the impurities, and the deepest and most lasting peace followed the interior revolution. One small cupful drunk during the day in three portions, is quite sufficient.

The second receipt for this tea is the following:

Two tablespoonfuls of pounded fennel, three tablespoonfuls of crushed juniper-berries, three tablespoonfuls of powder from dwarf-elder-roots, one tablespoonful of Fœnum græcum, one tablespoonful of aloe-powder.

This tea does not exclude purging effects; still its districts are (instead of the stomach and bowels,) more the kidneys and bladder; it drives the morbid matters out through the urine. Those who feel uneasiness in the abdomen (in the vicinity of the bladder) or difficulty in making urine, burning in the bladder and the kidneys, those who are in the first stages of dropsy, may calmy use this second tea. In the application the same rules are to be observed as with regard to the first receipt.

57. Valerian, common.   (Valeriana officinalis L.)

That something especial must be hidden in valerian, is proved to us by the cats, which are so attracted by it that they roll themselves among it.

We use only the roots, which are either cut up for tea or pounded for powder, and which (both as tea and as powder) are taken in small quantities only.

Valerian-root relieves head complaints, and removes spasms in a similar manner to rue; it operates upon both complaints as it removes their principal cause, viz. the gases.

58. Violet.   (Viola odorata L.)

This pretty little fragrant spring-flower shall fill our apotheca also with its salutary perfume.

When, in the beginning of spring-time, the children get bad coughs in consequence of the frequent changes in the weather, the anxious mother boils a handful of green or dried violet leaves in half a pint of water, and gives the children two or three spoonfuls of such tea every two or three hours. (The roots of the plant may be used too; but they must be crushed before boiling.) Adults are cured of whooping-cough by taking a cup of this tea three times a day.

It likewise relieves the cough of consumptive people and assists in loosening the phlegm. It serves as a medicine and should be taken as such, i. e. three to five table-spoonfuls every two or three hours.

This tea serves further against headache and great heat in the head. A piece of linen is moistened with violet-leaf-tea and bound across the forehead; or better still. the head, especially the back of the head, is washed with such a decoction.

For a swollen throat this tea is a tested gargle; at the same time the throat-bandage may be applied, dipped in the decoction instead of pure water.

Valerian
(Valeriana officinalis L.)

Those who suffer from difficulty in breathing, which, however, is more the result of gathered gases and morbid matters in the stomach and bowels, should undertake a little course of violet-tea, i. e. they should drink daily for some time two larger or smaller cups of this tea.

Crushed violet-leaves bound as a compress on inflamed tumours have a cooling effect; if boiled in vinegar, they will heal gout.

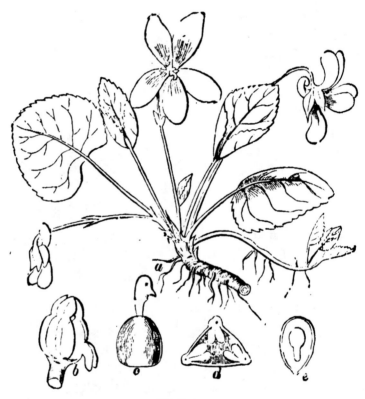

Violet.

(Viola odorata L.)

a. plant in natural growth, b. flower, c. flower from a side, d. and e. fruit.

Rejoice at the fragrance and the lovely blue colour of many a little bunch of violets; but keep also a little supply of this medicinal herb in your home-dispensary, that it may still breathe its fragrance for those who are sick, at a time when the little spring-flower has long since faded!

59. Wild Angelica. (Angelica silvestris L.)

There grows on damp meadows, or wet woody places a plant with a stalk from about twenty to forty inches high. The stalks are hollow, and the lads like to make whistles of them. This plant bears the name of Angelica. It is, like many others, not known in its salutary effects on the human body.

If any one has taken unwholesome or half-poisonous food, tea made by boiling its roots, seeds and leaves, is an excellent remedy for removing these injurious matters.

As the blood is prepared from the different kinds of food, and as these are not all good and wholesome for the system, this tea leads the bad matters out of the blood again.

How often does it happen that an uncomfortable coldness takes possession of the stomach! A cup of tea made from such roots, brings more warmth to the stomach again. It is best to divide such a cup of tea into three parts, and to take the first in the morning, the second at noon, and the third in the evening.

If there are morbid matters in the stomach and bowels, or if gripes are caused by gases, this tea is again an effi-

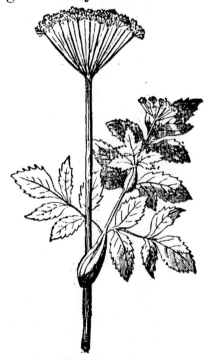

Wild Angelica.
(Angelica silvestris L.)

cacious remedy, especially if half wine and half water are taken for the tea.

Thick phlegm on the lungs and chest, heart-burn, phlegm in the wind-pipes, are by this tea especially, most easily removed.

The angelica can be highly recommended as an excellent home-remedy, and country people ought to gather a good quantity of it, for the whole year, in their meadows and woods, dry it in the air, and keep it in a dry place. These roots, seeds, and leaves, well dried, may also be made into powder, and a good pinch of such powder taken twice or three times daily will supply the place of the tea.

I caution those who have little knowlegde of plants, against gathering angelica lest they should carry home hemlock (poisonous plant) instead. I was urged to give this warning by the fact that cases of such most dangerous mistakes have repeatedly occurred.

60. Wormwood. (Artemisia absinthium L.)

Wormwood ranks among the best known stomachics. It leads the wind out of the stomach, improves the stomach juices, and so effects a good appetite and good digestion, whether it is taken as tea or as powder.

For a bad smell from the mouth, if it proceeds from the stomach, wormwood is of excellent effect.

Whoever is suffering from liver complaint (melancholy), let him take the little box of wormwood-powder instead of his snuff-box, and put a pinch of its contents into his first spoonful of soup, or sprinkle it like pepper on his food once or twice a day. The decreasing yellowness of the skin will soon show the improvement of the gall, and the patient, whose

Wormwood.
(Artemisia Absinthium L.)

breath has been, as it were, laced up by the foul air

and often still more foul juices — real dung-hills of the stomach — will breathe more freely again.

Wormwood can also be used as a tincture, which may be preserved for a long time. As a single little corn of incense glimmering on the charcoal will fill a whole room with perfume, so a little leaf of wormwood is sufficient to give a bitter taste to the contents of a whole spirit-bottle, — a sign of the virtue of the tincture and its effects.

Travellers who are much troubled with indigestion and nausea, should never forget to take with them as a faithful companion their little bottle of wormwood-tincture.

Wormwood-tea, used as eye-water, has often rendered the best services in eye-complaints.

Contents of a little home-apotheca.

I. Tinctures
of

Arnica
Bilberry
Gentian
Juniper-berries
Rosemary
Succory or Chicory
Wormwood.

II. Tea
from

Althea
Bark of oak
Bog-bean
Brier
Blackthorn - blossoms
Camomile
Centaury
Colt's-foot
Common elder
Common nettle
Common yarrow
Cowslip
Dwarf-elder
Eyebright
Juniper-berries

Lime - tree - blossoms
Lungwort
Mallow
Mistletoe
Mullein
Mint
Ribwort
Rosemary
Rue
Sage
St John's-wort
Shave-grass
Silver-weed
Strawberries
Succory or Chicory
Sweet wood-ruff
Tonic laxative
Valerian
Violet
Wild angelica
Wormwood.

III. Powders
from

Alum
Aloes
Colt's-foot
Dwarf-elder

Eyebright
Fennel
Fenugreek
Linseed
Mint
Sage
Sandal
Valerian
Wormwood
Wild angelica

further

Bone-dust
Chalk-dust
Coal-dust.

IV. Oil
of

Anise
Camphor
Fennel
Juniper-berry
Rue

further

Almond-oil
Oil of Cloves
Lavender-oil
Salad-oil.

Several kinds of strength-giving food.

Recipe for the preparation of bran-bread.

Get your miller to grind your wheat together with the bran. Millers, as a rule, do not like to do this for well known reasons;* therefore the flour returned from the mill should be well inspected.

Of this flour take 2, 4, 6, or 8 lbs. (according to the number of persons for whom the bread is going to be made), put it in a kneading pan, and make it into dough with hot water. Put the dough in a rather warm

---

* Those who on account of larger consumption of bran-bread, are able to buy one of the grinding-machines especially made for this purpose, will be best off; they can never be cheated. — I knew a professor in the Tyrol, who had a serious stomach complaint, and as he could only take the smallest quantity of food, his strength became very much reduced. He was advised to get such a little machine and take bran-bread. He, at once, ordered one from Vienna, and was himself the miller and the donkey too! He ground his own wheat, and his wife baked the bread for him. He became so healthy and his stomach with him; that the latter henceforth refused its services to no kind of food whatever.

place, where it should remain during the night. Neither leaven, nor salt, nor any other spice may be mixed with it.

The next day little loaves, or rolls, are formed out of the dough, and baked in an oven heated as for ordinary bread; they are left in the heat for an hour and a quarter to an hour and a half.

As soon as the bread is taken from the oven, it is thrust into boiling water for 3 or 4 seconds, then put at once into the oven again for a short time to dry.

I learnt this latter manipulation from a Trappist prior, who said that he had long tested the baking of such bread in different ways, and had found that this manner of baking was the best, as thereby all the nourishing substance, in particular the sugar substance is drawn from the bran.

I know many who have eaten this bread with particular liking, who eat it still, and say that it renders excellent and special service for complaints of the stomach, digestion, and particularly for hemorrhoidal complaints.

There are others whom I have known, who at first found this tasteless and unspiced bread remarkably insipid, but afterwards they have taken it with an almost passionate liking.

The bread is kept in a cool place and, should the crust be too hard, covered with a damp cloth.

The strength-giving soup.

Of this I am convinced: if the soup is known and used, a great number of miserable people can be made happy.

The strength-giving soup is not only to be recommended on account of its extraordinarily good nutritious substances, but also because it is very cheap and easily prepared.

A gentleman of position, who became acquainted with it, bought of a farmer two great loaves of black bread

(The black bread, as is well known, is prepared only from rye-flour, so carefully ground for the country people, that only a little of the bran is left, and consequently all the nourishing substances of the rye are used.) This gentleman ordered the two loaves of bread to be cut up in small slices, put on tin plates, and placed upon the hot hearth, in order to dry them as much as possible. Dried quite hard they were pounded in a mortar to a coarse powder. If he wanted a strength-giving soup, he stirred two or three spoonfuls of this bread-powder in boiling broth, and put in very little, or no spice; he also used but little salt. In two minutes the soup was ready. It has a pleasant taste, gives good nourishment, and causes no, or at least, not much gases. — Instead of broth, the gentleman often took milk, and when this was boiling, he stirred in the bread-powder. In two minutes this soup, too, was ready. The latter soup is even greatly superior to the former, because milk contains more nourishing substances than even broth.

If the gentleman happened to have neither milk nor broth, he ordered water to be boiled, and stirred the bread-powder in it while boiling, then a little spice and beef-dripping was added. This soup also deserves the name of strength-giving soup.

One day this gentleman entered a house where the farmer's wife was baking bread made out of spelt, which is similar to wheat. (This grain, too, is ground by the country-people with all possible care.) He bought two such loaves, and proceeded as with the black bread. Then the bread-powder obtained was mixed with that before named, and he had soup made from this admixture in the same way, as was explained before. He, thereby, obtained six different kinds of soup, which are also different in strength-giving property.

This strength-giving soup is particularly excellent for very weak children, because it is easily digested, very nourishing, and causes no gases. It is also to be recommended to young growing people, to improve the blood through the poverty of which the body suffers so much.

This strength-giving soup is, further, good for invalids, because it brings much nourishing substance to the weakened system. Lastly, it is especially to be recommended to the aged. When the teeth fail for well masticating solid food, one should keep to this soup. There ought to be no family into which this strength-giving soup is not introduced. I once recommended it to a person in high office, who afterwards assured me that he knew no more wholesome, or more nourishing soup.

Preparation of Honey-wine.

(Very recommendable for the healthy, and the sick.)

The ancient Germans had little or no wine. The brown beer was unknown to them, because there was no such thing. Their food was very simple, and yet nevertheless they were a powerful race; they attained a great age and enjoyed an extraordinary health. They attributed this great age and this extraordinary health to the "mead" (honey-wine). It is a great pity that this good drink is so little known, and that its place is now occupied by the everywhere-known brown beer, which is often so much spoiled by art that it can no longer be considered a wholesome drink. In the larger works on the breeding of bees, recipes are generally given for making honey-wine. But the complaint is often heard, that one has tried to follow these recipes, but has never arrived at a good result.

I generally prepare it as follows: I have from 60 to 65 quarts of soft water put in a very clean copper. When this has become rather warm, about 6 quarts of honey are stirred in it, and then it is left to boil quite gently for an hour and a half. From time to time, the scum is removed from the top. When the time for boiling has expired, the honey-water is emptied out into tin or earthen vessels, and when it has cooled (to a temperature a little higher than that of water heated by the sun), it is put into a thoroughly clean cask. The bung is put on, but not fastened. If the cellar is rather warm the fermentation begins after five to fifteen days. After about fourteen days fermentation, this new fermented honey-wine is drawn off into another cask. The dregs, of course, are left behind. In the second cask, the fermentation lasts from ten to fourteen days, and when the wine becomes quite calm, so that nothing more is heard in the cask, then the bung-hole is closed. After three or four weeks, it will be clear, and fit for drinking. If it is then drawn off into bottles, and these well corked and put into sand, it will effervesce in a few days rather strongly. This beverage is very cooling, and is therefore liked by those ill with fever. When sick people cannot drink either beer or wine, such honey-wine is a cordial for them. But it is also a good drink for the healthy; it ought, however, to be drunk in small quantities only, otherwise it causes disgust.

Part the third.

Diseases.

Benedicite universa
germinantia in terra Domino.

Introduction.

The following cases are no imaginary ones. They are tales of human misery which rest on facts, and I am ready to guarantee for every name mentioned.

It is perfectly well known to myself that this part of my book has many defects, and that my list of diseases is by no means a complete one. This must be attributed in part to want of time; in part to my intention to give hints and instructions on symptoms of, and remedies for, diseases in an entertaining manner, certainly the most suitable one for those readers to whom I wish to address myself before all others.

I selected among the various diseases those by which we are visited most frequently, and the individual cases of the different illnesses were again chosen with a view to make this part of the book as instructive as possible. Whether the execution of my plan quite answers my intention, I will not decide myself; but I think that whoever reads the book with good will and without prejudice will be able to discover at least some grains of gold in it.

With regard to the repetitions, which occur frequently in this part of the book, I must add that they were made for the sake of clearness which, although always of importance, is particularly so, when the various applications are spoken of.

Diseases are crosses, dear reader! Every one of us will sooner or later have to bear one of these crosses, perhaps unto death. We are allowed to lessen the weight of these our crosses, or did not the Prophet tell Naaman, the Syrian, to go and wash seven times in the Jordan that he might be cleansed from his leprosy?

May the Lord bless my intention to alleviate the burden of many a cross-bearer!

Complaints in alphabetical Order.

—◆◇◆—

Abscesses.

Inflammation is an inseparable companion of the various sores. Wherever fire breaks out, people hurry to the place. A somewhat similar gathering takes place as soon as the smallest spot on the surface of our body is inflamed. One blood globule tells the other and the curious ones that obey the calling, are soon burnt themselves. If a small ulcer has formed on the toe, be it not larger than a lentil, the pain of it is felt not only in the whole toe, but in the foot and the leg. These painful inflammations always remind me of a match which, when lighted in the dark, sheds brightness over a large space.

Ann has a very bad thumb. There is little to be seen; the thumb is swollen a little and is of a darker red hue than the other fingers. Not only the thumb, but even the shoulder, pains dreadfully. Mind, in a short time, your whole body will be suffering. Ann's father thinks that something must be the matter. Yes, certainly, there is something the matter.

The girl wraps her thumb well up, and has now been waiting 3 to 6 days for what might ensue. The thumb swells, the hand too. A big abscess begins to form; the girl feels acute pain in her finger, arm, and body: it is as if a comediant were playing at ball with knives. Only after a long time, the matter will be entirely removed, and the thumb healed.

What ought the girl to have done? As soon as she felt the pain, not caused by any accident, she ought to have done what her mother uses to do when she wishes to put out a small flame on the hearth. A gentle application of water might have suppressed the evil in its germ.

If it is not the hand only but also the arm that pains, the inflammation can no longer be compared to a small flame which may be extinguished by a mere sprinkling of water. May the girl now hold her arm under the spout of the well to put out the fire? By no means! There is not only heat to be cooled, there are also poisonous matters to be dissolved and thrown out.

The suffering part is wrapped up in an arm-bandage (piece of linen dipped in cold water), and this bandage is to be renewed viz. to be re-dipped in water every time it begins to be hot. The finger must indeed become "a bad finger", viz. the abscess must burst, but all that has been extracted by the bandage need not turn into matter and it is, no doubt, a great advantage if the abscess only swells to the size of a hazelnut instead of that of a walnut.

If the feeling of uneasiness extends to the whole body, we prescribe for some time the daily application of the Spanish mantle, and the general health will soon be restored.

One kind of abscesses is well known under the name of whitlow. The ill treatment to which such fingers are frequently exposed, affords new proofs for the foolishness of men. They behave as if they had completely lost their common sense. Every one knows a new ointment which will infallibly cure the finger, and where the ointments end, superstition begins to do its part of the work. I know of people who use as a remedy in such cases a living mole which they keep in their hands until it dies,

believing that their whitlow will cease to torment them
as soon as the poor animal's life is gone. After much
ointing, smearing, talking, and lying, the healing process
ends with the bursting of the abscess and a profuse
discharge of matter which is, of course, nothing but the
happy result of the ointments used and of the death of
the mole.

Can there be greater foolishness than this?

What is a whitlow? Nothing else than an abscess,
to be treated in the way prescribed to the above mentioned girl. Since this kind of abscesses generally appears
when much unhealthy matter has accumulated in the
body, the cure ought to extend to the whole system. The
local treatment consists in the hand- and arm-bandage.

The finger is swathed in a threefold piece of linen
previously dipped in a decoction of shave-grass to prevent
the affection of the bone; hand and arm are wrapped in
a twofold bandage dipped in a decoction of hay-flowers.
This bandage is to be renewed as often as increased pain,
or heat is felt. The whole body is worked upon by the
Spanish mantle and the short bandage which should be
alternately applied, every day for one hour. After the
first week, the application of bandages may take place
every second or third day. I recommend cautiousness
with regard to upper and lower showers which ought not
to be applied, before much dissolving and evacuating has
been effected. As soon as the finger is "mature", viz.
shows a bluish hue and becomes soft on one side, it
should be opened at once, and there is no reason for fear
if blood flows out along with the matter. This blood
would otherwise have turned into matter and if it is
spared this process, the healing of the finger is accele-
rated. Fear about opening an abscess too soon, is out of
place where water-applications are used; it may be
well founded, however, when an abscess is treated with
ointments.

There is still another way of healing whitlows which,
for the sake of its being shorter, I have often applied
myself. The hand and the arm up to the elbow, are
bathed in an infusion of hay-flowers, 2 or 3 times daily

for half an hour. The bath should be warm, but by no means hot. The above mentioned bandages for finger, arm and body are applied in addition to the baths.

The thumb of Andrew, a gardener, was in a terrible state. Dreadfully swollen, the whole finger was without skin resembling a mass of raw flesh covered with matter. The bone was to be seen in several places.

The physician had declared that amputation would be inevitable. I examined the hand and said to myself: If I could only save that poor man's hand.

Then I reflected and came to the following conclusions. The visible bone (and that was the principal thing) has an appearance of soundness and seems in no way affected. The dreadfully swollen disgusting thumb is like a cess-pool in which the body pours its good-for-nothing juices. These acrimonious matters increase the suppuration, destroy the flesh and poison everything. Therefore, I must work on the half corrupted thumb, and still more on the body that it may cease to kill its own member. My reflections were followed by action. The thumb and the whole hand were wrapped in a bandage dipped in hay-flower and shave-grass infusion (both kinds of herbs were boiled together); this bandage was renewed 4 or 5 times a day. The sick body received daily a short bandage and, 3 times a week, the Spanish mantle. To the finger, I applied daily diluted alum-water to wash away matter and dirt.

Four weeks had not past, when finger and hand were saved. A new thumb began to form round the bone which was, indeed, not affected. The new thumb had, the nail excepted, an entirely normal appearance. The man could attend to his work as formerly and lived many a year after.

Apoplexy.

Paul has been stricken by apoplexy. The right side of his upper body is paralysed, his mouth dreadfully distorted, his right eye sunk in, the eye-lid stiff, his voice broken, all his courage gone. The physician, who had been called immediatelly, declared that nothing could

be done and that the patient should daily drink some
"Bitterwasser" (mineral water impregnated with some
neutral salt). This prescription did not satisfy the patient, he began directly to try water-applications, and in
12 days he was well again. This happened 13 years ago,
and the robust, although elderly, gentleman delivered his
lectures for many a year after.

How was this cure effected?

As soon as the work of a watch is disturbed in its
order by a fall or a shock, a stand-still takes place. May
be none of the little wheels is injured, but perhaps there
is something between them that hinders their course, or
they press and prevent each other from keeping their regular pace. The disturber ought to be expelled, the little
workers reconciled in order to make every part serve the
purpose of the whole. In the same way the human body
is sometimes troubled by inward disturbers of peace, perhaps by one of those conglomerations which occur especially in advanced years, when the wheels of the work
viz. the organs are rather worn out. Mouth, eye, or
tongue, these delicate wheels, are not injured but have
been pushed, as it were, out of their proper place. Expel
the disturber, and order and peace will soon be restored.
I will try to assist you in the proceeding.

A head-vapour followed by a shower, will do its
dissolving work in the upper part of the body, a foot-vapour will produce the same effect in the lower part.
The patient should then take a warm bath followed by
a cold one, or by a cold ablution. This application, besides working in a dissolving manner, will diminish the
determination of blood to the head. As soon as the conglomerations are thus removed and the circulation regulated, it will be good to proceed to the oiling of the
machine which is done by a nourishing strengthening
fare — not too much at a time, however. Strong wines,
spirits, and spices ought to be avoided as well as mental
exertion and agitation.

A pastor was stricken by apoplexy. One hand, one
foot, one whole side of his body was totally paralysed,
voice and consciousness were also gone. Remedies were

applied for several days, but without success. The physician declared that the one side would remain paralysed as it was and that a second stroke was likely to follow the first and put an end to the poor gentleman's life. I thought that, in this case, an experiment with water could do no harm. The cold foot and arm were vigorously washed with cold water; two warm foot-baths with vigorous washing of the feet and 4 ablutions of the upper parts of the body were the applications of the second day. On the third day we perceived that there was still feeling and life in the two paralysed limbs. This gave us courage. On the fourth day we applied a lower bandage to the awkward body and put the feet twice into a warm bath with salt and ashes. We continued in the same manner for a fortnight. Then the patient began to assist us with the healthy hand and foot and showed to his own great satisfaction that he was able to lift the paralysed hand a little. For the following three weeks whole-ablutions were applied alternately with head- and foot-vapours, weekly one of the vapours and daily one ablution of the upper and lower body. New life seemed to animate the body that had been so suddenly struck down; the appetite increased. The applications for the next 3 weeks were: every week one warm bath followed by a cold one, one head-vapour, one foot-vapour, and 3 half-baths with ablution of the upper body (during 1 minute). The cure was concluded by upper and lower showers applied alternately with the Spanish mantle. It was indeed no easy work, but the gentleman recovered his former health insomuch as to be able to say Mass daily, and to sing it occasionally, to visit the sick, and to attend to his correspondence. His tongue, however, had been affected so much that a difficulty in pronouncing certain words always remained and rendered him unable to preach. It is now 10 years since, and the pastor still lives and enjoys good health.

A man, 45 years old, was stricken by palsy. The right hand and foot were completely paralysed and without any feeling; appetite was wanting entirely. The patient took daily ablutions of the upper body and the feet;

the water used was warm and mixed (in equal quantities) with vinegar. Three times a day he took 30 drops of extract from wormwood, sage, and bog-bean. After a fortnight, normal warmth and feeling had returned to hand and foot, and the man was able to walk in the room. The appetite increased, the paralysed side recovered its strength, and after a few days more, the man was perfectly well again. It is worthy of notice that this man had indulged in the drinking of brandy, and that the stroke must be attributed to this cause. To secure a complete cure and recovery of strength 8 to 10 baths of a decoction from oat-straw or pine-twigs should be taken, the temperature of the bath being 30—32° R., the duration of it 20 minutes. As usual the warm bath is to be followed by a vigorous cold whole-ablution, or a half-bath with washing of the upper body.

Some general remarks about strokes may find a place here. Whenever a person has been stricken by apoplexy and is partly paralysed, recourse should be had to cold washings immediately. Back, chest, and abdomen should be vigorously washed twice to four times daily. Salt or vinegar may be mixed with the water. In the same way feet and arms must be washed in order to distribute the blood equally to all parts and produce sufficient warmth in them. All ablutions must be performed as quickly as possible, their duration should never exceed 1 minute.

If the effects of the stroke are only slight ones, and the patient is able to sit, the best application will be a head-vapour (for 20 minutes) succeeded by a vigorous washing of the upper body. After an interval from 4 to 6 hours, a foot-vapour (also for 20 minutes) should be applied, followed by an ablution or lower shower. Then, the above mentioned ablutions may be made use of.

I caution against the application of the larger bandages in such cases; the natural warmth is too weak and cannot be roused by these stronger remedies. I know of a case in which a physician attempted to cure the patient by swathings. The first bandage did good; but after the second one had been applied, the person remained cold,

14*

and the whole body assumed a bluish hue. Only application of warmth could bring him round again.

A man is stricken by apoplexy. One side is completely paralysed as well as the tongue. The patient is unconscious. So he remains for ten days. The physician who attended him, declared that nothing could be done, and that a second stroke would soon follow. The first application, which I prescribed in this case, was the head-vapour. The sick man was lying in bed; a basin half filled with boiling water (a few handfuls of hay-flowers had been added), was placed on a stool near the bed; the patient was laid near the edge of the bed and his upper body, which was exposed to the vapour, covered with a blanket. In 10 minutes the man was bathed in perspiration and continued so for 15 to 20 minutes, the water running down in drops. Thereupon, the upper body and the head were vigorously washed with fresh water and vinegar and laid to rest. On the same day the washing was once repeated but without vapour-application. On the second day a foot-vapour was applied (for 25 minutes), the patient being still unconscious. Profuse perspiration of the whole body was effected by this vapour, which was followed by a whole-ablution. On the third and fourth day respectively, we applied head-vapour and foot-vapour; on the fifth day consciousness returned and the patient was able to move his paralyzed limbs. On the next three days a whole ablution with water and vinegar was taken twice a day. Then the patient partly recovered his voice, but three weeks passed, before he could speak freely again.

From this time the patient began to make use of 3 applications: a) whole-ablution, b) covering with wet sheets and c) lying on wet sheets, alternately in the morning and in the afternoon. In a few days the patient felt so much stronger that a knee-shower could be applied every morning, and an upper shower every afternoon. Besides these applications whole-ablutions were taken and as soon as the patient could walk, this application was substituted by half-baths, and upper shower with knee-shower.

The effect of the cure was so good that the man, even now after twelve years, is perfectly able to attend to his business.

Asthma.

A gentleman relates: "I am 46 years old. For 20 years I have suffered from asthma. I had recourse to several physicians; they declared my disease to be incurable and prescribed some remedies to relieve me a little, but without any result. I thought myself doomed to bear this heavy cross to the end of my life. Especially during the night my difficulty in breathing reached sometimes such a degree that I spent whole nights at the open window, exposed to the cold of winter. Such attacks lasted several days. To add to my affliction, I lost all appetite and felt my strength go so fast that I could not but expect to be soon delivered from all earthly sufferings. At last God had mercy on me. The book "My Water-cure" came into my hands as a helper in great need. In 8 days I was cured. It is hardly to be believed how water can effect so great a change in a man's system in the brief space of 8 days. The applications were: 1) Upper shower, then knee-shower, walking in water; 2) shower for the back, thigh-shower; 3) sitting-bath, upper shower, half-bath; 4) upper shower, shower for the back, walking in water; 5) half-bath, upper shower, sitting-bath; 6) whole bath, upper shower; 7) thigh-shower, upper shower. Moreover I walked barefoot in the grass, daily for 1 to 2 hours. It was summer, and I felt better from hour to hour."

A priest makes the following statements: "I am well built and have always been healthy and strong; for nine months, however, I have been so obstructed with phlegm that I have great difficulty in breathing, and when I have to cough, I fear to suffocate. I had formerly an excellent, sonorous voice, and now I can scarcely make myself understood; I feel also so tired that I am hardly able to walk. Several physicians whom I consulted declare my disease to be catarrh of the wind-pipe or catarrh of the chest."

Applications: Daily three or four times an upper shower and twice daily walking in water to above the calves of the legs this to be continued for 4 days. During the 5 following days, 2 upper showers, 1 shower for the back and 1 half-bath daily; besides these applications, the shawl was used 3 times a week, and walking in water took place daily. After these 5 days, the patient took a half-bath, a shower for the back, an upper shower and a knee-shower daily. These applications were continued for a short time and effected the secretion of a great quantity of matter. Day by day, the patient's appearance improved, his breath became easier, his voice clearer, his temper more cheerful. His complaint had been chiefly brought on by too warm clothing and want of exercise.

Bed-wetting.

Not only children of both sexes, but also grown up people are often afflicted with this complaint. It is a pity that such unfortunate children are often treated with cruelty or that remedies are applied such as those advertised in almost every newspaper. I was once told that in an institution for children the bed-wetters were punished every night before going to bed. No wonder, if fear and anxiety prevents the poor creatures thus treated from falling asleep immediately; but this is not all, they will afterwards fall into a faster sleep, and the dreaded accident is sure to happen. The cause of this unpleasant complaint is weakness of the system; if the latter is braced, the former will soon disappear.

I advised 6 children, from 8 to 13 years old, to walk for 3 to 5 minutes in a bath with so much water as to reach the calves of the legs and then to take brisk exercise either in the room or the open air. After 5 days only 2 of the 6 children wetted their bed, in a few more days these also were cured. After the walking in water they made every time use of the arm-bath, holding their arms in cold water which was of great efficacy not only against the defect in question but also against their unhealthy appearance. The applications prescribed for children will suffice for adults as well. Only when the juices or the blood are much affected through weakness, it is advisable to take a cupful of tea from common yarrow, half of it in the morning, the rest in the evening.

For the applications the coldest water proved the best. I made an attempt with warm water in such a case, and the result was increase of the complaint.

Births.

A young woman had given birth to 3 dead children. Her sadness and discouragement became extreme when the physician declared that she would never be able to bear a child alive. I consoled her and gave her hope if she would make use of water-applications in order to strengthen her system. She began with the easiest means of hardening, accustomed herself by and by to stronger ones, until she kept at last to half- and whole-baths. Within three years she bore the happy father 3 healthy and strong children.

A woman was ill of typhus; the headache made her almost despair. Her relations brought her from the town to the country that she might there die quietly. The poor woman was about to become mother. I was consulted and prescribed short bandages which were applied directly. The headache abated. For the sake of security the relations of the patient sought the advice of the physician, who had attended her, about the short bandage. His verdict was that the first bandage would cause an untimely birth. Unfortunately for his advice, six bandages had already been applied, when the message reached us. The patient became quite well again herself and gave birth to a healthy child.

Bladder, catarrh of the.

A gentleman relates: "I am 30 years old, for 3 years I have been afflicted with a catarrh of the bladder; I attribute this complaint to over-exertion and especially to undue retention of the urine. In the beginning I still attended to my ordinary occupation, although under great pain, until I broke suddenly down at table with weakness and pain. For 4 months I kept my bed and became so miserable that I resembled a skeleton; the weight of my body being reduced to 41 kilo. The physician prescribed Wildungerwasser (mineral water), of which I drunk no less than 100 bottles, and sitting-baths. A violent catarrh of the stomach and bowels added to my sufferings. In spring things went on better. In summer my pain was bearable, although very great at times; my urine was very often, almost daily, of a dull colour. In winter my pains always increased and in summer I became better again.

In the winter of 1887, the pain in the bladder grew more violent, the urine became always more scanty and dull, and I had to keep my bed for 3 weeks. My strength was going so fast that it was believed consumption would soon bring me to my grave. The lower parts of my body were always cold, and I was shivering in a very well warmed room dressed as I was in 5 pair of trowsers and 3 pair of stockings. The physician only prescribed keeping warm and several kinds of mineral water of which I took 150 bottles. At last, encouraged by many, I resolved to go to Woerishofen, as soon as the weather would permit."

The patient looked very ill and emaciated, but he did not cough. I gave him hope for recovery. On the third day already the colour of his face had improved, the pain decreased, the urine became profuse and clear and after 4 weeks the patient declared: "Now I am again the cheerful and healthy man I was formerly — this has been effected by the water."

The result was extremely good. A physician who had made bladder complaints his special study, declared the gentleman completely recovered and was greatly astonished on seeing the result of the cure.

The applications were: In the beginning sometimes a nightstool-vapour with a decoction of shave-grass; then for 3 weeks, upper shower and walking in water in the morning and in the afternoon; later on, daily sitting-baths and upper showers alternately; besides this, tea from shave-grass and juniper-berries.

Bladder, complaint of the.

A teacher says: My disease has been declared by physicians to be "nervous irritation of the bladder and the bowels." For 15 years I have suffered more or less from difficulty in making water. In spring this year the disease appeared in an unusually high degree. Sometimes I had to discharge my water 15 to 20 times a night. The considerable sediment contained salt-crystals and later on mucus. 1 was also afflicted with winds, constipation, a feeling of chill and trembling (especially of. the lower body) during the night, sometimes with convulsions in the legs. Complete loss of appetite and sleeplessness rendered me very weak.

The applications were the following ones:

1) every night whole-ablution (for which the patient got up after lying in bed for some time);

2) one day a short bandage, the other day a shirt dipped in warm salt-water;

3) daily a cupful of tea from shave-grass, in which 20 crushed juniper-berries had been boiled: all this to be continued for 3 weeks.

In a short time appetite and sleep returned, and one symptom of the disease disappeared after another. There remained only debility and pain in the legs. Against these we applied:

1) an upper shower in the morning;

2) a knee-shower in the afternoon;

3) a half-bath from time to time.

The last symptoms of illness soon disappeared.

Blood, decomposition of the.

On my return from a journey, I visited a parish-priest of whom I had heard on the way that his end was expected. I entered and found the gentleman sitting in an arm-chair. He gave me the following account of his sufferings: I have 25 holes and wounds in my body. You see in my face 5 little plasters; of these I have 20 on my body. The little pustules form quickly and contain a brown fluid. If I put on a plaster, it will stick to the pustule for a day and, when taken off, some putrid flesh will come off with it. In this manner I have suffered for months, and I fear there is no longer help for me. More

tormenting even than the wounds on my body is for me
a foul taste in my mouth which is disgusting beyond
description. If you, dear brother in Christ, have some advice for a wretched man like me, give it speedily. I
prescribed 4 to 6 spoonfuls of tea from sage and wormwood to be taken every 2 hours to remove the bad taste
from his palate. Then I left him, convinced that I should
only see him again in Heaven.

Five days after this incident, a messenger brought me
the news — not of the priest's death — but that the
tea had effected the desired change in the priest's taste,
and that he even felt appetite for food. He now asked
me for a remedy which would complete his cure. I prescribed a whole-ablution to be taken daily for a fortnight,
the washing to be performed as quickly as possible. Again
the news arrived that the patient's health was improving
and the appetite increasing. I now advised him to make
use of the Spanish mantle and the whole-ablution alternately, every day for some weeks. After a fortnight the
priest said Mass for the first time after a long interval.
From that time he took every week a hay-flower-bath
(28⁰ R.) to conclude with a cold whole-ablution, and every
day cold half-baths (with ablution of the upper body)
alternately with whole ablutions. The good priest's recovery was a perfect one, and he lived for 24 years after
this cure cheerfully attending to his office as pastor.

A man comes and relates: For 2½ years I have been
ill, and nobody can help me. 2 years ago both my feet
swelled and became quite blue up to the knees. 2 holes
formed on each foot, out of which ran much matter and
blood. When the feet became a little better, the right
arm swelled, became likewise blue and holes formed on
it. The arm is now better, but I have a tumour and pains
in the back. Sometimes my abdomen is swollen, and I feel
great pain there. But much worse than my bodily complaints are my mental sufferings. People say that I sometimes speak confusedly. If it were allowed, I should have
committed suicide long ago. They also say I was
bewitched. Whether this be true or not, I cannot become
more wretched than I am.

I prescribed: Boil oat-straw, dip a flour-sack in the oat-straw-water thus obtained and slip into the sack, as you would in a pair of trousers up to the arm-pits. Then have yourself wrapped in a blanket, and remain so for 2 hours, after which you can go to work. The second day dip a coarse shirt likewise in such hot water, wring it out, and put it on, then the blanket, as the previous da . The third day you take a short bandage dipped in oat-straw-water, for 1½ hours. Thus continue for a fortnight. After this time all tumours had disappeared, one foot was cured, the other one had still a little hole; the appetite came back, and the peasant had to make use of one of the 3 applications every third day. After 3 weeks, body and mind were completely restored.

Blood poisoning.

A house-wife had scratched her finger a little, and not minding, the trifle went to bed without examining the injury; it seemed her too unimportant. In the night she wakes up, feels cramp in her finger, great nausea and a tendency to vomit. The injury was on the left hand, and she felt pain and cramp in the right foot. The hand, and the arm up to the elbow swell, become of a bright red, and within 10 hours the excessive pain extends over the whole arm. The veins up to the elbow swell and become dark-coloured. There was no physician in the village, and there was evidently the greatest danger.

Boiling water was poured over hay-flowers, and in these hot hay-flowers the whole arm was wrapped up. The arm, wearing the bandage, was then laid in the hot hay-flower-water for eight hours. These hay-flowers acted like a vesicatory on the whole arm and drew the poisonous matters out of the blood. This incident shows how necessary it is to procure speedy help in cases of blood poisoning. Perhaps in 1 or 2 hours this house-wife might have been dead. It is worthy of notice that even the tongue of this poor woman had already a bluish colour. After 36 hours the skin on the palm of the hand was so completely detached from the flesh that it could have been stripped off. As soon as the cramp in the finger ceased, the nausea, was gone.

Joseph killed a cow and, by accident, wounded his own thumb with the bloody knife. He paid no attention to it until he began to feel excessive pain, and his hand swelled so that he could scarcely move his fingers. The heat increased, and before long yellow and blue spots appeared on finger and hand. A physician gave him some remedy with which the hand was to be washed and bandaged. But the pain, which had got hold of the arm up to the elbow, became more unbearable than ever; the poor man felt that the inflammation inside was making continual progress.

I was sent for and, having examined the case, I prescribed vapours for hand and arm 4 times a day, each one of ½ hour's duration. During the time when the arm was not exposed to the vapours, it was wrapped up in boiled hay-flowers (to above the elbow).*

Every 2 hours i. e. as often as the pain increased, the bandage was renewed. This proceeding brought not only relief but complete cure. The spreading of the inflammation ceased on the evening of the first day, and after 4 days the inflammation was entirely removed.

A gentleman cut his corn which was inflamed. In a few days the inflammation made so rapid a progress that he could no longer doubt about blood poisoning having set in. Many, who had some experience of the matter, thought him lost. The patient took daily 2 foot-baths of boiled hay-flowers (these being left in the water for the bath) and daily the feet were wrapped in cloths dipped in a decoction of shave-grass (every hour to be re-dipped in it). These bandages were to be applied several times a day, each time for 2 hours. Since there appeared other symptoms of blood-poisoning (sickly appearance and want of appetite), general applications were added to the above-

---

* Hay-flowers are soaked with boiling water, then squeezed and spread on a cloth. On this the patient puts his arm and has it wrapped up in such a manner that it is quite surrounded by the damp warm hay-flowers.

mentioned partial ones. A lower bandage of 1½ hours' duration and ablution of the upper body were applied daily.

In a few days the gentleman was out of danger, and in 10 days he was perfectly well again. He took daily 2 cupfuls of tea from wormwood and sage (both herbs mixed).

Such small foot complaints require great precaution. I know of no better preservatives than walking barefoot (be it only in a room e. g. 15 or 20 minutes before going to bed) and frequent cold footbaths; for weak persons the latter may be lukewarm. Great care for the cleanliness of the feet is an important means for the preservation of general health.

A stout parish-priest tried to give his thick throat a normal shape by means of iodine, prescribed by a physician. In order to produce the desired effect in as short a time as possible and get rid of this goitre he was rather extravagant in the use of iodine. In a short time the strong gentleman emaciated so remarkably that he lost half the weight of his body. The physician gave him up, because the iodine had poisoned his blood.

In such cases the Water-Pfarrer is always good enough to make up for other people's imprudence! I wish this remark to be regarded as a mere joke which I write down without the slightest feeling of bitterness! The patient took warm baths with a decoction of pine-twigs (28— 30° R.) followed by a cold, but quick ablution; he lay on, and was covered with, wet sheets; there were further applied to him: the upper and lower shower, the lower bandage dipped in a decoction of pine-twigs, every day 2 applications in the given order. Besides this, he walked barefooted in the dewy grass.

He took daily a saltspoonful of chalk-dust or slacked lime dissolved in ½ pint of water, to be divided into 2 to 4 doses; likewise daily 1 or 2 spoonfuls of Provence-oil whilst he lived on simple, nourishing household-fare. Also in this case the water did excellent service.

Blood vomiting.

Whenever blood is spit or vomited, it is of the greatest importance to ascertain whether it comes from the lungs or the stomach. It is sure to come from the lungs when it is thrown up in a fit of coughing like phlegm, and when it is foamy and of a bright red hue; if the blood is coagulated and of a dark brown colour and the eva-cuation resembles ordinary vomiting, it may be concluded that it comes from the stomach. Blood vomiting is always frightening and requires great precaution, since it is infallibly accompanied by a greater or lesser danger. If the blood comes from the stomach, who knows, what little vein may have been injured, if and when the vomiting will take place again. Carelessness might have serious consequences. Therefore the injury ought to be healed as speedily as possible.

Blood vomiting from the lungs is by far more dangerous and should be attended to immediately.

For both kinds of blood vomiting tea of shave-grass is, on account of its contracting property, an efficacious remedy. If the blood flows from the nose, such tea ought to be drawn up by it; if it comes from the mouth some spoonfuls of such tea should be taken every 2 or 3 minutes. As a rule it stops the bleeding quickly. The tea should be taken for some time after the cessation of the bleeding. I do not know of a single case in which shave-grass has failed to bring about the desired effect.

If a person is repeatedly troubled with blood vomiting, the causes of the complaint should be investigated. It is then either the lungs which are affected and the patient is consumptive, or a too strong determination of the blood to the head takes place (s. congestions), or the bleeding proceeds from ulcers on the stomach.

In passing by, I will say a few words about bleeding of the nose. Many people have frequently bleedig at the nose and do not mind it at all, because they feel "well" after it. Yet their state is not a normal one, and sooner or later a severe disease is sure to ensue. Poverty of blood, weak blood and their attendants: anxiety, fear, scruples of various kinds are the inevitable consequences of this frequent loss of blood. I do not approve of the various ways in which people attempt to stop bleeding at the nose. There are some that pour water over the neck of the patient, others try to stop the bleeding by suddenly frightening him etc.

The only thing to be aimed at, seems to me the regularity of the circulation. The blood which overfills the head ought to be drawn down to the abdomen and the feet, which, with such people, are generally poor of blood, and it is just this poverty of blood that will cause many complaints later on.

The following water-applications will prove of excellent effect in this leading downwards of the blood: in the beginning a warm foot-bath with ashes and salt, for 15 minutes twice or three times a week; walking on wet stones, likewise twice or three times a week, and 2 or 3 short bandages. When the system has thus been strengthened, upper and lower showers and half-baths with ablution of the upper body will render very good service; one of these applications will be sufficient for the week.

There is one kind of bleeding of the nose which is not only serious, but really very dangerous. A girl of 15 bled to death within 2 hours. The blood flowed from the nose as if discharged through a pipe, and the bleeding only ended with the girl's death.

A girl of 16 years of age discharged through the nose 3 basinfuls of pure blood within 1½ hours. The increasing paleness and drowsiness seemed to indicate her approaching end. At 2 o'clock a. m., I was called to prepare her for death. All home-remedies had been unavailing; a physician was not to be had. Without delay, I had the contents of half a watering-can poured over her head, the other half over the upper part of her back. The bleeding ceased almost instantaneously. The girl lay for several hours quiet but on account of her weakness more or less unconscious. She had scarcely recovered herself a little when the bleeding of the nose began again. The gush was repeated and had the same effect. In order to gain new strength, the patient took 2 or 3 spoonfuls of milk every half hour — appetite and thirst being entirely wanting. After 2 days, she began to take strength-giving soups alternately with milk, but in very small portions. The upper shower was taken daily. The bleeding did not return and a very good appetite made itself felt instead. In about 6 weeks, the patient was quite well again, but although her appearance was as healthy as formerly, the girl felt the consequences of the attack (great internal weakness) for not less than 6 months.

Bloody flux.

A house-father comes and relates the following: "My wife has had bloody flux for some time and is dying; she may be dead, when I come home. There is no medical help for her. Is there no help at all?" My advice was the following: the woman should take 2 to 3 spoonfuls of tea from shave-grass every ¼ hour, later on 2 spoonfuls daily. She should put a cloth, dipped in half water and half vinegar, on the abdomen; the cloth ought to be renewed every 20 minutes and applied for 2 hours. The flux soon ceased, and the woman had to make use of the compress only twice after the first application and each time for ½ hour only.

To repair the loss of blood, she took 2 tablespoonfuls of milk every hour besides the ordinary household fare. After 4 weeks this woman was able to do the work in the house as before.

I must, however, remark that such applications should only be resorted to in cases of need, until a physician can be had.

Bowels, complaints of the.

A priest, 45 years of age, asserts:

"For more than 25 years I am suffering from an obstinate costiveness, and for some years, too, from stomach complaint. About 8 years ago I undertook a cold-water-cure, which improved the stomach, but the costiveness remained. In the year 1885, disease of the kidney's came on with surplus formation of urine acidity and formation of gravel, against which the doctor ordered a grape cure and after this a ten days' course with Glauber's-salt, which courses, however brought as a consequence a very violent catarrh of the bowels. After having undertaken every possible cure in vain, it was declared that my disease was incurable, that I could be relieved, but not cured. I was tormented with sleeplessness, want of appetite, lassitude, heaviness in the legs, dislike to work, pain and pressure in the vicinity of the kidneys, and costiveness in a high degree, with swelling and stretching of the abdomen, with a sensation of chill in my feet and great heat in my head, whilst the other parts of my body perspired easily and profusely. In this state I made up my mind to try the cold water, against which I had been so much warned."

The following was prescribed for the gentleman:

Daily an upper shower, a shower for the back, a sitting-bath, besides, according to need, a half-bath, knee shower, walking in water. But the Spanish mantle operated the most powerfully, and has become a dear friend to this gentleman. After a course of 12 weeks' duration, his digestion was perfectly regulated without any special diet, the bodily weight had gained 30 lbs.

Bowels, inflammation of the.

An overseer relates: "For years I have suffered from violent, almost unbearable pain and cramps in the bowels. I can scarcely eat anything without pain and succeeding diarrhoea. I have taken a great deal of medicine, but obtained only little relief for a short time. The appearance of this man in his best years, is very sickly. He is emaciated, pale, and his eyes are dull. What could bring him help?

1) This man took 3 sitting-baths weekly;

2) He washed chest and abdomen vigorously with water and vinegar, every morning and evening.

In 4 weeks the poor man was freed from his sufferings. He had also taken 12 drops of wormwood extract in warm water, twice daily.

Brain, disease of the.

A brew-master of about 33 years of age has been suffering greatly for 11 years. In May 1877, one morning as he rose from bed, he fell suddenly prostrate half insensible and remained in this state for 2 hours. This attack was the precursor of serious typhoid fever which lasted six months. Great giddiness with vomiting and faintness tormented him daily. The giddiness began with a beating in the brain; then it threw the man to the ground, often full length. This state continued mostly from 5 to 10 minutes, and returned daily 5, 8, or 10 times. After these six months he was able to work again, but only for 2 months. Thereupon, the attacks set in again so frequently and with such force that he was obliged to keep his bed for 8 months. In the course of these 11 years, he was every year 6 or 7, even 8 months confined to his bed. The disease increased to such an extent, that, when he was not in bed, the attacks of giddiness and falling returned every two or three days, especially after any mental exertion, after quick motion, at every turn of the head. The attack always announced itself by a beating in the head, and if he were able quickly enough to cling to a table, or in the open air to a tree, it shook him and threw him hither and thither until at last he came to the ground. He did not lose consciousness, but his sight went.

For 9 years the attacks were always accompanied by vomiting, which ceased since the last year. The whole time, for above 10½ years the unhappy sufferer felt a constant pressure on his head as if a heavy weight were lying there. For 5 years he has had a continual humming in the ears and a difficulty of hearing with his right ear. He was scarcely ever able to sleep at night until one or two o'clock on account of a feeling of weight and fulness in the head, and this for 9 years. From May 1886 to October 1887, the man was, with a very slight interruption, bedridden. He took a whole host of medicaments from the 14 doctors who attended him in the course of his long illness, several of whom declared him incurable.

Most of them gave the opinion that through a former hurt on his head — a cask had fallen on it — the skull was cracked, and since then a splinter of bone pressed upon the brain, thereby causing all his sufferings.

In my opinion, there was an extraordinarily strong determination of blood to the head, and the following applications were prescribed:

Upper shower, walking in water, gush for the back, thigh and knee-gush, foot-vapour, as well as the Spanish mantle. The result of the five weeks' course, from July 28th to September 2nd, was a particularly excellent one. Even on the fifth day, the patient declared himself free from the pressure on the brain.

On the second day he had an attack after rather long mental exertion (letter-writing), — it was the last. From day to day his health improved to his great joy; the next 4 weeks he felt as "born anew, so free and so light in his head," and his sight relieved too. For these five weeks he slept the whole night through. The man is overjoyed, and returned, as it were, to life. At home he had simply to continue daily with one of the above applications.

Brain, inflammation of the.

The blood has always a determination to those parts where an inflammation has arisen. It speedily flows to these heated spots and leaves other parts, and especially those at the greatest distance from the inflammation, more or less bloodless. When the brain is inflamed, the blood must be led to the extremities, but also the inflamed part must be worked upon. The applications are the following: Feet and legs up to the knees, are to be bandaged in cloths dipped in water mixed with vinegar. Should the feet be very cold, the cloths might be dipped in hot water first, but as soon as they become hot, cold water is to be taken for renewing the compress. The hands and arms should be likewise bandaged at least to the elbows; then, the patient may lie on wet sheets. After $\frac{3}{4}$ hour, the cloth must be re-dipped in cold water. If the heat does not give way, these applications should be continued. A twofold coarse cloth dipped in water and laid on the abdomen, will greatly assist the other applications in leading the blood downwards. As a more direct application to the affected part, a wet cloth may be tied round the forehead or round the neck. The latter application is almost more efficacious; both have to be renewed every $\frac{1}{2}$ hour. The shawl also does good service in

15*

such cases, but it, also, must be renewed every $\frac{3}{4}$ hour.
These applications, when used alternately, will prevent
the fever from attaining a high degree, and the inflammation will be quickly removed. Fresh water is the best
remedy for interior use but not more than 1 or 2 spoonfuls should be taken at a time. An infusion of Foenum
graecum may also be taken instead of water.

Burns.

A peasant's house burnt down. The peasant burnt
his face and hands in such a manner that he was not to
be recognised. The physician put several plasters on the
injured spots. From the fingers and from half the arm
skin and flesh hung down in strips. Almost despairing
with unspeakable pain, the unfortunate man longed for
death to come and release him. The physician declared
the recovery of the patient an utter impossibility.

The absence of the pastor of the parish, in which
the accident occurred, proved providential for the poor
man. I was called to his bedside, and on seeing him in
his intense suffering, I tried to find out a means of re-
lieving him in order that he might die quietly. I had all
the stiff, sticky little plasters removed, then I quickly
stirred with a pen raw white of egg, linseed-oil and sour
cream to a paste which was applied to the suffering parts
in such a manner as not to allow the entrance of the
air. Over the paste I put worn out, wet linen rags, and
over these again a dry cloth. After every 2 hours the
dry cloth was gently removed, and the damp cloth carefully moistened again to prevent the so painful sticking
of it to the wounds. In the morning and in the evening
the moist cloth, too, was removed and a layer of fresh
paste added to the old one. It is incredible in how short
a time the patient was cured. The first application already had the effect that the fearful pain gave way and
the cramps, the approach of which had been announced
by the well known ominous writhing, were prevented.

As internal cooling remedy, the patient took one spoonful of salad-oil twice daily. Under the paste which closed
the wounds completely to the air, the new skin formed

remarkably quickly. The strictest cleanliness — after the first few days, the matter was washed away with luke-warm water several times in the day — helped to promote the cure which was almost accomplished after 14 days. The physician himself declared this patient's recovery almost a miracle. He had never believed in the possibility of healing such injuries.

A man-servant was grievously injured by a camphine-flame. One half of his upper body was so terribly burnt that one arm, half the chest, and one side of the head were covered with black, yellow, and red spots, and the skin could be everywhere stripped off. He offered a dreadful sight, and the unfortunate man suffered agonizing pain. Exactly the same treatment as the above mentioned saved him and gave him back to his vocation and his master.

Protection from the outer air, dampness of the cloths applied, regularly renewed application of the cooling paste, and great cleanliness are the chief requirements for, and conditions of, a rapid cure of burns.

Sauerkraut (pickled cabbage) is a good house-remedy for slighter burns. It must be fresh from the tub and is bandaged round the injured part. Also the water produced from Sauerkraut by pressure, may be employed in a similar manner. Some prefer scraped potatoes, others linseed-oil. All these little remedies are good.

A cook had the misfortune of scalding her hand and her arm up to the elbow with boiling water. Medical aid was immediately on the spot, but in spite of the most careful treatment, the wound did not heal for weeks. Now the person had recourse to the remedies prescribed by me which alleviated her pain almost instantaneously and eventually effected her complete cure.

The applications were: 1) The whole wound was painted with white of egg and oil and bandaged with a wet cloth; for the first few days the bandage was renewed twice daily. 2) Injurious juices and dirt were extracted by a bandage of infused hay-flowers. During the cure, several ulcers formed. To heal these, a decoction of Foenum graecum (or fenugreek) was applied. By means of these remedies which were alternately made use of, hand and arm were completely cured.

Cancer.

A very frequent disease of the present time is cancer. There is hardly a part of the body which may not be destroyed by cancer, or cancerous injuries. If it happens that this evil has already spread, I dare not attempt anything with water; blood and juices are already too corrupted.

Cancer is hereditary, especially if blood and juices of an individual are already disposed to that kind of decomposition. I knew a married couple who visited a cousin suffering from cancer in the tongue. Without any misgiving, they were both terrified as they perceived the horrible ravages of the dreadful disease.

Within three days, the half of the woman's tongue had swollen in a morbid manner, and the man's under lip became inflamed and sore. "We have taken the disease" they came lamenting to me. I tried to encourage them; for they were frightened to death, and did all I could to dissuade them from their firm assertion. At the same time I advised them on the one day to wash out their mouth, especially the affected part, with alum-water about 4 times, the second day to repeat the washing with aloe-water, besides taking every second day a head vapour, and alternately with the head vapour to put a bandage round the neck.

The two persons were quite cured of the disease. I myself could never have believed that terror alone could have the effect of giving so frightful a disease. I heard later that a doctor had really said they had taken the disease.

I have treated several cases of cancer in the first stages, also smaller advanced cancerous injuries. They are easily cured. All applications aim solely at the purifying of blood and juices.

Caries.

A gentleman of position got a bad toe; he thought the nail had been a little hurt, and did not consider the matter worthy of any further attention. In the meantime the toe became inflamed, and made it necessary to call in a doctor, who, during several weeks, prescribed different remedies. The toe was all right, he thought, although the inflammation had gained in extent, the whole foot was greatly swollen, and he could neither stand on, nor walk with it. The patient suspected nothing until one day two little bones came out through the skin. Then he began to mistrust his foot and all those who had until now considered and pronounced it quite excellent.

The gentleman knew me and asked me to inspect it. Caries had set in. I at once ordered shave-grass to be boiled in water, and the foot as far as the swelling reached, to be bound in cloths dipped in the decoction. Within quite a short time, the swelling and the still young caries were removed; the foot healed up again, and its master used it as before.

After about a year, the unhappy disease announced itself again, this time on the other foot, and indeed just on the big toe again. During the healing the patient experienced on his other foot a continuous pain similar to that which he had felt before the appearance of the first attack. The healing of the toe progressed in the meantime and was at last declared complete and successful, although the cut and healed toe remained half as thick again as it should have been and rather red. The energetic gentleman could walk and work, and what more would he have? As one who does not keep the truth behind a mountain, but always speaks his mind straight out, I was avoided and questioned no further. That was agreeable to me, for my reply would have been: the disease is partly, but not en'irely removed. The consequence will be, that sooner or later the caries will penetrate further. I had not deceived myself; for so it happened. How had this foot to be treated? Necessarily both feet must receive treatment at the same time, so long, until no spot of particular redness is to be seen, and not the least pain is to be felt. They are to be treated with foot-bandages dipped in a decoction of oat-straw, in such a manner that the feet are wrapped up a few times daily, and the bandages reach a little above the diseased and painful places.

The perfect and real healing will not take too long a time. How is it then that in our case the caries should have settled itself just in the feet? Why not, e. g. in the hands or arms? — This gentleman had formerly had a serious and tedious illness, which left a great weakness behind it, especially in the feet. Possibly morbid poisonous matters lay there. One thing is certain that, with the then convalescent gentleman, the feet on account of the hard work (they alone always carry the body, and often what a body!) could never properly recover themselves, and so as the weaker part, easily succumbed to the attacks of the poisonous matters.

The gentleman is still living. He must take great care if he does not want to be visited again by caries. At the least sign, he would do well by following my friendly and well-meant advice, and not delay with the compresses of shave-grass or decoction of oat-straw. Sero venientibus ossa! The gentleman is a latin scholar, he will laugh and understand me. They who do not know Latin need not rack their brains, or let their hair turn grey because, against my usual custom, I have, this time, not translated the foreign words. I pass over other cases of cured caries, as they concern younger persons, with whom, in the beginning of the disease, the cure is easily and quickly effected.

Catarrh.

Most catarrhs owe their existence to a rapid transition from the open air or a cold room into a well heated room. Also draught to which one has been exposed, may cause catarrh. It generally makes itself felt by a sensation of contraction in chest, throat, and nose. It is a feeling as if there were a little dumpling in one's throat. If this swelling is overlooked, it settles and spreads. Great susceptibility for catarrh is caused by effemination of the body through too warm clothing. It would not be difficult (I say it boldly) to remain free from every catarrh if the body was not "barbarously" but reasonably hardened, as emphatically recommended in other passages of this book.

What must we do in order to be spared?

An example shall show it us. I have been walking for an hour at a rather quick pace. It is pretty fresh, as the peasant says while rubbing his hands; we have 12^0 R. below zero. Immediately I enter a room where the thermometer shows 14^0 heat. This change of temperature amounting to 26^0 cannot remain unrevenged. It would have been better if I had walked slower for the last 20 minutes and remained in the cool passage for some minutes (taking some exercise) before entering the warm room. In this manner the heat of the body would have been decreased and the perspiration arrested. To make the change of temperature completely harmless, I might have walked up and down for a while in the heated room itself.

If you feel the consequence of your imprudence, the little dumpling in your throat, return to the open air and take some exercise. This will dissolve and remove all superfluous matter in your throat within $\frac{1}{2}$ hour.

Hoarseness is nothing else but catarrh extended to the organs of speech. The silver-bell, when tied up, gives no sound, the most sonorous voice is mute when the organs of speech are swollen. Remove the catarrh, and its companion, the hoarseness, will follow it without hesitation.

On this occasion I insert a remark about coughs which will render good service to many. There are people who have a tendency to cough a great deal. Every trifle e. g. the tickling of the fresh air in their throat calls forth this barking. Such people cough for years without the slightest pain. This disposition is generally inherited from the parents and therefore difficult to remove. This kind of cough is of no consequence, whether it proceeds from the throat, or from other organs. Such people may derive comfort from the German proverb: He who coughs for a long time will live for a long time. Other hereditary defects are not so innocent in their consequences, but well worthy of attention, as consumption, phthisis etc.

There it wants acting on the maxim: Principiis obsta! Meet the first beginnings decidedly, but with all prudence and precaution. A slight catarrh, in a family where phthisis is hereditary, can like the bark-scarab which ruins the strongest pine-tree, destroy the most vigorous constitution. Therefore be careful! By prudent treatment even hereditary defects may prove without serious consequences and not destroy altogether the hope for a long life.

Chlorosis (Green-sickness).

The whole body derives its strength, the formation and growth of its parts and its capability of endurance from the blood; good and sufficient blood is, therefore, the first condition of health. He who has good blood enjoys good health; he who has much blood is enduring, and where little or bad blood is prepared, there is a liability for all possible diseases.

Good, wholesome air, much light, nourishing food, and suitable exercise are essential for the formation of good blood. If these necessary conditions are wanting, the blood will fail, and if the food is not sufficient in quality, unhealthy blood will be formed.

Poverty of blood can also be caused by loss of blood through wounds, by bleeding etc.

He who is poor of blood is also sick or at least ailing.

Those who suffer from chlorosis (or green-sickness) offer a true picture of the effects of poverty of the blood. The face is pale, white, often yellowish, brownish; the lips and gums are especially livid, and in the whole person weakness, emaciation, want of vital heat, drooping stature prevail. Further consequences are: palpitation, heavy breath, especially when mounting stairs, headache, pains in the back, fainting-fits, cramps and bad digestion. Such people have frequently a strange craving for unsuitable food.

Persons afflicted with this illness should be in the open air as much as possible and if they are in the room, this should be but sparingly heated. Their clothing should be only moderately warm and not closely fitting the body, in order that air may penetrate everywhere.

The food of such patients should be good and digestible and consist chiefly in milk, good bread, bread-soup, and simple farinaceous dishes; they should eat but little at a time. From 2 to 4 spoonfuls of milk taken frequently are the best food for them since the juices of the stomach are scanty and much food at a time cannot be digested by them. Exercise and work in the open air (provided that the patient's strength is not overtaxed) will aid the formation of blood.

The water-applications suitable for such patients are: To take a whole-ablution from bed 3 or 4 times a week; to stand in water to above the calves of the legs for one minute; directly after this the arms, too, are held in water, about twice or 3 times a week.

If the chlorotic person is very week and has very little vital heat, warm water should be taken in the beginning for the ablutions as well as for the baths; the water may also be mixed with salt or vinegar. To promote appetite it will be very good to take 2 or 3 tablespoonfuls of wormwood-tea, 3 times daily. An excellent remedy against chlorosis is pulverized chalk of which a salt-spoonful in 4 to 6 spoonfuls of water should be taken twice daily.

As soon as the general health of the patient has been improved through the above mentioned applications, half-baths may be taken twice or 3 times a week instead of ablutions and foot-baths; upper shower and knee-gush, if not used too often, will also render excellent service.

Poverty of blood in a child: A mother brings a boy, 5 years old. The boy is stout, well built and has a good stature, but his face is so pale that he resembles a corpse rather than a healthy child. The child has neither courage, nor appetite, nor strength, in a word the child is so poor of blood, and its whole organism so inactive that it seems an old man. Several physicians have attended to the child but nothing has brought it relief. Two physicians ordered much wine to be drunk; but the condition of the little patient remained the same since the child felt a great repugnance for wine as for all other food. What is to be done here?

1) Every day the child should put on a shirt dipped in a decoction of hay-flowers.

2) Every day the whole body of the child should be washed with water and vinegar.

3) The boy should, if possible, walk barefooted in the room; he should also go out in the open air. His food should consist in simple household-fare, chiefly in water and milk (but always in small quantities, 2 to 3 tablespoonfuls), this to be continued for a fortnight. After this time:

1) To walk daily in moderately cold water to above the calves of the legs, for 3 to 5 minutes.

2) To take a whole-ablution with water and vinegar, daily.

3) To put on a shirt dipped in salt water or in a decoction of hay-flowers, once or twice a week.

These applications are to be continued for a fortnight and after this time to be made use of half as often.

Cholera.

How much dreaded is cholera! Two years ago several countries were visited by this terrible epidemic and numberless where those who fell a victim to it. To protect a country against inundations dykes are erected and rivers regulated. When a forest is on fire, ditches are digged to prevent the destroying element from spreading. Such a dyke and ditch against cholera, this terrible foe of human life, is water. It saves us from danger and surrounds those by whom it is rightly applied with a dyke or ditch.

With regard to cholera the prevailing maxim is: If profuse perspiration is produced, the patient is saved; if not, he is lost.

One night I was called to a poor maid-servant. She had vomited 20 times, and just as many times she had made use of the close-stool. The physician lived at a distance of 6 miles. The poor girl wanted to be prepared for death; for she felt herself that her death must be at hand. Her hands and feet were as cold as ice, her face pale, her features sunk, the symptoms of imminent dissolution were there. I directly sought to produce perspiration seeing that on the effect of this procedure everything depended, life or death. The housewife brought speedily 2 large coarse sheets. I dipped them in hot water, folded and wrung out, and with this almost hot compress chest and abdomen were covered. Underneath on the skin a single cloth dipped in hot vinegar was laid. The wet hot compress was covered and closed to the air by a feather quilt as warm and as heavy as the patient could bear. Violently did the heat penetrate into the body and in 15 minutes the whole body was warm; when 20 minutes more had past, the perspiration rolled down in pearls from the face. I had the compress redipped in hot water. In a very short time the cramps ceased and with them the vomiting and the sensation of sickness. To meet within, the heat working from without, the patient took a cupful of hot milk with fennel (one spoonful of ground fennel boiled in milk for 3 minutes). Profuse perspiration being thus produced, the girl was saved.

The time of convalescence is in such cases of the greatest importance. The convalescent should lie on wet sheets, for an hour daily, and be covered with wet sheets for the same time daily. For the first application the sheets should extend to the length of the spine, for the second they should cover chest and abdomen. The patient just spoken of, did so and was cured in 10 days. A second case was treated in the same way and with the same result.

As soon as the symptoms of this disease, violent diarrhœa, vomiting, cramps etc. appear, the person so affected should be laid in bed. Country people are often too hard against themselves in this respect; this is want of prudence. As interior application a warm drink may be given. If cramping pain sets in, or the feet become ice-cold, a warm compress should be applied to the abdomen, for not longer than about three quarters of an hour. For the same time the patient should be laid on wet sheets. As often as the cramps return, the compresses may be repeated. As soon as heat and perspiration set in, the patient is saved.

Great precaution with regard to food and drink should be used until health is completely restored. Of the usual simple fare the lighter kinds of food should be chosen. The best beverage is milk which is remedy at the same time.

When cholera rages in a place, be not over-anxious, but trust in God. Wash chest and abdomen vigorously with cold water every morning and every evening, chew 10 to 12 juniper-berries daily and if you cannot have these, buy pepper-cakes; for 3 d. you will get a good many of them. Five pepper-cakes, taken twice a day will warm the stomach, assist the digestion and lead out gases.

Cholerine.

Almost in every place, there are some cases of cholerine every year. Cholerine is cholera in a diminutive form, a very unpleasant guest, though not so much feared. Its attendants are violent diarrhœa, vomiting and sometimes more or less violent cramps.

My applications for cholerine are exactly the same as those for cholera, modified in number and degree according to the stages of the disease. I had once no less than 40 persons afflicted with cholerine under treatment and, with all of them, the happy result was complete cure.

Colic.

Colic accompanied by diarrhœa or sickness often appears suddenly without an apparent cause. It may be caused by cold, by over-heating or by some particular food or drink.

A patient of this kind should be laid in bed without delay and a warm cloth (perhaps also a hot-water bottle)*

---

* Poor people will find a substitute for the hot-water bottle by making a brick hot and rolling it up in a woollen cloth.

put on the abdomen, then he should be covered so as to prevent the entrance of the air. As a lenitive the patient should be given ½ pint of milk in which fennel or cara-way-seeds have been boiled. This simple household-remedy will be sufficient.

Regarding the diet of the patient, as long as he continues in this condition, the food should be very simple and very digestible, with very little salt and spice. Water and milk are the best beverages for such patients; water and wine (mixed) can also be recommended.

Congestions.

An officer lamented in the following manner:

I suffer from heavy breath, cramps in the neck and very violent headache. Often I spend whole nights sleepless on account of congestions and pain in my head. No evacuation of the bowels takes place unless it be pro-duced by remedies. Moreover I have much cramp in the chest, and sometimes it extends to the bowels and causes me great suffering. I know not how to protect myself against the cold; my hands and feet are generally cold. My station in life is a pleasant one, but I am constantly tormented by these sufferings. I went to several bathing-places but obtained no relief. I was formerly corpulent, but now emaciation has taken the place of corpulence. If the water brings me no help, he concluded in a sad tone, I shall be lost.

The treatment was the following:

1) The patient walked barefooted in the grass and on foot-paths every morning and evening for some time. This brought him indescribable relief and led the blood off his head.

2) 2 short bandages weekly.

3) Once the Spanish mantle.

To promote the evacuation of the bowels, he took for several days a spoonful of water every ½ hour, and if there was greater difficulty, he took every hour a spoon-ful of warm water in which a piece of aloe as large as a pea and half a spoonful of sugar had been dissolved.

Consumption.

Like a serpent in the grass or among stones lying in ambush for its prey, consumption often begins to do its destroying work in some part of the system before it shows itself openly. Its beginning is a decomposition which takes place in some part and by formation of matter spreads and destroys organs of the body. The chest, the lungs, the pleura, the abdomen, the intestines, the kidneys the throat, the windpipe, the larynx, the noblest and most important organs may be thus affected. Wherever such a decomposition takes place it is quickly followed by disturbances in the circulation. A person afflicted with this malady is like a tree whose leaves fade before the time. Sun and fresh air are of no avail there. The same may be said of a consumptive person. The blood, this fluid on the condition of which life depends, decreases like the sap of a decaying tree and the patient resembles a light growing weaker and weaker and becoming eventually extinguished through want of nourishment.

If consumption is so far advanced that an organ has been destroyed by it, then all human help is idle; but if it has only commenced to affect one or the other part of the organism, cure by water is easy. It is a sad thing that the symptoms just of this disease seem of so little consequence. The patient coughs a little, the cough causes no pain and is not even accompanied by expectoration. If the cough is worse from time to time, the patient considers it a slight catarrh which comes to trouble him sometimes, but which will soon be over again. Even when the body begins to be more languid and a decrease of strength is distinctly felt, there are always excuses. This time the catarrh lasts a little longer, but still I can attend to my duties. At this stage of the illness, a person has generally already suffered more than he himself believes. Blood and juices have decreased, and the decomposition has gained in extension.

If, then, the patient seeks for help, it is generally too late, and remedies applied at this period will often but serve to shorten his life. I say all this to caution people against neglect of so-called catarrhs. In cases of advanced consumption I do not even attempt to cure by water* (I declare this also to all such patients who consult me); for there, nature is too much weakened as to take up the combat with the fresh water.

The symptoms of advanced consumption are: frequent coughing, much expectoration, heavy breath, and want of appetite. As long as the phlegm swims on the water (make the experiment) there is no need for giving up all hope; if it sinks, hope for human help is generally in vain. The patient should resign himself to the will of God and should quietly prepare for his last hour.

On the other hand I can prove by many examples that water is the best and safest remedy in the first stages of consumption. It refreshes and revives the languid body by working like oil poured between the wheels of a machine; it produces a quicker circulation and infuses new life into the weakened organism. Moreover it winnows the bad juices as a sieve does the poppy-seed by throwing off what is injurious. The applications, however, should never be such as effect violent dissolution and evacuation. Strengthening of the organism must be the chief aim in order that invigorated nature itself may throw off injurious matters. Any application which is likely to weaken or destroy the vital heat should be carefully avoided. That would be promoting the disease.

Only very short applications must be used. I would not venture to make use of an application extending to the whole body, if there were symptoms of rather advanced consumption.

If the disease has its seat in the upper part of the body, the upper shower followed by the knee-gush will be of excellent service (the latter to be applied for ½ minute only). If the weather is favourable, walking barefoot in wet grass is a practice surpassed by no other; it braces

---

* Countless experiments have always led to the same result; the condition of the patient can be relieved, but he cannot be cured.

the system, and there is not the least reason for fear of its doing harm. Walking on wet stones is also good; it draws the blood downwards and effects a quicker circulation and, therefore, promotes the formation of blood in general. I will say one word more about the diet of such patients who are, more than all others, served with the ritornello: "Eat and drink well". The simplest fare is the best, no ardent pirits, no spiced or sour food should be taken.

The best diet for consumptive people is that which is most suitable for children and most conducive to their growth.

It is remarkable that such patients have a particular craving for salt so as to put it on their bread, to dip the meat in it; they also have a special liking for sour and spiced food. I regard this as one of the surest signs of the malady, and for me it has often been the decisive one.

I recommend milk as preferable to all other kinds of food, but if taken only without change of diet, it will soon turn distasteful to the patient. Strength - giving soups are also to be recommended, the preparation being sometimes altered, even if the sick person should have a particular liking for one kind. Simple farinaceous food without complicated or artificial preparation should also hold a prominent place in the diet of a consumptive person. The beverage which is least apt to cause repugnance is water, perhaps mixed with a little wine. Curdled milk is also good. I never recommend beer or wine.

In the more advanced stages of this illness, the patient often suffers from violent fever accompanied by profuse perspiration and followed by a sensation of chill. He may be relieved by a vigorous ablution of back, chest and abdomen.

A schoolmistress had been treated by a celebrated physician for a long time, but without result. At last she was no longer able to teach, and being dispensed from her duties, she obtained a pension for 9 months. When this time had elapsed, her condition was not much better, and the physician declared her incurable and therefore unable to follow her vocation. Some friends advised her to try the water-cure, and she took lodgings in a village near my parish. The patient was almost unable to walk 1½ miles, so great was her weakness. She used water-applications according to prescriptions, and after 5 weeks she was completely cured. She applied to the government in order to obtain her former office as teacher, but nobody would believe her cured. She presented herself in person to the minister (president of the comittee for education) who was astonished at seeing her healthy appearance and still more at the fatal epithet "incurable" in her certificate. She has now been teaching for 6 years since and enjoys the best of healths. What disease the physicians had found in this patient, whether decline or consumption, I don't know. The symptoms were those of consumption. Her brother had died of this illness, and sufferings similar to hers had preceded his death. It was high time to arrest the disease, but the water has arrested it. The remedies prescribed were: to be much in the open air, to walk frequently barefooted in the dewy grass in the morning, baths, from the lightest to the strongest, always cold. As interior remedy she took tea from herbs; her food was the simple strengthening household fare of the country people.

A gentleman of position relates: I was never very strong and never enjoyed so much health for a short time as many a person during his whole live. I could, however, finish my studies and attend to my vocation till about 2 years ago. Then a change took place. Wherever I go, I meet with ominous looks, and sometimes I heard my friends whisper to each other that I would not have to live much longer. The thought of death is no strange guest to myself since I cannot close my eyes to the symptoms of its approach. My strength has gone as well as the healthy appearance. The appetite, this best barometer of health, shows that my vital strength is fast giving way.

I suffer severely from difficult breath, still more from a cough the sound of which is really frightening. The doctors declared me consumptive. They have given me

16*

up, but advise me to go to Meran where the climate is milder. (Poor fellow, I thought, won't they even let you die at home?) On my journey to Meran I heard of the effects of water and inquired if it could be of any avail for my broken constitution. You can try it, was the answer. The beginning was not easy. I wore very warm clothing, and yet I felt always chilly. Now I was told that I must gradually disaccustom myself from woollen underclothing and part first with my flannel shirt, then with a woollen scarf which I wore round my neck. I was wondering what effect a clothing which was rather cooling than warming, would have on my illness and the cold water made me shudder. The practices by which I was initiated into the course of applications were very moderate and very cautiously applied. On the third day already I could leave off one of my woollen shirts, on the sixth day I sacrificed the second, and, after a few days more, I parted with my woollen scarf.

Through the water-applications I got a very pleasant sensation of vital heat which increased from day to day; the difficulty in breathing disappeared, the cough, too, gave way. The improvement of my humour kept pace with that of my bodily health. The course of applications lasted 5 weeks. Against all expectation, I was now on the way not to eternal repose but to a new life, as it were. I thanked God, my Creator, for the restoration of my health as well as for having given us so effective and so easily obtainable a remedy as water. Would I could make it known to all men and exhort them all to appreciate the water and its effects. How many sufferings would they escape on their pilgrimage through life, how much better would they fulfil the duties of their vocation!

You will be desirous, dear reader, to know what applications I made use of. Like a young shepherd whose constitution is hardened by many a shower, my upper body received 2 showers daily. First the jet played on my back for half a minute only, after some time for 1 minute. Daily I walked in the wet grass and on wet stones. According to the general prejudice, I feared that all possible complaints would ensue; but I soon took the greatest pleasure in it. Winter was at hand, and snow fell. I walked for a minute in the freshly fallen snow. The result was more favourable than I expected. I was allowed to repeat this practice frequently, and I can assure every one afraid of water, that I never felt so thoroughly warm as after these snow-walks. The feet burn for 2 or 3 minutes on account of the snowy cold; but, then, a warmth develops which makes one forget the snow. In a few days I was able to continue my brisk walk in the snow for 10 minutes or $\frac{1}{4}$ hour. It was just the walking in snow which brought on an extraordinary increase of strength, and which greatly diminished my difficulty in breathing. Of catarrh there was not the least idea. If somebody had told me about this practice before, I should have thought it madness and the ruin of health. I continued walking barefoot for a fortnight, then the applications were limited to upper and lower showers applied in a more vigorous manner, twice daily. After 3 weeks my system was regulated again, and in 3 more weeks I had entirely recovered my former strength. Instead of going to Meran in order to die there, I returned to my dear home to attend to my vocation with renewed vigour.

A man comes and relates: "There is something the matter with my throat and my chest. It began with a very bad catarrh, then I lost my voice almost entirely; for weeks I felt violent burning in throat and chest, and I have often attacks of fever. I have had several physicians and have inhaled a great deal. The result was always a little relief, but no perfect cure. Now I am emaciated, and for a long time I have not been able to work. My feet are always cold, my appetite is better than formerly."

Applications: 1) A knee-shower or walking in water twice daily; 2) an upper shower in the morning and in the afternoon daily; 3) to drink 2 small cupfuls of tea from foenum graecum daily; 4) a cold sitting-bath for one minute every second day. These applications to be continued for 3 weeks.

Costiveness.

If there are many people who frequently suffer from diarrhoea, there are a far greater number who are tormented with costiveness and, therefore, must seek help in remedies which certainly operate on the bowels, but the end of which is, in most cases, destruction. One can boldly say: The longer any one uses such remedies, the more the whole constitution suffers. Who could name the innumerable remedies which are applied for purging and for assisting the evacuation of the bowels? I know a man who is renowned far and wide for his laxatives. What did he do? He very frequently took goose-dung, boiled it, and with this decoction served his honoured customers. There are other instances I could give, if desired. *Mundus vult decipi!* The world wants to be deceived! But still that concerns chiefly the "stupid country-fellows." The genteel world is treated otherwise. Innumerable bottles with different mineral waters are driven daily through the body, and indeed they do effect the most copious evacuations. A patient once brought me an enormous quantity of quicksilver which he had just taken from the close-stool. It had been given to him as a laxative. How many Morison's pills were taken at his time, and how many people found an early grave through them! There is scarcely a disease that is operated upon and tried in so many ways and so unsuccessfully as costiveness. And in most cases the consequence is, that, the more and the longer the remedies are taken (and at last there is no evacuation without a laxative), the greater will always be the difficulty. A man, entirely forsaken by medicine, complained to me, that not one day passed by, on which he was not obliged to apply a clyster or some drastic remedy to obtain the necessary evacuation. So far had he been brought by these tiresome remedies (?), and the man was not near 40 years of age.

It is a great improvement in the medicine of our time, that all violent medicines have been scouted, and many doctors — it must be said to their renown — have chemically analysed hundreds of so-called secret-remedies and exposed the deception to all reasonable people. Nevertheless this ghost of secret-remedies still creeps into a thousand families and does mischief.*

When the evacuation of the bowels is irregular, in most cases the whole organism is not in order, not only the stomach or some other particular part; and I am of the firm conviction, which a great number of cases have always confirmed, that again the water is the surest and most harmless remedy to be found on the earth. It helps by being applied interiorly, and by being permitted to operate exteriorly.

One of the first questions which the doctor puts to the patient is: are the bowels regular? If this is so, one has the first sign of health; if they are irregular, it is the sign of the commencement of an illness, and if this evil is not remedied, the patient goes to meet an illness, sooner or later, perhaps an early death.

When no rain has fallen for a long time in summer, the earth becomes dry and splits. When the necessary moisture, the fluids are not properly worked up in the body, and heat arises somewhere, dryness with its unavoidable results sets in likewise in the body. Already many years ago refuge was sought in water, in drinking of water for the curing of this disease. I myself have known people who drank from 6 to 10 pints daily. Was that a good thing? It was too much of a good thing, and the greater number of these boasting heroes did themselves more harm than good. The body could not long endure this water-torture. My principle is: who operates in the mildest manner with water, effects the surest and best of cures.

Those suffering from costivenes should take from breakfast to midday, every half hour, a spoonful of water. They will obtain greater effect by this small quantity than if they took half a pint, or more, at once. In the afternoon also, the patient can take a spoonful of water

* Several calendars, also newspapers and periodicals of the last years have given lists of hundreds of such remedies and warnings against them. Many of them have been condemned as a swindle, which the buyers, the cheated ones, often buy at dear rate with both money and health.

every half hour, **or** every hour. This constant, though sparing, pouring operates in a cooling manner and increases the juices. Besides this the patient may drink water, when he is thirsty. A great number of teas which are obtained from plants very easily found will serve the same purpose. Who does not know the blackthorn-blossoms? Their tea operates excellently. Tea from elder-flowers is cooling, dissolving, and takes away the interior heat; if 3 or 4 grains of aloe are mixed with it, it is a cleansing, cooling, dissolving and leading off remedy; 6 to 8 elder-leaves gathered green in spring and summer time and boiled as tea, are likewise cooling. Half a cup is drunk in the morning, and half a cup in the evening. No house-apotheca should despise this harmless little medicinal plant, especially as Almighty God, the chief doctor and apo-thecary, lets it grow for all of us gratuitously.

To the interior application of water should be added exterior ones. The patient, when rising or when going to bed, washes the abdomen vigorously with a handful of water. This remedy is most simple and nevertheless operates well, for many (weaker natures) it is sufficient. Those for whom this application is too easy may, from time to time, pour fresh cold water on the knees for 1 to 3 minutes (knee gush), an excellent application for producing the evacua-tion of the bowels.

If this is not sufficient and great heat is in the in-side, the patient should, a few times in the week, lie on wet sheets; covering with wet sheets is also of good effect. In the same way a cold sitting-bath operates power-fully; it may be taken twice or three times in the week. A cold whole-bath, if taken for a very short time, is not to be despised. All the named applications will arouse the sleeping organism, animate it, bring it into new ac-tivity, strengthen it. The wheels are oiled anew, the whole machine runs well again, and the desired effect will surely not be wanting.

Nothing surpasses the harmless and sure water-remedy, and what is easier than to drink water, to wash with water?

In this place, there is still a word to be said about

emetics. The drastic purging with minerals and poisons, whether it be in the form of powder, pills or anything else, appears to me against nature. But still more against nature is all that is taken to cause vomiting, alas! often again poison. Such an ill-treated and martyred creature affords a pitiable sight.

It will be noticed that I have not given the well known and generally used purgatives, such as rhubarb, senna-leaves, Epsom-salt, Glauber's-salt etc. And the reason? These in themselves harmless remedies are nevertheless too strong for me; help can be obtained by milder means. No one would chase a gnat or a flea with a gun. Much more do I decidedly reject all the insufferable emetics, whether they are called water-emetic, or tartar-emetic, or bear any other kind of title. If one must vomit — and there are such cases — then do as the farmer did: when he felt a great inclination to do so, he put his finger down his throat and was soon relieved. With strong inclination for vomiting, operate only on the regularity of the bowels. My strongest remedy for this is the "Tonic laxative". This tea has the peculiarity, that while it effects a copious evacuation of the bowels, it will also stop diarrhœa (try it with half a cupful!) It seeks after the morbid matters in the body and leads them out. If there are no more in it, if all have been removed, its operation ceases of itself. Therefore the twofold effects. Quackery — many will say disdainfully! But whether they do, or do not, it is all the same to me. The fact remains firm.

That is just the reason why the powerful laxatives are so weakening, so bad and injurious in their results, because they do not drive out the morbid matters only, but everything without distinction.

The battle begins and ends with the overthrow of the juices which are most precious and necessary for the propagation of bodily strength. Who has not already experienced this himself? Therefore the great weakness, the quick and enormous decrease of strength after such courses. How foolish, how laden with consequences! *Sapienti sat!* Injuries make one wise or at least ought to do so.

Cramps.

I was called to a sick person whose whole body was trembling so violently that she was thrown about on every side; the patient could not speak herself, but her mother related: "My daughter has always a dreadful headache, a great oppression on the chest and in the vicinity of the stomach; hands and feet are always ice-cold and wet with a greasy perspiration. My daughter has been married for nine months; for ten weeks she was quite well; then this state began in a slight degree, and has been increasing to this height. She cannot eat and at the most only take a few spoonfuls of plain broth or coffee. Everything which doctors gave her, and also injections applied to force her to sleep, only made her condition still worse." —

To this patient I gave the following advice:

Twice daily to put her feet, and as far as the calves of the legs, into cold water, at the same time washing them with a sponge or towel; directly afterwards to put hands and arms up to the shoulders, in cold water for one minute, washing them also at the same time; then hands and feet must come under the warm bed covering; every morning and afternoon the patient must take about 12 camomile drops (see apotheca) in 6 or 8 spoonfuls of warm water. As nourishment she should take 3 or 4 spoonfuls of milk from time to time, or drink malt-tea; it is especially recommendable to take the milk and malt-tea alternately.

After 12 days this person was so far advanced that an appetite set in for the usual household fare; the cramps had disappeared, and the oppressive pains in chest and head had ceased; the headache had gone, hands and feet were warm.

The further applications were: every second day to put the feet into cold water as above; twice in the week to take a warm foot-bath with ashes and salt for 14 minutes, and once a week to rise from bed to take a whole ablution, and directly to go back to bed again. Instead of camomile-drops she took wormwood and sage-drops, each time 10 to 12 drops in warm water; the patient was so far restored that she was able to go to church again, and to attend to her household work, and needed in order to become perfectly healthy and strong, only to wash twice a week with cold water; half-baths would be of more powerful service still.

Croup.

A father comes and laments that his daughter, of 4 years of age, has croup. "The child", he says, "has it just like the 3 other children who died. They died suddenly; this child will do the same. The girl can now scarcely breathe and ceased to cough because she is no longer able to do so. Her head and body are swollen. What shall I do? It will take me 4 hours to fetch the doctor and till then my child will not live." The answer was: "Good father, go home directly, and get some hot water mixed with vinegar, dip a towel in the mixture, wring it out, and put it round the child's neck. Cover this swathing with a dry cloth, and leave the compress on the child's neck for $\frac{3}{4}$ hour. Then dip the cloth again in water and vinegar. Continue thus for 6 hours, wetting the compress every $\frac{3}{4}$ hour anew. Then take the compress off and cover the neck lightly. Hereupon apply to the child a short bandage for which you may use the same towel redipped in water and vinegar. Over the short bandage put a dry cloth and cover the child well but do not put too much on her. Thus the child is to rest for one hour. After an hour remove the cover and let the child lie in bed with her usual covering. Should there be heavy breath or cough after 6 or 8 hours, you can renew the neck-bandage and put it on for 1 to 2 hours. If the cloth becomes very hot and the child feels great difficulty in breathing, dip the cloth in afresh. You will experience the effect."

The father did as he had been told and after 30 hours the child, who had been thought lost, was quite well again. In this case the cure could also have been effected, by dipping the cloth in very cold water (mixed with vinegar in equal quantities) and renewing it every

¼ hour. If this application had proved insufficient, its effect might have been increased by a foot-bandage reaching to above the calves of the legs.

Debility.

A blacksmith, 46 years old, came and complained: "It is now 2 years since my hands have become so weak that I can hardly manage the hammer. As my arms have lost two thirds of their strength, they have also lost more than half their thickness; otherwise I am pretty well. Only for the last half year I have felt my feet also getting much weaker, and they pain me too, particularly towards evening. The appetite is pretty good, but not so much as formerly. At the small of my back I often feel a powerful strain."

The veins on the thin hands are scarcely seen; it is evident that the arms are not nourished, therefore the weakness, stiffness, and cold. Accumulations of blood in the nape and its vicinity may be the cause of the blood not being able to flow in all directions.

The blacksmith held his arms in a bath of hay-flowers for half an hour daily, and once at another time of the day for 2 minutes in cold water, besides this the shawl was applied 3 times weekly. Thus he continued for a fortnight. Even during this course the arms became firmer, the veins swelled, the accumulations were dissolved.

After a fortnight, an upper and lower shower were taken daily, a warm hay-flower-bath, and a cold-water-bath for the arms, twice in the week. The man continued with these applications and became again able to do his work. He also took during the course 20 drops of wormwood-extract in warm water daily.

Decline.

We often see people become corpulent in a comparatively short time. It is the well founded opinion of many that such persons will not live much longer. There are others, men, women, and children who suddenly begin to lose their strength and healthy appearance. The remarkable side of the matter is, that such persons do not feel any particular suffering. They generally complain about languor, bad humour, and either very great or very little appetite. If help does not step in soon, such half-withered plants die gradually, or may be an acute illness suddenly brings on the end. Sick people of this kind seem to me — to use a picture from every day life — like a house in the building of which bad material was employed and which begins to decay before its time. He died of Bright's disease, people say. This is only a different designation for what I call the breaking down of a friable, weak body. Good eating and drinking is of no avail there. Throw a tubful of mortar on the wall of a decaying house and every sensible person will smile at you. Decline differs from consumption in as much as the latter disease affects one particular organ be it the lungs, the chest, the larynx or any other organ from which it proceeds and spreads, whilst the former consists rather in a general dissolution, in a ruin of the whole body. Decline has been supposed to originate in the kidneys, in the abdomen; but in most cases a decision as to its origin is impossible; the surest signs have often proved deceptive, when the dissection of the corpse revealed the real cause of the disease.

A rather corpulent gentleman enjoyed the best of healths. His mode of life and his diet were well regulated. Suddenly he observed that his corpulence and his strength were giving way. He suffered from giddiness and was hardly able to stand without support. Six weeks had scarcely past when he had lost 72 lbs. in weight. The tall, handsome man of late tottered and staggered about, reminding one of a broken reed or a withered tree. All medical remedies were of no avail; the patient looked forward to his approaching end with certainty, but also with great sadness. He was a dear acquaintance of mine, but when he came to see me, I did not recognise him. I had great doubts about the possibility of recovery; I advised him, however, to make a last attempt with water.

Nature which was occupied in destroying itself had to be strengthened, the progress of the disease to be checked.

The patient walked barefoot in wet grass or on wet stones twice or 3 times a day. Every other day he lay on wet sheets and was covered with wet sheets, once a week he made use of the Spanish mantle. These applications were succeeded by the following: weekly, 2 half-baths, 1 short bandage, lying on wet sheets and covering with wet sheets. After some time the half-baths were replaced by whole-baths, cold ones for one minute and warm ones with twofold change, one of each kind to be taken in the week; he likewise took a whole-ablution once a week. To complete the cure and prevent a relapse I precribed a cold whole-bath, and an upper shower with knee-shower, to be taken every week and the Spanish mantle, to be applied from time to time. The patient had been used to drink from 4 to 5 glasses of beer daily; their number was reduced to 2; I further ordered the diet to be simple and nourishing.

At the close of the first week, an improvement was already noticed in the state of the patient; after 8 weeks he could attend to his duties. He continued to increase in strength and corpulence and is, to this day, a healthy, portly, and strong man.

A mother lost in a few weeks her blooming appearance and all her strength. She was generally believed to be doomed to die shortly since all medical remedies remained without effect. In her distress she had recourse to water.

Twice a week she put on a wet chemise and enfolded herself in a dry woollen covering in which she remained for an hour; she also took 2 half-baths in the week and continued both practices for a fortnight. Her health improved. Instead of the former applications she now made use of the short bandage and the whole-ablution from bed, applying each once a week. Complete health was given to the mother and the healthy mother was restored to her rejoicing children.

Sufferers of this kind are often apt to take too much food. Since this cannot be manufactured in juices, blood, bone, flesh etc. by weakened nature, such consequences as abnormal formation of muscles, conglomerations of blood or juices must necessarily ensue. The well calculated water-applications dissolve and lead off injurious matters, regulate the circulation and strengthen the whole organism.

Another cause which may bring on decline is the following. Food is taken and, without profiting the body, evacuated again. The organs are weak, inactive, and unable to work. In this case, too, great disturbances must arise in the body, and its health must be undermined. Cut the roots of any plant, and it must die. The organs resemble the roots. The water strengthens and refreshes them.

How many young people are now-a-days carrying about sick bodies, real corpses. I wish with all my heart that they may find the source of help and health at the right time.

Delirium tremens.

A man 36 years of age, had drunk much beer, eaten little, and so had lived pretty well on beer alone. For a short time after drinking it, he always felt very strong, but as soon as the beer-vapour had gone he complained about enervation.

Delirium tremens had already developed so strongly that even young people noticed that he was no longer right. At the same time he complained particularly much about rheumatic pains, spasms and occasional headache. Although the passion for drinking is extremely difficult of cure, nevertheless this patient had a good will, and wanted to be freed from his misery, no matter at what sacrifice. Within 3 weeks the following applications perfectly restored him: Every day he understook 2 or 3 applications in the following order: 1st day: a) upper shower and knee-gush, b) standing in water, walking in water and putting the arms in water, c) shower for the back. 2nd day: a) half-bath, b) upper shower with knee-shower. 3rd day: a) sitting-bath, b) upper shower. 4th day: a) half-bath, b) whole-bath. He thus continued until he was cured; all morbid conditions ceased, the appearance was perfectly improved, good appetite had come, and the passionate desire for drink had entirely disappeared.

It must be emphatically remarked that, during the course
of applications, many eruptions appeared on various parts
of the body by means of which the poisonous matters
where removed.

Diarrhœa.

There are people who get diarrhœa without any special cause. The repetition can be regular, e. g. at particular times, once or twice a year, or it can be irregular.
Those seized with it feel quite well both before and after
the attack. The regular diarrhœa is caused by strong
nature throwing off all the accumulated superfluous matters. How calmly a man can work when a safety-valve
is on the steam-boiler. How calm one may be, when
nature like the boiler throws off what is too much and
unwholesome!

Against this kind of diarrhœa I have nothing to
prescribe; on the contrary, I give a warning not to wish
to do anything against it.

Generally these attacks occur in autumn or spring,
and it appears that the air, the temperature is of good
influence and assistance.*

The irregular diarrhœa which appears with, or without, pains is more worthy of notice. It is a warning for
such people that morbid matters have accumulated in
their body, which, if they are not removed, frequently
occasion destruction. Indeed experience teaches that people
afflicted in this manner suffer from some organic defect,
that they generally die early or at least never reach a
particularly old age. Often diarrhœa is the forerunner
of a serious illness. To effect its cure, before all, the
bowels must be operated upon, but always alternately

* Those who read the newspapers see what part the
blood-purifying pills, herbs etc. play, especially in spring and
autumn, but to some extent at every season. I should never
recommend such things. Those who will absolutely take
something (and there are such people), let them take once a
week on the one or the other day, every half hour a tablespoonful of fresh spring-water for 5 or 6 hours. This remedy
assists nature, many others may as well destroy it.

with applications for the whole body. Sudden stopping
of diarrhœa is never to be recommended; the foul matters
should be gradually removed and the interior organs so
strengthened that nature may not allow such foul matters to form without trying to get rid of them at the
right time.

For the interior, tea is taken made from wormwood
with sage, from centaury with sage, or from common
yarrow with St. John'swort, one or two small cupfuls daily,
or 6 to 10 juniper-berries are taken daily. All the
above mentioned remedies assist the digestion, increase
the stomach-juices and, at the same time, contain
nourishment.

If the diarrhœa is violent and of longer duration,
half a spoonful of bilberry-spirit should be taken (in warm
water) twice daily. As exterior application 3 or 4 compresses on the abdomen weekly, each time for 1½ hours
and a short bandage likewise weekly, will be sufficient.
(The compresses should consist of a fourfold cloth dipped
in water with vinegar, or in a decoction of pine-twigs,
and laid or bound on the abdomen.) This is continued
for a fortnight. After this time there may follow 1 or
2 half-baths with washing of the upper part of the body
weekly, and also 1 or 2 whole-ablutions weekly; for the
latter application the patient should rise in the night.
This should be continued for the 3 or 4 weeks following
in order to increase the strength of the whole body. If
then it were made a rule never to let a week pass by
without taking at least a whole-ablution or a cold half-
bath with washing of the upper part of the body, the
whole organism would become stronger and healthier, and
the diarrhœa (unless it has a deeply rooted cause) would
not return.

A man of 48 came and complained:
"I have constant diarrhœa, already this morning I
have been troubled 7 times while on the journey; at
home 1 to 6 times daily. I have been suffering from
this complaint for 9 months." The appearance of this
man was very good, neither thin nor too stout, the colour
fresh. This patient took:

1. every morning and every afternoon an upper shower;

2. every morning walking in water, and every afternoon a knee-gush.

The effect of these applications was that, after 5 days, the bowels were moved for the first time. He had taken nothing except 6 to 8 juniper-berries daily. But why, many a reader will ask, were these applications given here? they are so entirely different from the usual ones. Answer: Because this man looked healthy and strong, his eyes also looked fresh and well; this was a proof that there was still good natural strength; if, then, this is supported, and still more warmth produced by the water-applications, the interior evil will soon be removed by the natural strength itself. I would recommend as further applications: twice or 3 times a week a half-bath, or just as often an upper shower with knee-shower.

A gentleman, aged 48, says: "For many years I have had diarrhœa with very little interruption; I have tried all kinds of diet; I have taken a great deal of medicine, also used many housebould remedies, have been sent to several bathing-places, but — all in vain. The diarrhœa is particularly violent when I drink, whether it be water, beer, or wine. Very dry food suits me best. But because everything goes from me too quickly and too little digested, I have never got any strength; and if I am not quite emaciated, my muscles are nevertheless without strength."

The applications were the following:
1. twice daily an upper shower,
2. once daily walking in water, and
3. once a knee-gush.

In the second week:
on the one day, upper shower and walking in water,
the next day, half-bath.

After these two weeks the patient felt stronger, fresher, and better, but the diarrhœa remained.

In the third week he had:
1. daily a fourfold cloth dipped in water mixed with a little vinegar laid on the abdomen for 1 1/2 to 2 hours;

2. the one day upper shower and shower for the thighs;
3. the next day half-bath and upper shower.

After this week the action of the bowels was entirely changed.

A further week:
1. every day a half-bath;
2. every second day a cloth on the abdomen, as above.

For the further preservation of health and strength, the following applications proved sufficient:
1. every week 2 half-baths, and
2. every week once or twice a wet compress on the abdomen as described above.

For interior use were applied:
a. Wormood-drops,
b. Juniper-berries, alternately.

Some one might ask why just this succession was observed in the application.

The reply is:

The applications of the first week, begun from above and below, sought to strengthen the body;

those of the second week strengthened both the body in general and the interior organs;

those of the third week operated chiefly on the strengthening of the stomach and bowels.

In this way the whole body was repaired. The applications of the fourth week embraced the whole organism in all its parts, and so in this case, too, the cure was a successful one.

Diphtheria.

Those who are seized with Diphtheria must take care:
1. to loosen the accumulated morbid matters as soon as possible. 2. to operate upon the whole constitution, that the irregular flow of the blood and juices, shown by the barometer of the fever, may be restored to order again. Such a patient should be given first the head-vapour, and after every 20 to 24 minutes the whole body should be washed. After 6 to 8 hours he should put on the shawl for $1\frac{1}{2}$ hours, redipping it in fresh water every half hour. Then the patient should take a foot-

vapour, directly afterwards a half-bath (quite cold) with washing of the upper part of the body. The time given to the latter applications should be 1 minute at most. Then follows the shawl for 1½ hours, as given above. When these applications have been undertaken, they should be repeated from the beginning, allotting one to every half-day. At the same time the patient must diligently gargle his throat with shave-grass-tea, at least 4 to 5 times daily. The dreadful disease will very soon disappear.

All the given applications are perfectly harmless.

If the patient (this is a general rule) is at rest at night, if sleep comes on, he must, by no means, be disturbed. For good sleep is a proof that nature is returning to order (to rest) again, and its strengthening effects assist the applications in obtaining a good result.

Here it may be remarked, that if during any application for which lying in bed is prescribed, the patient falls asleep, he must never be awakened. When the application has made its effects, the patient regularly awakes himself.

A father came to me and related: "My child, 11 years old, cannot swallow at all, and for 3 whole days can scarcely breathe. He is full of heat and is delirious. I have put a wet cloth round his neck, but he does not get any better. What shall I do that the child may not suffocate?" The lamentations of the grieved father and still more the failure of the application induced me to accompany him to the sick-bed. There lay the child, a picture of misery, to all appearance lost. For there were already signs which hardly allowed a thought of recovery. Well, let us venture it in God's name! Every half hour during one day, the back, chest, and abdomen were well washed with cold water. As the fearful fever-heat would not give way, there was applied to the abdomen nothing further than a cloth dipped in cold water. On the following day the father came again and said: "The child is already able to swallow a little, but on both sides of the head the cheeks towards the jaws are swelling rather greatly. His speech is scarcely to be understood; yet I am unspeakably glad that the little one can talk again." The father was advised to bind up the swellings with a cloth dipped in water mixed with vinegar, and to renew this compress every half-hour.

Besides this the child should be washed, as given above, chest, back, and abdomen as often as he felt hot and anxious. On the third day the little one was out of all danger. The washing was continued for a short time, as often as the heat began to increase.

Gargles with tea made from Fœnum græcum (1 teaspoonful of Fœnum græcum boiled in half a pint of water, and often given by spoonfuls to the child sitting in bed) had excellent effect. Tea from mallow, common yarrow, mullein, would render the same service. Three or four teaspoonfuls of salad-oil taken daily is also very good. This takes away the interior heat remarkably quickly.

The child was saved and, at the present day, enjoys excellent health.

Dropsy.

When the rain continues for a long time and the sun shines but little, in many places the water does not sink into the earth, neither is it drawn up by the sun. Then there form little pools of water which later on become sour and foul and are of bad effect on the plants which grow near them.

Almost the same thing happens in the human body at the time dropsy commences, which is most frequently developed in those organisms whose blood and juices are too watery, which no longer possess any normal, any life-nourishing blood. All the organs and constituent parts of the body feed upon the blood; it is the source of power and strength from which each draws that which it needs for its purpose. But from a bog, from unhealthy puddles, from morbid blood nothing strength and life-giving can be taken, hence the flabby flesh, the inactive bowels, therefore the accumulations, sure forerunners of dropsy.

The complaint can be detected even by the exterior: young people suddenly appear old (he or she, people say, has quickly become old,) the complexion fades, the muscles and nerves, like broken strings, hang withered on the bones, little bags of water already form on different parts of the body particularly under the eyes. You have only to touch them, and the water-globules spring from under your fingers. The whole body soon shows a number of such little bags, just as if it were begging for good blood; but it only receives water.

There are different kinds of dropsy. If the accumulations arise between the skin and the flesh, we have skin-dropsy. If the bowels in one or in several places are like a sea, as it were, this is called dropsy of the bowels. If the blood-pump of the body, the heart, is flooded with water, it is called dropsy of the heart, etc. Dropsy also arises readily after many diseases and then, as a rule, all is over before long. For very many it has been a messenger from death and the grave, or it was, as it were, the last heavy wave that foundered the bark of life, already a wreck. It appears particularly after scarlet fever, if this has not been thoroughly worked out, if poisonous matters still remain and the weakend body has not strength enough to throw them off. The whole body then begins to swell.

If dropsy has already spread, reached a high degree, then in most cases nothing can be done on account of deficiency of blood. In the beginning (with not yet advanced decomposition) help can be obtained very quickly, if one strives to pump out the foul water from within and from without at the same time.

Some examples shall make it clear.

The whole body of a peasant woman about 48 years of age begins to swell; she is scarcely able to walk. The enervation is already great, breathing a great burden. I advised her immediately to put rosemary in wine and daily to drink two wine-glassfuls of this rosemary wine, altogether about half a pint. The wine strengthened her exceedingly, as she said, and drove out a great deal of water. Exteriorly she used daily for several days the short-bandage for 1½ hours; for a longer time (about 4 weeks) daily two half-baths of one minute with washing of the upper part of the body. The peasant woman got well and was able to attend to her work entirely and unhindered.

A boy had had scarlet fever, and according to everyone's opinion grew strong again. After six weeks he got dropsy. The whole body swelled A shirt dipped in salt water and worn for 1½ hours each day according to prescription for three successive days, perfectly cured him.

A woman, 54 years old, became dropsical. The feet and the body, so I was informed, were frightfully swollen. Two pinches of dwarf-elder-root powder were put into a pint of water and left to brew for 3 minutes, the patient then drank this tea at two or three intervals. Besides this she had daily for 3 days a lower bandage for 1 hour. For the following 10 days the bandage was applied every second day, and the 14 days following again every third day. — The patient recovered perfectly and that even after 3 weeks. I learned later that the water went off in great quantities as urine.

Dwarf-elder has always proved the best interior remedy for dropsy of the belly,* as rosemary has done for pectorial dropsy and dropsy of the heart.

An excellent exterior application in cases of dropsy of the heart, is lying on wet sheets and covering with wet sheets once daily. Interiorly 2 glasses of rosemary wine are drunk daily.

The body of a young man, of 36 years of age, swelled within eight days in a remarkable manner. Head, neck, hands, and feet showed swellings and under the skin a quantity of water. For eight days he put on the Spanish mantle twice a day, for nine days further once a day, the last ten days after every three days. "I have become quite a Spaniard", the man said laughingly, "the

---

* As household remedy juniper-berries will do, boiled and drunk as tea. This tea operates well but always too weakly: The effects of dwarf-elder-root are much more powerful and enduring.

climate, although not particularly Spanish, has done me good. I am quite restored."

One remark I must not forget here, as it is just in this disease that every beginner with water could easily deceive himself and others.

In cases of dropsy the water may never be applied warm, neither in the form of vapours, nor of warm baths.

The evil would thereby gain ground in an extraordinary manner as the warm water causes inactivity and languor, and the torpidity of the organs, their inactivity is one of the worst features of this disease. The coldest applications are the best here; but they must never be used for too long a time or in any other way than that prescribed; where there is weak blood, there is little vital heat.

A man relates: "My whole body is already rather greatly swollen. The doctor says I am getting dropsy. I have taken a great deal against it, but I get worse from day to tay. My left leg, particularly the thigh, is very much swollen. The right leg too begins to get thicker. I have great thirst; if I drink beer, it gets worse still, and water does not help either. Must I die, or is there still help for me?"

I replied: "Use the following: 1) Every day an upper shower and a knee gush; 2) three times a week a short bandage, the cloth being folded from four to six times, for 1½ hours; 3) every night rise from bed, and take a whole ablution, and then return at once to bed without drying. Continue thus for three weeks, then send a report."

This was very favourable. Thereupon I ordered the following applications:

1) Every week three half-baths for one minute; 2) every week three showers for the back; 3) twice the Spanish mantle for 1½ hours; 4) daily to drink one cup of tea made from crushed juniper-berries and a little shave-grass, boiled for 10 minutes. This to be drunk during the day in three portions.

After six weeks the patient was perfectly well again. Besides sleep the best appetite and full strength returned again. This declaration was sent to me three months after the course of applications. The man is fifty years old.

Dysentery.

Dysentery is a sister of cholera. They resemble each other very much. This disease begins as a rule with dreadful spasms in the bowels, violent diarrhoea accompanied by bloody flux from the rectum.

The quickest way to cure dysentery consists in the application of a twofold cloth which is dipped in very warm water and vinegar and laid on the abdomen. A small glass of bilberry-spirit will be of great effect on the interior; this spirit is easy to prepare and should not be missing in any house-apotheca. Twice a day 2 tablespoonfuls of this spirit should be taken in hot water; the refreshing drink will be relished by the patient. If he is not better on the second day, the compress on the abdomen should be renewed and the same dose of bilberry-spirit taken.

Joseph lay in his bed bent like a worm. Sometimes the spasms turned him round like a globe. He screamed with pain. The stools contained more than a pint of blood. 2 spoonfuls of bilberry-spirit taken in the morning and in the afternoon cured him in a short time.

Anna, a woman of more than 50 years, moans in terrible spasms. Diarrhoea accompanied by much blood made her fear that her case was cholera in its worst degree. The vinegar-cloth on the body and the bilberry-spirit in the interior have restored her in 1 day. If bilberries cannot be had, milk in which fennel has been boiled will also render good service.

Ears, diseases of the.

Who could enumerate the manifold causes in which diseases originate and the various ways in which diseases work upon individual organs causing them to suffer even, when the original disease has disappeared. The more delicate an organ, the more injurious is the disease that affects it and the more difficult the cure of the same. One of the most delicate organs of the human body is the ear, and very often the sense of hearing is lost through illness or through a disorderly mode of life.

A mother comes and relates: "My daughter has had the scarlet fever of which she has been well cured. Since that time she has never been quite well. Now she complains of this, then of something else, but the hardest thing to bear, is that she has lost her hearing almost entirely. All remedies applied have had no effect."

This girl has not been cured entirely, and the hard hearing is but a consequence of it, which might just as well have laid hold of any other part of the body. If the girl is cured of all injurious consequences of the scarlet fever, her hearing will be restored to her. We have therefore to work upon both the hearing and the whole system.

By the following applications the best result will be obtained: 1) To put on a wet chemise for $1\frac{1}{2}$ hours. 2) To put on a shawl for $1\frac{1}{2}$ hours (to be re-dipped in water after the first $\frac{3}{4}$ hour). During these $1\frac{1}{2}$ hours each foot to the calf of the leg is wrapped in a towel dipped in warm water — foot-bandage, for $1\frac{1}{2}$ hours. 3) To rise from bed, take a whole-ablution, and go to bed again without drying, special attention being paid to the back of the head and the ears. 4) To bind a piece of linen dipped in warm water on the ears and the parts near them for 2 hours; the bandage to be re-dipped in water every half hour. 5) To take a head-bandage (s. bandages).

These 5 applications should be made use of for some time, every day at least one application. A warm oat-straw bath (28 to 30° R.) taken for 25 minutes every week would also be of good effect. It should be followed by a quick ablution with cold water to brace the system. These applications will restore thorough health to the weakened body; the warm bandages on the ears may be continued for a longer space of time.

Ears, humming in the.

A person had very often loud humming in the ears, weak nerves, trembling of the hands and feet, pale complexion and sunken eyes. This person had been attended to by several physicians. The one said the humming in the ears came from the nerves, the other attributed it to a suppressed cold in the head, the third declared it a contraction of the tympanum etc.

Applications: 1) Walking in water for 2 to 4 minutes daily, then exercise in a warm room or weather permitting, in the open air. 2) Every other night whole-ablution from bed with water and vinegar. 3) Twice a week the shawl for 1 hour.

To be continued for a fortnight or 3 weeks. If further applications are required a whole-ablution may be applied once a week and walking in water every second day.

Epilepsy.

I never let this kind of sufferers give a report of themselves. I simply ask them how long they have been afflicted with this disease, if they, each time, perceive the attack and its symptoms, how old they are, if the mental powers are still fresh or already in a very low state.

According to my conviction this disease also has its principal seat in the blood, whether it be caused by poverty of blood, morbid blood, corrupted blood, or irregular circulation of the blood. My opinion is supported by the often recurring facts that the enticed eruptions on the skin, as it were, the evaporations of the blood, have always brought such patients lasting and certain help, that further these so-called incurable people are always known by their being puffed up, their blue colour (these are accumulations of corrupted blood).

If the answers to my questions are favourable, which occurs, as a rule, with young people at the age of 8 to 20 years, I look upon the so-called "falling-sickness" as a spasmodic condition similar to St Vitus's-dance, and as curable. I have been able to bring help to very many, even to such as had inherited the disease from their parents.

If particularly the question regarding the perception of the signs of the attack is answered negatively (sign that the powers of the mind are gone), if the evil is old, and has caused more or less imbecility, then the poor sufferers, who happily never feel their misery deeply, have nothing to expect from me.

According to these principles I have ever arranged the manner of treatment, which always aims at improvement of the blood and the regulating of the circulation of the blood.

Before all I sought to lead the patients to hardening, particularly to going barefoot very diligently. In summer I occasionally ordered them to take a cold bath, never longer than one minute, in winter this bath (lasting one to two minutes) was warmed a little. Besides this they had once a week a wet shirt, dipped in salt water.

The eruption, which through the last application often made its appearance, was treated according to the rules given in their proper place (see Eruptions). I have always strongly advised young people to accustom themselves to simple, sensible, not effeminating clothing, and especially the girls to give up the blamable, unnatural and disease-bringing lacing up. Their daily food must be plain. All spirituous drinks, as wine, beer, etc. and also coffee, must be carefully avoided. Their work should never be above their strength, but always suitable to their abilities.

Eruptions.

Under this head I class all those innumerable and undefinable impurities of the skin that often come and go the same day or the same night. Little importance is generally attached to them, nevertheless, they become sometimes very troublesome and torment the chest, back, arms, legs, or other parts of the body. For years this burden may be borne without causing any particular illness or even any particular trouble. Yet, I know persons who were afflicted with attacks of insanity every time, when the eruptions disappeared, and I remember 2 cases where raving madness set in, in consequence of suppressed eruptions. Applications such as indicated for tetters and ulcers enticed the eruptions out again, whereby those mental disturbances were immediately removed. These trifles are indeed not to be trifled with. They may have serious consequences, when neglected, especially in matters of cleanliness. Besides mental disturbances, consumption, liver and kidney complaints may ensue; for these destroying fellows will do their devastating work wherever they take root.

Every one tormented in this manner should, as long as he feels none of the above mentioned consequences, make use of a few easy water-applications, such as the whole-ablution, the Spanish mantle and the short bandage. It would prove sufficient if one application were taken every third day. There is no reason for fear if the eruption seems to increase after one or the other of these applications. This is an excellent proof of their effect and ought to encourage their continuation.

Who follows this advice will surely see that the result of the whole cure will be as good as that of every single application. Every impartial person may judge for himself whether it be better to use for such cures those horrid and abominable ointments called beauty-milk, wonder-balsam etc., or the pure, clear water. What stuff may they contain, those ointments now-a-days advertised in every newspaper? Many a gentleman and many a lady would blush with shame if it were known to their noble relations and acquaintances that they, too, were found among the quackers. But such considerations, I know, are of no avail. The world has ointed, and the world is ointing. *Mundus vult decipi* i. e. the world will continue ointing and smearing. *Habeat sibi!*

A farmer relates: "For more than 2 years I have an eruption on my face and on my whole body. Sometimes there is not much of it to be seen, sometimes more. I am otherwise healthy; but if this eruption grows in extension, as it seems to do, I don't know what fate will befall me. I have used many and various remedies, but all in vain."

Applications: Weekly 2 warm oat-straw-baths with 2 changes, every time 15 minutes in the warm bath and one minute in the cold bath or vigorous whole-ablution. 2) 3 times a week, whole-ablution, with cold water either from bed during the night, or in the morning when rising. 3) Daily a saltspoonful of white powder, as described in the apotheca. This to be continued for 3 to 4 weeks, after which time a whole-ablution or a half-bath should be taken once or twice a week.

Erysipelas.

"My husband is getting erysipelas; his face is swollen and as red as fire; he has violent fever; the red colour spreads over the whole face; there are blisters in many places, and he is screaming with pain" — these were the complaints of a wife. I ordered a shawl to be dipped in warm water and put on the patient for ¾ hour; then the cloth should be re-dipped in fresh water and put on again, the same should be done a third and fourth time. 3 to 4 hours after, a fourfold cloth should be dipped in fresh water, wrung out well and laid on the abdomen for 3 hours; the cloth should be renewed (re-dipped in fresh water) every hour. Three hours after the removal of the compress, the patient is laid for an hour on a cloth which has been dipped in cold water, wrung out and folded several times. These 3 applications can be thus alternately renewed until the heat is cooled and the injurious matters led out of the body. To the suffering parts of the face nothing is applied except washings with lukewarm water from time to time, when the extension of the skin is too painful. If the patient is very thirsty, water or sugar-water is always the best drink, but it should be given in small portions. Another course of water-applications for the cure of erysipelas is the following:

Twice daily the shawl should be put on the patient for 3 hours (re-dipped every hour); during the rest of the day back, chest, and abdomen or, which is better, the whole body should be washed with water and vinegar, every ¾ hour; the duration of this washing must not exceed 1 minute. When the fever begins to decrease, it will be sufficient to undertake an ablution every 2 or 3 hours, later on once a day. In the beginning warm water mixed with vinegar is to be used, later on fresh water only. The swelling on the face may only be washed from time to time and with lukewarm water. — By these two courses of applications many have been completely cured from erysipelas.

Josephine, 22 years old, healthy and strong, is seized with violent fever. Her exterior is full of heat, interiorly she feels chilly and cold; she suffers from great, thirst and has no appetite. As often as the heat was great, her whole body was washed in the beginning with warm water, then with cold water; this was done for 3 whole days. Then the cold gave way, the whole head was swollen, and the erysipelas appeared in an unusually high degree; the face showed large blisters, and the mouth was greatly swollen. For 4 days the ablutions were applied from 6 to 10 times a day; also the shawl was put on twice a day; twice warm, then cold. After 3 days, Josephine began to perspire profusely and continued so for 2 days; then she was cured. The ablution was taken twice a day during the time of perspiration. The perspiration came by itself, and the ablutions promoted it a great deal. The whole cure lasted 8 days; the patient took no medicine whatever. To the head nothing was applied; only during the last 3 days the face was washed with lukewarm water, twice a day.

Erysipelas is caused by a poisonous matter which gathers between skin and flesh and seeks to escape through the former. Feet, arms, head, any part of the body may be affected by it. Wherever it appears, the skin is extended as if ready to burst. Sometimes erysipelas causes great pain before it appears on the surface of the body. At its breaking out little blisters containing a brown fluid form in great numbers; they are so poisonous that whole portions of the skin are destroyed by them. Erysipelas may be dangerous and even cause death, and this is generally the case when instead of appearing on the outside of the body, it poisons the blood, the flow of which is especially attracted by the inflamed part. It often happens, too, that erysipelas although developed on the outside, leaves its original place and seeks another in the interior. These cases mostly end fatally.

I knew a man-servant who had erysipelas on the arm. He attached no importance to the complaint, calling it a woman's disease. The erysipelas disappeared, but took post in the brain and the patient died soon after.

I also know a priest who had erysipelas on a foot. What remedies he applied, I do not know. The erysipelas disappeared, and the patient thought himself liberated from his enemy. But before long the unpleasant guest reappeared, this time on the upper arm. Again it sought another place and attacked the head. Within 4 days the priest died.

Every one who has carefully observed cases of this illness, will be able to tell of many a case where neglect of it was revenged by an early death.

In the cure of erysipelas, the first care must be to prevent its wandering from one place to the other. On the spot where it first appears, its spreading ought to be hindered, and the poisonous matter led off. Also the afflux of blood to the affected part should be prevented by all means.

Whoever has erysipelas on the foot should take a short bandage. This will extract those matters which would otherwise increase the inflammation. After the short bandage, the leg upwards of the affected part may be likewise bandaged. Erysipelas can also be worked upon on the spot. This is done by putting on the fiery place a soft, worn out, linen cloth which has been dipped in warm water. The wet cloth must be covered with a dry woollen one. This compress will dissolve and lead off the poisonous matter.

If somebody gets erysipelas on the arm, he may, as in the previous case, prevent its spreading by the application of a short bandage. Then he should put on the shawl which ought to be renewed in proportion to the heat. Here also the affected part may be brought under immediate treatment.

If erysipelas affects the head, covering with wet sheets will lead the poisonous matter downwards and a neck-bandage will soon diminish it. When these applications have been made use of, the affected part itself may be treated first with warm water, until the greater part of the unhealthy matter has been led off (which is known by a decrease of the swelling and redness); then with cold water. These applications consist in linen-compresses or bandages; if the head is the suffering part, the head-bandage is applied.

Eyes, cataract of the.

An official brought to me a boy of 9 years who had diseased eyes. Both pupils were so badly affected that the poor boy could hardly walk alone. "How do you come to me?" "My child," the father replied, "has been in a medical establishment for diseases of the eyes, but he was dismissed and declared to suffer from incurable cataract. That is dreadful: to be blind at the age of nine!" The one eye was already so dull that the pupil could scarcely be distinguished; it was utter darkness for the little one. On the other eye, there lay a cloud which covered all but a narrow strip of the once so lightsome eye.

At the first sight of the boy, I had noticed that not his eyes only were suffering. The whole of his little organism was weakened, so miserably enfeebled that whosoever saw him could but think: that child is ill through and through and, as it seems, declining fast. There was no appetite, no life, the body emaciated, the skin dry and scurfy. Let us first seek to cure the body, perhaps the eyes will, then, cure themselves.

We began after having first removed the spectacles hitherto worn by the little sufferer. The boy walked as much as possible barefoot in wet grass or on wet stones; back, chest, and abdomen were vigorously washed once or twice daily. After some time the ablutions were replaced by half-baths, then by whole-baths, never for more than 1 minute's duration. Whilst the course of these applications was going on, he also had from time to time a bandage or a wet shirt dipped in salt water and applied for $1\frac{1}{2}$ hours. All these applications aimed at infusing new life, new activity into the body, i. e. to cure and strengthen it.

As special remedies for the eyes, i. e. for their cleansing and strengthening, I employed several eye-waters. First I used aloe water (a saltspoonful of aloe powder boiled for a few minutes in $\frac{1}{2}$ pint of water); with this the eyes were well washed, 3 to 5 times daily. Aloe dissolves, cleanses and heals. Later on I used alum-water (2 saltspoonfuls of alum mixed with ½ pint of water); with this the eyes were vigorously washed, 3 or 4 times daily. Alum is corrosive and cleansing. Later still I took honey-eye-water (half a spoonful of honey boiled for 5 minutes in ½ pint of water) to wash the eye 3 to 5 times daily. The boy began to thrive so well that his strength increased from week to week; his appearance became fresher and healthier, and in the blooming face shone the bright eyes to the immense joy of his parents. His eyesight is as good as that of his companions and nobody would believe that the child had ever been so wretched.

I am firmly convinced that the impaired eyesight was only a consequence of the more impaired body. It is but natural that there should be diseased eyes where the whole organism is diseased. A decaying tree bears blighted leaves, but when the tree again is able to put forth fresh sprouts, it will soon be adorned by new leaves and blossoms.

Eyes, catarrh of the.

A celebrated military physician said to me about 30 years ago: Catarrh is a disease from which every possible malady may spring, as mucous fever, nervous fever, typhus, dysentery, consumption, etc. It is, therefore, of the greatest importance to be armed against catarrh, and this should be done by reasonable hardening of the body. He who has a catarrh ought not to rest until it is perfectly cured.

If total blindness is one of the greatest misfortunes that can befall man, the various complaints of the eyes, which are so often its forerunners, are certainly well worthy of notice. We have only two eyes. What an irreparable loss is it therefore, if only one of them refuses its service: Be careful, and guard both of them well! There are sufferers from complaints of the eyes of every age, but little children, and especially schoolchildren, are most frequently troubled by them.

The source of the complaint is mostly to be sought in the body. A healthy body throws off superfluous fluids by means of perspiration, respiration and in other ways. Marvellous is the working of this most wonderful of machines. A different process takes place in the diseased body. The fluids which are not secreted by the enfeebled organism collect in the body, in the head, or elsewhere. If they gather in the head, they generally choose the eyes for their outlet. The secreting fluids are corrosive, the eyes, however, and all parts of them extremely delicate. This accounts for the violent burning regularly caused by the secretion of the fluid. This burning is also a sign that the eye and its parts are affected by this acrid secretion. Whenever this fluid finds no issue, the eyes become inflamed, they often become red, and the weakened eye can no longer bear the light. Cure is impossible unless the fluid is secreted as soon as possible. The eye and its parts are healthy in themselves, the corrosive matter alone causes its disease.

There are some persons suffering from diseased eyes who can scarcely see at all, or they see everything through a veil or a mist, as it were. Others have an impression as if flies or gnats were flying about before their eyes; others again see fiery bunches and other things. All these evils flow from the same source, they are all blossoms of the same poisonous plant; they all originate in the same poisonous matter. Remove this, strengthen the affected eye, and it will be cured. An example will explain this.

Little Antonia, 5 years old, looks very pale. Her face is puffed up, her whole appearance unhealthy, her eyes inflamed, and she can no longer bear the light. She also suffers from want of appetite and sleeplessness, and cries a great deal. What is to be done? Every day the child should be bandaged from the arm-pits downwards, the bandage being previously dipped in lukewarm water in which oat-straw has been boiled. Should the bandage be applied at a time when the child usually sleeps, she will soon fall asleep. If she does so, let her rest until she awakes; if she does not go to sleep or awakes soon, she should remain in the bandage for an hour. This process is to be repeated daily for a week. In the second

18*

week a warm oat-straw-bath (24 to 26°) should be prepared in which the child must remain for 15 to 20 minutes. In the last minute the contents of a small watering-can of not too cold water should be poured over the child, and then she should be dressed immediately. This refreshing shower is of the greatest importance after a warm bath for all children. The warm bath dissolves and leads off unhealthy matters; the cold shower closes the pores and strengthens. The first time the child will cry and lament, as children use to do, but as soon as it has gone through the process a few times, it will, encouraged by its mother, gladly enter the bath. This bath is to be repeated every second or third day. The child will soon feel fresher, stronger, healthier; the eye, too, will become clearer. Should the careful mother wish a remedy more directly for the eye, she may take a piece of alum as big as 4 barleycorns, dissolve it in ¼ pint of water and wash the eyes of the child 3 to 4 times daily with it. After the removal of the evil, the mother should not neglect to wash the child once a week in the aforesaid manner and to give it a bath, likewise once a week.

If the little patient is not 5 years but only 5 weeks old, the careful mother must not be frightened if I recommend the same bandage and the same bath also for this very little one.

Little Anthony, 4 years old, is scrofulous, has eruptions on the head and about the mouth, his eyes are inflamed. His mother always thought the child would die; he suffers, but dies not. The little one should have put on a shirt dipped in salt water; then the mother should take him to bed and envelop him in a blanket. If she does this every day in the first week, every second day in the second week, every third day in the third week and once in the fourth week, and if she gives little Anthony a saltspoonful of powdered chalk in his food or drink, the boy will get well, and the mother will rejoice in the health of her child.

Bertha goes to school but looks very poorly; she has almost every week "bad eyes," wherefore she cannot read. The eyes are quite red and cause violent burning.

The child should put on a wet chemise 6 times within 10 days, and if this application is not sufficient in its effects, the mother should prepare baths of about 24° R. mixed with a decoction of pine-twigs. The warm bath should always be concluded by a cold shower. As eye-water she may use aloe-water (a saltspoonful of aloe put in a glass and poured over with hot water) with which the eyes are washed 3 times a day. The latter remedy heals the inflamed eye and strengthens it.

William, a boy of 9 years of age, had diseased eyes. He could no longer read and scarcely distinguish persons, the poor little one was more than half blind. His parents had spent about £ 20 for the cure of these eyes but without result. The whole body of the child was just as impaired as the eyes. His hands and feet were always cold, his stomach without appetite, his body emaciated, his stature drooping and depressed. Wretched are not only the eyes, wretched is the whole little man. Blue spectacles and the leader were openly confirming my statement.

In 4 months William was restored to perfect health of body and eyes. The little one had to take 2 warm baths weekly. 4 times weekly I had a shirt dipped in cold salt water and put on him. He remained in it for 1 to 1½ hours. Moreover I let the boy walk barefoot in wet grass or when it was raining. After the first 4 weeks William took 3 to 4 baths of 15° R. every week; the baths were of only 1 minute's duration and always followed by exercise. They were continued for several weeks. The boy also washed his eyes twice daily with alum-water (a saltspoonful of alum in ¼ pint of water). As the body revived and recovered his health, the eyes, too, became better. At last they shone in the blooming face of the boy as if they had never suffered from the least disease.

Christina, 24 years old, has a fresh and healthy appearance but is always afflicted with complaint of the eyes. She has too much blood in the head, too little in the feet, and therefore always cold feet.

Christina takes every second day a lukewarm foot-bath with ashes and salt. This draws the blood from the head downwards. 3 times a week she takes a half-bath (½ minute) reaching to the armpits. She is much barefoot when working. The determination of the blood to the head is diminished, ceases gradually, and the disease of the eyes disappears.

Agatha comes and complains: "For 3 years I have been tormented with violent headache so that I often could not sleep for whole nights. My feet are constantly cold; when the headache gives way a little, I feel such a pain in the back that I am quite stiff. I have consulted many physicians but none could help. For the last half year my sight has become so weak that I can scarcely see the houses. If it goes on like that, I shall soon be blind."

Agatha made use of the following applications:

1. Twice weekly she put on a wet chemise dipped in salt water, enfolded herself in a blanket and remained so for 1½ hours.
2. Twice a week she took a short bandage which had been dipped in a decoction of hay-flowers (warm) for 1½ hours.
3. Daily she had a knee-gush for 1 minute followed by exercise. These applications were continued for 2 weeks.

In the third week she took daily in the morning an upper shower and a knee-gush, in the afternoon a half-bath, she also walked in water for 3 minutes daily; she continued in the same manner during the fourth week. After the fourth week the determination of the blood to the head disappeared, her sight was restored because the cause of the complaint was removed; her feet were warm, in a word, the patient was cured.

As further applications Agatha took 3 half-baths weekly to brace the whole system.

Fever.

Anthony comes into the room and relates: "I had to make such an effort to mount the stairs. My strength is entirely broken; I have fallen down twice. I have also a fearful headache, I am sometimes as cold as ice and then very hot again. Sometimes I feel a piercing pain as if lightning was darting about in my body. I have noticed it for some time; but it is now 5 or 6 days since I feel worse and utterly unable to work.

Application: Go home, Anthony, and lie down in bed at once; as soon as you are quite warm, wash your whole body with cold water and, without drying it, go to bed again. In the same manner wash every 2 hours, and when you begin to perspire profusely and have done so for ¼ hour, wash again.

Anthony comes on the third day and reports: I feel much easier, I have perspired profusely several times. The sensation of cold and heat has disappeared, the headache, too, has ceased. Appetite is coming back again; I feel well, but tired. Anthony took about 10 whole-ablutions during a fortnight, and then he enjoyed perfect health. He is about 40 years old.

Giddiness.

A priest, in his best years, felt a continual decrease of strength, especially in his legs. Only with the greatest effort he could walk for a quarter of an hour, and even such a walk caused him a feeling as if his legs were broken. Moreover he suffered so much from giddiness that he could not stand for any length of time without leaning on some firm object. If he wanted to turn at the altar, he was always obliged to hold himself by it. Whenever the sensation of giddiness decreased, he felt great pressure on the chest and an anxiety as if he was about to be stricken by apoplexy.

The patient used much mineral water and medicaments, but without any result. His appearance was very good, his appetite also, but he did not sleep well.

Result: For 3 weeks he walked daily much barefoot (in grass, on wet stones, and in water up to the knees); he had in the beginning daily two upper showers and a knee-shower, later on half-baths, and baths taken when in perspiration. At the conclusion of his course he made an attempt to walk 12 miles in one day which he did without fatigue. He now felt quite well and disposed to cheerfully fulfil the duties of his vocation.

A gentleman, 74 years old, relates: "I suffer a great deal from dizziness, and I sometimes feel great pressure on my head; my feet are often cold, and whenever my head is free from suffering, I experience great discomfort in the abdomen.

Unless remedies are applied, no evacuation of the bowels takes place. The book "The Water-cure" has induced me to ask if at my age water-applications could be used with success. If not, I am resigned to my fate, but if water can still be applied, I shall go into the cold element like the youngest."

In 3 weeks the old gentleman was so well that he repented of having given up his office to another.

The applications were as follows: 1st day: To wash the upper body in the morning with water and vinegar and afterwards take a knee-shower; in the evening a warm foot-bath with ashes and salt, for 14 minutes. 2nd day: In the morning upper shower with one can, immediately after, walking on wet stones (for 5 minutes); in the afternoon: a cold sitting-bath for 1 minute. 3rd day: In the morning, to walk in water, for 2 minutes, directly after to hold the arms in water. In the afternoon an upper shower, towards evening a sitting-bath, 4th day: In the morning walking in water up to the knees, for 3 minutes; immediately after to hold the arms in water, for 2 minutes; in the afternoon a shower for the back. 5th day: In the morning a shower for the back, in the afternoon a half-bath, for one minute. In this way the latter stronger applications were continued. The giddiness disappeared entirely, the bowels became regular, the injurious gases were removed, the normal warmth returned: thus the machine was in order again. The old gentleman enjoyed henceforth the freshness of youth and the best of humours.

People will be surprised at the fact that to this aged man not more than one warm application was prescribed. The reason was that he still possessed pretty much strength and vital heat; else he would have been advised to take whole-ablutions from bed with warm salt-water or with vinegar and water in order to increase the vital heat. Old people prefer the cold water as soon as the temperature of their blood has been raised by warm ablutions, and the first trial has been given to cold ones. They see that the effect on the vital heat is much sooner obtained by cold applications than by warm ones.

A priest, 78 years old, suffered so much from giddiness that he could no longer look upwards nor was it safe for him to walk; he was rather corpulent. His whole appearance made the impression that the poor old gentleman was lacking sufficient vital heat. Although it seemed as if water could be of no avail in this case, his appearance changed in an astonishing manner, he seemed to have become young again, the giddiness disappeared as well as his fear when walking: the aged gentleman was like a lamp which, having received a fresh supply of oil, begins to burn anew.

If a very aged person reads this, he will ask, what was done to him. Answer:

On the first day his whole body was bandaged from under the arms, the cloth having been dipped in hot water in which hay-flowers had been boiled; this for $1\frac{1}{2}$ hours. In the afternoon an ablution with vinegar and water, quite warm. On the second day: in the morning a foot-vapour, for 20 minutes, directly hereafter a quick shower of fresh water; in the afternoon a whole-ablution as on the first day. On the third day: a head-vapour (20 minutes) with following upper shower. On the fourth day: in the morning a cold upper shower followed by a knee-shower; in the afternoon a wet shirt, for $1\frac{1}{2}$ hours. On the fifth day: in the morning a warm foot-bath with ashes and salt; in the afternoon, upper shower and knee-shower. Henceforth only cold applications were used, viz.: in the morning, upper shower and knee-shower; two hours later, walking in water and arm-bath; in the afternoon, only upper shower. If these applications have been continued for 6 days, it will be sufficient to take a whole-ablution from bed once or twice a week. At home the patient had only to walk in water and to take an arm-bath twice a week, and to take a sitting-bath once a week; the latter could also be taken warm. The only interior remedy applied was tea from fennel, common yarrow, and sage.

Gout.

If you go into the *Allgäu* (district in the southern part of Bavaria) in autumn, you will see now and then people manuring the field. Lately they have invented a new method which is quite apt to rouse the indignation of any true farmer. They do not distribute the food to the hungry soil in an equal manner, as it was formerly done, but with an un-heard-of carelessness they give 2 or 3 portions to one clod and let another fast the whole year long. The whole work resembles the play of the mole. There must be in spring foul swamps, on which this ill-concerted prodigality has produced a luxuriance which looks strange enough beside other spots where stunted and crippled stalks accuse the owner of, and punish him for, the stepmotherly treatment which they experienced.

This picture will assist me in conveying a true idea of what the gout is.

Food has to do the same work in the human body that manure does in the field. Is there anything like equality with regard to quantity and quality of food in the various stations of life? Do not many enjoy super-abundance while numberless others have 365 days of fasting every year?

What must be the inevitable consequence if a person supplies his field (his body) with so much food that poor nature cannot master it? The bones want sulphur and lime for their structure. What must arrive if the body by means of very nourishing and strengthening food is supplied with so much building-up material as would suffice for the construction of 2 or 3 new bodies? What must arrive? Swamps (thick blood) will form in one place, bogs (bad juices) in another, and the bones will be encumbered by heaps of sand, lime, and stones.

The ankles swell, become inflamed and cause lasting and dreadful pain until these cartilaginous knots are burnt, as it were, by the pain itself or by other means. And in spite of so much suffering the poor corpulent podagric is scarcely pitied by any one. That is not becoming a christian, yet it sometimes appears to be very natural. People say : he has had the enjoyment, let him now also bear the consequences of it. Poor people, however, are also sometimes afflicted with gout; even the poorest are visited by it. Once a poor, but very diligent, domestic presented himself to me; he suffered from gout in its highest degree. The reason was that he had entirely neglected the care of his health from too great zeal for his service. Broken bellows do not work the air into the pipes of the organ but out of the holes. Weakened, unhealthy organs often work on tumours instead of the sound flesh, on the kernel instead of the bone.

Gout may also be caused by over-exertion, dampness and cold. Gout in a high degree torments many, gout in a lesser degree torments numberless persons. With some it has its seat in the toes, with others in the head, with some in the extremities, with others again in interior parts of the body.

People who are simple and not too much weakened, who obey cheerfully and do not shrink from every little pain I cure willingly and mostly very easily. With regard to podagrics of the nobler kind, I never give way to delusions. They are a cross for me and, as a rule, not to be cured by water; for they do not obey because they are bent under the double yoke of effeminacy and dread of water, else they would be curable as well as all others afflicted with gout.

A gentleman of high rank had suffered from violent pain in his feet for about 4 weeks. His acquaintances called him jokingly a new member of the confraternity of podagrics. Sweating cured him for this time. But the following year the complaint returned, and he had to keep his bed for 12 weeks. There was much burning and as much sweating; but this water alone did not cure him a second time. He consulted me and declared that he was ready to do everything, if only that fearful disease did not return. In a few weeks the principal part of the cure was over. The swellings disappeared under the various water-applications and later on the patient repeated one or the other practice from time to time. The complaint has not troubled him for some years since. The reader may learn the applications from the following case.

A priest sent me a message, letting me know that his feet were burning as if containing real fire and that his condition drove him almost to despair. I advised him to have hay-flowers boiled, squeezed out of the hot water and put on a linen cloth; into these hot hay-flowers he should lay his feet and tie the warm hay-flower-bandage round them. After 2 hours the hay-flowers were to be re-dipped in the infusion, squeezed and put on again. It is of no importance whether the hay-flowers are cold or warm for this renewed application. The sick priest continued thus for some days. After the first few hours the chief pain already ceased and in 2 or 3 days the patient was completely free from pain.

If hay-flowers cannot be had, oat-straw may be used in the same way instead. This grass is also of excellent effect in such complaints.

I beg to call the attention of the reader to the fact that in the cure of gout I seek to effect the cure especially by warming or rather dissolving.

I must in this place caution against a delusion. As soon as persons afflicted with gout feel no longer any pain, they believe to be perfectly cured. It would be a great mistake to discontinue the water-applications as soon as the pain has ceased. The foot-bandages must be followed by at least some applications in order to remove from it all unhealthy matter. The Spanish mantle put on twice or 3 times a week will render excellent service for the first 3 weeks. For the month following some warm baths with decoction of hay-flowers or oat-straw (changing 3 times) are recommended.

A workman was seriously afflicted with gout. He went 3 times a week into the sack which had been dipped in a hot decoction of oat-straw; moreover he took every week 2 baths with a decoction of pine-twigs (33 to 35° R.) changing 3 times and 2 cold whole-ablutions from bed. After 3 weeks he was pretty well cured; he continued, however, for some time to make use of the sack twice in one week and of the warm bath once in another week. He was soon able to take up his work with renewed strength and has attended to it ever since.

A well-sinker showed me the swellings on his fingers and his toes which, so he said, were sometimes burning in an almost unbearable manner — the complaint had been brought on by dampness.

Every other day he took the above mentioned warm bath, every third or fourth day he went into the sack; these applications completely restored the man in a short time. During the night his hands were bandaged with boiled hay-flowers.

A poor housefather got a piercing pain in the joints. He did not know whether it proceeded from gout or from another cause; he only felt dreadful pain which rendered him unable to attend to his business.

It was just the time of haymaking. I advised him to go on his haystack, which was then fermenting, to make a hole in the hot hay, to lie in this hot hay-grave and to cover himself with hay so as to let only the head look out. He did so, and after $\frac{1}{4}$ hour he was swimming, as it were, in perspiration. The peasant ascended his haystack and descended into the hay-bath 6 times within 10 days and was completely cured.

I should not advise every one to do this; but only he who has experienced it, knows the extraordinary dissolving virtue of such a hay-vapour. Very old and deeply rooted diseases can be led out by such a harmless vapour. The hay-vapour will be most effective if it is immediately followed by a cold half-bath with ablution of the upper body. The latter application is exceedingly strengthening.

Two gentlemen of high rank improved their health so much by 15 of these hay-vapour-baths that it seemed to them incomprehensible how by such simple means and in so simple a manner a recreation of the organism could be effected.

I venture to say that rheumatism in its weaker forms and cramps, generally remains of severe diseases, can be cured by 2 or 4 such hay-vapour-baths.

You see, my dear countryman, what treasures your house encloses. It only requires a trial. In summer when you return home from the field, throw a few handfuls of hay or hay-flowers in hot water, and let it cool. Such a foot-bath will draw every sensation of fatigue out of your limbs.

And whenever you feel something like burning or a piercing pain, be sensible. You give the wholesome herb every day to your quadrupeds. Let your own body, too, profit by its salutary virtue.

An innkeeper relates: "I have often such racking pains in my head, especially when the weather changes, that I am unable to attend to my business. Sometimes I feel the same pains also in the back and in the thighs, and when they descend into the feet, I can no longer walk. If I drink a glass of beer, the pain makes itself felt in the head directly. For months it has been impossible for me to do any work, and life itself has become a heavy burden to me."

The applications were the following: 1) Weekly 2 warm oat-straw-baths, 30° R., for ½ hour followed by vigorous washing or a short cold bath; 2) every day an upper shower and a knee-shower; 3) every week 3 whole-ablutions, as rapid as possible, either when perspiring or from bed; 4) daily in the morning and in the evening a cup of tea prepared from 5 or 6 finely cut elder-leaves, boiled for 5 minutes. In 4 weeks this innkeeper was so completely restored to health that all his acquaintances declared his appearance being that of a much younger man than he really was. In order to prevent the disease from attacking him again he had to take the above mentioned whole-bath every month and the whole-ablution once or twice a week.

A tradesman comes and relates: "Both my feet are greatly swollen, quite stiff, and I am never without pains; sometimes I cannot sleep for one hour during the whole night; especially in the extremeties I feel violent pain; my arms are also quite stiff; I have appetite, but whenever I take something, it inflates me that I can scarcely breathe; I can hardly walk and especially when getting up in the morning I am so giddy that I hardly know where I am. I have been attended by many physicians, have taken a great deal of medicine, but, in my opinion, my condition has become worse, and I have often wished for death."

The patient looked pretty strong and resembled much more a well-fed brewer than a tradesman although he only took simple fare and did not drink much. He is about 50 years old. The physicians had declared fatty degeneration of the heart to be the cause of his sufferings.

In 5 weeks the patient was freed from his many complaints and enjoyed perfect health. What was it that cured him?

His feet were bandaged in hay-flowers for 2 to 3 hours, first every day, then every other day, and later on every third day. 2) every second day and later on every fourth day, he put on a shirt dipped in a decoction of hay-flowers. When the swelling on the feet had almost entirely disappeared, the patient was given an upper shower and a knee-shower every day. He also took half-baths. These applications were continued for 5 weeks.

Hemorrhoids. (Piles.)

Hemorrhoids (commonly called piles) may be inherited or proceeding from certain modes of life. People who lead a sedentary life generally, and learned men especially, are often troubled with this complaint. The peasant who lives on a simple fare and never sees meat except on Sundays and Holidays, who drinks milk and apostle's wine (water) instead of beer and strong wines, who daily works hard in the field and at home, knows this complaint scarcely by name.

Hemorrhoids are a troublesome, though in the beginning and sometimes through life, harmless disease. The itching and burning is very painful, but more painful still is the effect of the complaint on the mind; they cause irritableness and depression. There are cases in which they embitter life in a most terrible manner and almost cause insanity.

Indifference and neglect are here out of place; great care should be taken to prevent the disease from increasing and from assuming a malignant character.

But what are hemorrhoids, and how are they formed?

Every reader has, no doubt, seen a turkey cock and the fleshy bags hanging from its neck like empty pockets. If the cock is in a passion, the bags become filled with blood and resemble red globes. Such globes, such bags filled with blood or mucus are the hemorrhoids, whether they appear in or on the body, whether they be bleeding or blind hemorrhoids.

The veins are elastic tubes. The more the blood flows irregularly to one place, the more the veins become extended, and they become so particularly, where the blood collects and forms little blood-pools, as it were. Small knots form, and these are filled with blood. From time to time these knots burst, and their contents consist in brown mucus, frequently, however, in pure blood. The bursting of the piles is a relief for the patient; when filled and in great number, they cause much trouble and pain.

The more numerous the piles are, and the more frequently they burst, the greater is the injury caused to the parts where they originate. It is therefore not seldom the case that incurable ulcers, cancer of the rectum etc. are the sad consequences of neglected hemorrhoids.

The sufferings caused by hemorrhoids are often increased by little worms (ascarides) that form inside the rectum. If there are great numbers of them, they seriously injure the rectum and occasion ulcers.

The treatment of hemorrhoids with water is easy and in most cases effective. The number of those cured by water-applications is very great, and I may add that in all cases the result was a happy one.

We shall first attack the ascarides, these leeches of the rectum. They betray their presence by a sensation of pinching, biting, gnawing, and itching inside the anus (the same feeling, however, always accompanies the re-filling of the knots).

Take 1, 2 or 3 cold-water clysters in quick succession, and let the water flow off again. As soon as the cold water enters the rectum, the ascarides interrupt their destroying work, like the leeches, when salt is applied to the bleeding spot; when then the water flows off again, it washes them away. If this proceeding is repeated twice or three times (it may take place twice or 3 times weekly) many of them, sometimes all, come away.

If only the hemorrhoidal knots have to be treated, it is important to remember that the blood which has a determination to a certain part of the body must be led off, that vessels which are too much extended must be contracted, that impurities must be evacuated.

To effect all this, the following application will render good service: A piece of linen is dipped in very cold water and prepared in bed as for the lying on wet sheets; the cloth must be so long as to reach from the neck to over the anus and so wide as to cover the back. On this compress lie down for $\frac{3}{4}$ hour, and repeat the application 3 or 4 times weekly. If the cloth becomes warm before the $\frac{3}{4}$ hour is passed, it should be wetted afresh. A further very recommendable application for such patients is the cold sitting-bath, which should be taken 3 or 4 times weekly. It may be repeated twice or 3 times during one day or also during one night when taken from bed, the duration never exceeding more than 1 or 2 minutes. If any one afflicted with piles makes use of one of these applications for 1 or 2 weeks every 3 months, he may be assured that if a complete cure be not effected, the evil will be at least prevented from increasing. Those who think these applications too troublesome can expect no further advice from me.

Kneipp, Water-Cure.   19

With regard to food I want to call the attention
of the reader to one point to which, in my opinion,
generally too little importance is attached. Many persons
afflicted with piles have begun to eat bran-bread instead
of ordinary wheaten bread, and they assert to have obtained great relief from this kind of diet. I wish this
bran-bread were eaten not by some individuals only, but
by all, for many reasons. I am sorry to say that the
bran-bread has already shared the fate of many other
articles of food; it has been falsified. In a large town
abroad, I once found bran-bread (the true bran-bread is
very heavy) just as light as ordinary bread. I cut the
loaf and discovered that it was ordinary bread, the bran
having been strewn on the surface only. The recipe for
preparing bran-bread has been given in the second part
of this book.

Head complaints.

A gentleman of high rank had a head complaint of
a very peculiar kind. The headache began regularly at
7 a. m. and lasted till the evening; it was so painful
that he could not even read easy things, far less was he
able to attend to his correspondence. At the setting of
the sun the pain ceased, and he was sure to spend a
painless night, unless he had had some mental exertion
during the previous day. The spot where he felt the
pain was on the left side of the forehead and had the
size of a crown-piece. The headache affected the whole
body in such a manner that the gentleman's appearance
became always worse and with the healthy appearance
his strength also went. The most celebrated physicians
were consulted, an establishment for water-cures had also
been visited but without any visible result. The physicians sent the patient to Meran for a last attempt, and
thence he returned, apparently cured, to his native city.
His relations rejoiced at his recovery, until the next
morning punctually at 7 o'clock the old unpleasant guest
returned and took post in its old place. Lamentations
filled the house as the sad news spread, that news which
seemed to destroy all human hope. The gentleman was

advised by some of his acquaintances to have recourse to my water-cure, and an attempt was resolved upon. The patient looked very ill and was rather emaciated. After having given a description of his sufferings, he added that he was seldom without catarrh, and that he had very little vital heat. All this had been attributed to an accident with which he had met in the previous year. "Whatever be the cause of my sufferings," so he concluded, "you know all about them, and you must cure me."

The sickly appearance, the low temperature of the body, the susceptibility for changes in the atmosphere, the emaciation, all these symptoms were as many credible witnesses which accused not the painful spot on the forehead, but the whole system of lacking health and strength. My prescriptions were given accordingly. The whole organism was worked upon, the local complaint was not deemed worthy of a single application. The simple means of hardening with some ablutions such as described in the first part of this book effected the cure i. e. regular circulation of the blood, good digestion, uniform perspiration and with these increase of vital heat, better appearance, in a word, complete health. It is always the old story which, however, cannot be told and re-told often enough.

The correctness of my opinion concerning the head complaint was proved by the result. In about 6 weeks the whole system was restored to health, nor did the much feared pain in the forehead ever return at the usual hour. The water gave the cure of this particular spot (without any particular application) in the bargain.

A gentleman relates as follows: "For 6 to 7 years I suffer from a headache which renders the performance of the duties of my vocation very difficult and almost impossible for me.

I often lost courage entirely. I feel pressure on the head and have a sensation as if something was swimming about in a fluid. Every step I take when walking increases my headache. As soon as I become warm through walking or working, I feel as if I were intoxicated.

8 times I have had colic of the kidneys caused by stone in the same. 12 physicians whom I consulted about the pains in my back have not been able to ascertain the nature of my illness. Only one of them relieved me a little. I have pains in the kidneys when I eat anything sour, or when gases accumulate, when I walk for a longer time and become warm; when I stand or sit for any length of time I feel pain directly. Sometimes I feel a great heat in my whole body, at other times I feel chilly again. In summer I suffer more than in winter. Formerly I suffered much from lethargy. I was healthy, very strong and well built, when I was younger; but for the last 20 years I have been so wretched that I believe nobody could be more so. I have also been to a medical establishment and obtained some relief, but no cure.

The applications were: 1) daily twice an upper shower; 2) daily walking in water and knee-gush. Moreover the patient had from 3 to 5 showers for the back weekly, sitting-baths frequently; he walked in the grass and on stones and took tea from juniper-berries, rosehips and shave-grass, but only for some time 2 cupfuls daily.

In 4 weeks the man was restored to health and now, after 6 months, it can be said that he is in the full possession of perfect health, of bodily strength, and mental vigour.

A man relates: "I am 35 years old, have a constant headache and sometimes such a sensation of weakness that I can scarcely bear it any longer. I have also pains in the chest and in the back, but most of all in the nape of the neck where I feel a constant cramp-like contraction. I have lost a great deal of my hair and if it continues falling out, I shall be perfectly bald in six months. My feet and hands are generally quite cold, and I have no appetite whatever.

Applications: 1) Wet shirt dipped in salt-water; 2) 3 times weekly a whole-ablution from bed during the night; 3) 3 times weekly a wet shirt; 4) daily a saltspoonful of white powder.

After 2 months this man presented himself and declared that he was perfectly cured, that there remained a slight pain only in those parts where he had suffered most. The weight of his body had increased by 10 lbs.

Two gentlemen, musicians, relate as follows: "We both have the same complaint; we suffer from constant headache, it is sometimes almost unbearable. We have little sleep and are restless during it. Congestions and giddiness almost drive us to despair. Our hands and feet are quite cold." Both of them were more than 50 years old.

For 12 days these companions of suffering used the following applications: every day twice upper shower and knee-gush; one day a half-bath, the other day a shower for the back; moreover once a week a head-vapour was taken. After these 12 days both were restored to health and assumed again the duties of their vocation.

In order to preserve their health and gain new strength, they made use of one of the means of hardening daily and took a half-bath twice weekly. According to the latest news, they continue in good health.

A gentleman from Hungary comes with the following statements: "For more than a year I am unable to attend to my vocation on account of violent headache and great giddiness. Over the whole body I feel intense itching and burning, which often deprives me of my sleep. In consequence of my complaint I feel melancholy and uneasy.

After a few weeks he was completely cured by the use of the following course of applications: 1) Upper shower directly followed by walking in water; 2) a half-bath daily. In the second and third week, 3 times a half-bath, daily upper shower and knee-shower; 3) later on whole-baths and upper shower with walking in water.

Heart complaints.

In our times, which may indeed be called times of excitement, there are innumerable persons who are said to suffer from diseases of the nerves, the stomach and the heart. Heart, stomach, and nerves are the scape-goats

to which most complaints are attributed. If a person
has enjoyed good health for 20 or 30 years, if he, so to
speak, never knew where his heart was and all at once
begins to feel ill, it must be a heart complaint that
afflicts him, perhaps even an organic incurable defect of
the heart. My experience — and I have treated innumerable cases of this kind — teaches me that real
defects of the heart are comparatively rare. Among 100
cases in which persons believed, or had been declared,
to have a defect of the heart, there were surprisingly
few of whom this could be said in truth. The heart belonged to the soundest organs of many of these persons,
but there were other unhealthy conditions which influenced
the heart and caused it temporary suffering. The
healthiest cat will scream if you pinch its tail. The best
clock will cease going if I take out its weights, but in
this case it would be foolish to say that the clock is
bad. The soundest heart can be impeded, disturbed in
its activity if an enemy inside throttles it, as it were.
This enemy must be sought, the draw-back removed, and
the last sign of a heart complaint will soon disappear.
It always rouses my indignation if I only hear people say:
heart complaint, heart complaint! People are alarmed
without a reasonable cause and new excitement is added
to that already existing.

A man, still in his best years, told me he had a
defect of the heart, the physicians having declared that
the heart was too much extended. I inquired if he had
ever been ill.

He answered negatively but added that he had an
eruption under the knee. That was enough for me.
Vigorous nature itself had here digged a canal through
which it secreted unhealthy matters. I had only to aid
it in its work i. e. to cause the injurious matter to be
thrown off as soon as possible. The heart was not worked
upon at all. The patient told me that as often as the
eruption increased in dimension, he felt his heart greatly
relieved and that whenever the eruption disappeared fearful palpitation of the heart set in. All this brought grist
to my mill. The man received weekly 2 short bandages,

1 lower bandage, 1 Spanish mantle, and 1 foot-vapour. The Spanish mantle worked in a dissolving and evacuating manner on the whole body, the short bandage in the same manner chiefly on the lower body. The lower bandage completed the work of the short bandage and the foot-vapour drew the still existing unhealthy matter powerfully down. In about 3 weeks the body secreted much, and I hope all unhealthy matter. The heart complaint had disappeared. Since there was neither a defect of the heart before the above mentioned symptoms first showed themselves, nor after the cure of the sick body, am I not right to conclude that there has never been a defect at all?

One night I was called to a housemother who was unable to speak on account of extremely difficult breath. The palpitation of the heart was so violent that the motion could be seen on the blanket and that the beating could be distinctly heard at a little distance. The patient had a sweet taste in the palate and was in great fear of meeting her death by hemorrhage from the mouth, her mother having died of such an attack the same year. The physician attending her declared her sufferings to be caused by various complaints but, in the first place, by a defect of the heart. Hands and feet of the patient were quite cold, and she was continually tormented by a tendency to cough.

Cold hands, cold feet, unusually vehement palpitation of the heart. What does this reveal? All the blood must have left the extremities to seek its original home, the heart, and thence it wants to escape again. Hence the beating and hammering as if it wanted to force the bolts and gates of the heart.

In 5 minutes the violent palpitation was considerably diminished by the application of a twofold wet towel on the abdomen. The blood, which is easy to treat, was soon led away from the heart, and after 10 minutes the beating of the heart was calm; the heart, the seat of the principal defect, was cured already. The patient now began a course of water-applications. On the first day she undertook 2 whole-ablutions in bed, on the second day she put on the Spanish mantle, on the third she had a head-vapour, on the fourth a foot-vapour. She continued the applications in the same succession for some time. The abdomen was the last to listen to reason, it had been the chief leader in the nightly attack. Its obstinate resistance, however, was at last overcome by water, and everything was right again, quite right, the heart not excepted, which, as far as I know, remained healthy ever after.

A gentleman of position had been indisposed for years and could only with difficulty attend to his vocation. A peculiar anxiety increased his sufferings. The least incident caused him palpitation, excitement, alarm. Those who lived with him had to be very cautious in communicating news; for sensations of joy or sorrow were always followed by irregularities in the pulsation of the heart. In summer as well as in winter, the rooms had to be heated, and it required constant attention to keep them in the right temperature. The most celebrated physicians were consulted, and they all agreed in the opinion that the patient, besides suffering from affection of the liver and lungs and from hemorrhoids, had an organic defect of the heart and that he would meet his death by a stroke. The gentleman died. On account of his peculiar complaints the corpse was dissected. And what was the result of the dissection? Lungs, liver, and heart had belonged to the soundest organs of the gentleman, but a mass of fat had formed round the heart and a layer of the same substance in the chest. The gentleman had died through want of blood. The blood had been entirely absorbed by the formation of muscle and fat. One of the physicians, who were present at the dissection, on relating me the fact added: "In this case science has been thoroughly deceived."

A girl complains: "Whenever I walk fast or get frightened, whenever I hear tales of misery or misfortune, I feel a great depression about the heart, and it beats so quickly that I always fear to die suddenly. At the same time my hands and feet become cold, and in the heart I feel great heat. I have a heart complaint; I was told so also by several physicians. A heart complaint, of course, what else could it have been?

If a child sits at the house-door and a big dog comes, the child screams, jumps up, flees frightened into the house and calls: Mother, mother! And if the poor heart is frightened through an accident, the heart cries out and jumps up in violent palpitation, and the blood flows from the house-doors of the body, from the extremities into the house, into the heart which beats then even louder and cries out so that it can be heard at a distance. What is there astonishing in this, and where is there a heart complaint? The girl should first of all leave off all unnecessary and hurtful clothing and muffling and then commence to make use of the lighter means of hardening. The delicate being will, then, cease to be frightened at the barking of a dog or at the whistle of the locomotive. She should hold her arms in cold water and stand in cold water to above the calves of the legs for one minute 3 times daily; these are excellent strengthening remedies. Should the water seem too cold the naive girl may breathe a little over it. *Probatum est.* These applications should be continued for a week. Then the patient may be washed from bed 3 times weekly, and once a week she should take a half-bath to under the arms with quick ablution of the upper body ($\frac{1}{2}$ minute). These practices occupy the second week. In the third and fourth weeks 2 upper and 2 lower showers should be applied to the patient daily. The latter practices must be followed by brisk exercise in order to restore the vital heat. In 6 weeks the girl was well, and all scruples about defects of the heart were washed away.

A young lady comes and asks for help. She relates as follows: "I have past the examination in music and obtained a first class certificate; for 6 years I have taught music in a convent school. I suffer so much from head-ache that I can scarcely bear the sound of an instrument, be it the organ, the piano, or the violin. Even the altar-bells cause me a piercing pain in the head. The physicians attribute my sufferings to a disease of the nerves and of the heart. Had I been healthy, I should have been

received in the convent, but now I am not only unable
to follow my religious vocation but even to earn my bread,
and I suffer unspeakable bodily and mental pain." I replied: "I cannot help you, you must seek help elsewhere."
On her question why I treated just her so harshly, I replied: "A town lady like you with such linguistic and
musical accomplishments will probably not do what I require; otherwise your deplorable condition is curable." She
answered resolutely: "In order to become well again I
shall do whatever you require." And she has kept her
word. I sent her for ten days with the maid-servants in
the field — it was in March — where she was to walk
barefoot. Daily she had a warm foot-bath and an upper
shower to accustom her to the cold. After 6 days she
knelt daily in water reaching to her stomach instead of
the foot-bath. She worked in the field for the sake of
exercise, as much as practice and strength permitted.
After 10 days the young lady returned to a benefactor
who had supported her during her studies and also advised
her to try the water-cure. She continued all the practices,
even the work in the house and field, which she now
liked. Instead of the violin and music books, she now
used spade and rake. In proportion as the body grew
stronger, the nervous and heart disease disappeared. After
4 months there was not the slightest symptom of any
malady whatever, and the young musician enjoyed the
freshness and health of her infancy.

A student of theology came and asked my advice
saying that he was suffering in many ways and among
others from a heart complaint. He wished to become a
priest but with so much headache, such palpitation of
the heart, and all the pressure and anxiety which accompanied it, there was no hope.

I advised the patient to harden his body in a reasonable
manner, which would do him no harm since he was well
built. After some weeks he resumed his studies, became priest, and for health and strength he was surpassed
by few of his companions. Every morning the young
gentleman walked for $\frac{1}{2}$ hour in the dewy grass, daily
he descended in the water up to his stomach and washed

his upper body at the same time. When rainy weather prevented him from his favourite walks in the woods, he substituted some easy work at home for the out-door exercise. Later on he used profuse upper showers, 1 or 2 daily alternately with half-baths to brace his system. Head and heart complaints disappeared as his bodily strength increased.

Hoarseness.

A girl, of 11 years of age, had lost her voice for several months and only with great effort could make herself understood in a croaking manner. Her colour was quite white, her eyes bluish, her body emaciated and without all strength. There was neither vital heat nor appetite except for a little beer or wine.

In 2 months the girl was completely cured and strengthened, and this was the result of the following applications:

1) twice to 4 times daily, she walked barefoot in the grass.

2) 2 or 4 times weekly, she put on the shawl.

3) 4 times weekly, she took a sitting-bath.

4) During the last 3 weeks, when the weather was warm, she took 3 baths in water warmed by the sun, each week.

Her diet consisted in simple household-fare, especially in milk, which was taken by tablespoonfuls every hour, for half a day.

According to the news arrived, the girl enjoys now perfect health.

A priest suffered from hoarseness every year from October to May. He tried everything, consulted several physicians, but in vain. The complaint remained the same for 14 years. At last he had recourse to me, and in a short time he found the desired help.

The gentleman had to stand in water to the knees daily; at the same time he held both his hands in water. Moreover he had to take whole-ablutions generally when rising in the morning, or during the night when waking up.

Already after 12 days the complaint, from which he had suffered for years, disappeared and in the 16 years since past he has never had a relapse.

Another proof of the thoroughness of the cures effected by water.

Hypochondriasis.

I always feel the greatest compassion for hypochondriacs as well as for scrupulous people. How often do you hear people say: "Well he is a hypochondriac, he is scrupulous!" A cheap and worthless saying. These poor people who are so much ridiculed, whose feelings are hurt so frequently are greatly to be pitied. Whenever I have to attend to hypochondriacs (I observe the same rule with regard to the scrupulous) I ask myself: Was this hypochondriac once a normal human being? Was there a time when he thought and worked like other rational men? If I receive an affirmative answer to these questions, it would be foolishness on my part to think that this man is in good health, and that he torments himself and others merely for the sake of the pleasure he derives from doing so. On the contrary, I must admit that a change has taken place either in his body or his mind i. e. that he must be very ill. Restore him to his former healthy condition, and he will cease to be a hypochondriac. Just the ablest persons who are much given to study are most frequently afflicted with this kind of mental disturbance.

In my opinion, the root of hypochondriasis, like that of any other mental disorder, is to be sought in the body, in the diseased body. Only a cure which proceeds from this point of view will be sure and successful. The treatment of such patients must tend to rouse them from indolence, to strengthen their weakened system, to restore the organs to their former activity: in a word, to promote the circulation of the blood, and the hypochondriac will soon be cured.

I knew a man of extraordinary talents. For many years he lived happily in his vocation doing with easiness and enthusiasm as much work as two others. Suddenly he became hypochondriac in such a degree that he had no longer the least care about his duties, shunning and fearing everything and flying from all society.

Instead of obtaining help and compassion of which he was so much in need, he was told daily and hourly that he was just a hypochondriac and that there was no help for him. Must not such treatment cause the greatest depression in the poor patient?

It is remarkable that this gentleman had already visited two establishments for water-cures and thereby only aggravated his sufferings. The applications had been too drastic and only apt to promote the destruction of his half-ruined body.

It was just this case that afforded me another proof of the efficacy of gentle applications. That such a complaint as this cannot be cured in a few days, is obvious.

Those who observe the ordinary rules of health (rational food, clothing, ventilation, recreation, cleanliness) will never become hypochondriacs and when symptoms of the illness first appear, it is easy to destroy it in the germ.

The most suitable water-applications for hypochondriasis consist in whole and part-ablutions, in half-baths, especially sitting-baths, in short bandages and finally in cold whole-baths.

Two more remarks may find a place here. It is the ruin of our time that spirituous drinks are held in such estimation that even young people are in the habit of drinking strong wines; such stuff can only do harm to our present weakened generation. People should strive to remain sober and simple and many a complaint which only of late made its appearance on the stage of diseases would soon disappear behind the scenes.

Another draw-back to health is, that so many want to live almost exclusively on meat, that the excellent food prepared from milk and flour, which gives the best blood and the best juices without acrimony, is so much despised and avoided. That is unnatural and must be of serious consequence. Only the teeth and stomach of the beasts of prey have been formed and adapted for flesh only. Man, for whose sake everything else was created, has had a wider range of food allotted to him.

Inflammation.

A little boy scarcely able to walk sees his mother strike a match and light the fire. He wants to imitate her and contrives to get one of those wonderful little wood splinters. He succeeds, and the little culprit lights a great fire with the little match. The whole house burns down and everything in it.

How many lie in the churchyards in whose bodies a little spark of morbid matter, as it were, was lighted; the spark became a flame. The blood flowing from all sides to the inflamed spot afforded fresh fuel. Perhaps no proper means were employed to extinguish the fire, and the wretched habitation of the human soul burnt down.

Thousands of animals are thus destroyed every year. Thousands of men perish in the same manner. And how quickly this is often accomplished! Your throat has caught fire, it is inflamed. A rough draught comes and serves as bellows; it blows the fire on, the veins supply it with fuel, and in a few hours your whole throat is on fire. Is it not so? What is to be done? What do people do when there is a fire? They give the alarm and seek to save whatever can be saved. If there is time to do so, they remove from the fire everything combustible, and then they continue spouting water on the fire. These hints we should understand and profit by them.

As soon as inflammation appears in any part of the body, the afflux of blood to this spot should be impeded, the not yet inflamed blood should be saved. In the same manner the inflamed part should be worked upon, in order that the blood there collected may be diverted and led off.

One night, not long ago, when I was just going to sleep the wood in the stove began to burn. (The fire had been laid for the next day.) How unpleasant, I thought, this crackling wood will deprive us of our best sleep. My companion was sharper than I. "Not the crackling," he murmured, "but my rest I will have. And what did he do? He took the wood, piece by piece, out of the stove, not minding that some of the pieces were burning already. It is clear enough that there was no longer a fire to trouble us with its noise.

Now let us return to the inflammation of the throat. Just feel the patient's feet whether they are not as cold as ice. The blood seeks the spot where there is most heat. It must away, as it were, from the feet to the fire in the throat. Swathe the feet in linen rags dipped in water mixed with vinegar. Soon you will feel great heat. The foot-bandage draws the blood down and thus deprives the fire of some of its fuel. Then seek to lead the blood further into the lower body. This is done by a compress dipped in water mixed with vinegar and laid on the abdomen. Re-dip it in water as often as it becomes hot. More combustible matter is withdrawn from the endangered neck by this second bandage than by the first. And now you can attack the neck itself, the seat of the fire. Dip a cloth in the coldest water and put it round your neck, but do not let it become hot;* renew it as soon as it becomes warm. If you allow it to become hot, more heat will be produced in the throat, and the blood which was partly led off will flow in the direction of the neck again and fan the inflammation afresh. Whoever understands this last point well, will soon be able to judge for himself when and how often the compress has to be renewed.

Influenza.

This disease is by no means a new one; it is the same kind of catarrh which has long been known under the name of "Grippe". With regard to this illness, people

---

* My 30 year's experience gives me a right to the following assertion. Every one who applies a Priessnitz compress for a whole night will make the unpleasant discovery that the inflammation is increased by it rather than diminished. This is generally attributed to a defect in the way of bandaging; the result, however, has a deeper cause. See neckbandage.

used to say that the patient must take great care of himself during the time of convalescence, lest another disease might follow the first. People in the country who were afflicted with it generally kept their bed, took 2 to 4 cups of hot tea, covered themselves well so as to produce profuse perspiration, and in 2 or 3 days they were well again and no fatal consequences had to be feared.

Water has often proved the best remedy also in this illness. If influenza appears, the patient should take a whole-ablution (cold water mixed with a little vinegar) every hour. After the second or third application, he will begin to sweat, and through this the morbid matters will be removed. I know of a peasant who began to take the ablutions at 7 in the evening and continued them till the following morning when he was perfectly cured. If tea from St. John'swort and milfoil or sage and wormwood is taken in addition to the exterior application, the cure will be even more speedily accomplished. Instead of ablutions, half-baths (of 2 seconds' duration) might be taken as often as the fever increases.

Anastasia relates: "1½ years ago I had influenza and have not been well ever since. I have used much medicine, but without any result. I was formerly pretty strong but I have now lost ⅓ of my weight, I seldom feel appetite and never sleep, I am almost unable to attend to my duties. What is there to be done?"

Answer: 1) Every night take a whole-ablution from bed to promote the vital heat; this will open the pores and produce perspiration.

2) Every day take a shower for the back and an upper shower. These applications effected the dissolution of the unhealthy matters and their evacuation by means of sweating; every third day a short bandage was applied which tended to produce the same effect in the lower body. 12 days after these applications the patient was considerably better. Several smaller and larger ulcers formed through which the morbid matter was led off. Further applications were made use of to brace the system, and after 4 weeks the patient was completely restored.

Why had she not been entirely cured before? Answer: Although many remedies were used, there was none which dissolved and evacuated the morbid matter in the whole body. The medicaments which were taken went through the whole body, but what had collected between flesh and skin was left untouched by them. This had to be removed by perspiration. Thus our ancestors were right when they sought to cure influenza (under its old name) chiefly by profuse sweating.

Insanity.

How fearful it must be when the night of insanity spreads its dark wings over the human mind, when man seems no longer man and bears more resemblance to the irrational creature than to the supreme Creator to whose image he was made. 50, 40, 30 years ago, cases of insanity were rare; now-a-days their number increases in a terrifying manner. The medical establishments for the insane, however numerous they may be, are overfilled. Outside great cities, whole suburbs are built for the purpose of lodging these most wretched of human beings. Besides those that have completely lost the use of their intellect, there are thousands who suffer intensely from greater or lesser disturbances of the mind and receive comparatively little help. In truth, I may say that a great number of these unfortunate people had recourse to me for relief and cure, and that I always felt a particular love and care for these comfortless people. They were generally unable to attend to the duties of their vocation, although their mental derangement had not reached such a degree as to make them fit for the mad-house. Unspeakable, innumerable, and manifold are the torments of these wretched people. Some of them hate their formerly cherished vocation, others will no longer fulfil their religious duties. Fear and hatred of their fellowmen has taken hold of some, hatred of their own person of others; they wish to commit suicide etc. The heads and their contents are of so many different descriptions as the poor individuals themselves.

In all cases of mental disease which I treated during 30 years, I have found out the cause of the derangement which was either hereditary or proceeding from bodily ailment* or sometimes from the patient's mode of life.

I caution against a delusion to which people are often subject with regard to insanity. Their heated imagination makes them see supernatural conditions and diabolical influence where there is nothing but a wretched body affecting the poor mind. Even in cases in which it seemed evident that Satan had taken possession of the patient, the simple cold gush drove him out.

In my whole practice there has not been a single case in which natural means, rightly employed, have not effected the cure. I cling firmly to faith and to the supernatural as to a life-boat, and God forbid that I should give up as much as one atom of my convictions, but on the other hand I would never offer a handle to the enemies of faith and so make faith itself an object of derision.

Those whom this concerns will understand me. An example: A brother brings his sister who declares that the evil spirit is dwelling in the middle of her chest, that she knows a great deal about him whilst he knows all about her, even her most secret thoughts, that she is completely ruled and guided by him. She further asserted that her brother was a fool, the curate being more stupid still and the physician the most stupid of all. Why? "Because they always say I must put on another head, do away with my follies, and obey them. If the devil has taken possession of anybody," she concluded, "one is no longer master of one's own head." It is not to be told in how violent and wild a manner the poor girl raged against the aforesaid three individuals.

Had they only been silent (since they knew before whom they were speaking), they would not have caused

---

* "Mens sana in corpore sano" says the proverb of the ancients. A healthy mind only dwells in a healthy body. Here it may be considered how great an influence the country has on its people, the palace or the poor damp cottage on their inhabitants. Should it be otherwise with regard to soul and body which are moreover so closely connected as to form one whole?

so much excitement in the patient, and my task would have been easier. With such patients everything depends on the manner of treatment. Instead of contradicting her, I only said: "Yes, indeed, your interior is in a bad condition." This answer satisfied her, and I had won her over to my side. Her answer showed that my reply had inspired her with confidence. "If anyone will not believe that I have the devil in me," she replied, „he will not be able to drive him out."

This confidence means for me as much as: the patient is already half cured and my work more than half done. The girl took what I gave her; she punctually applied the water according to prescription. In 6 weeks she was perfectly cured. It will be interesting for many to hear what was the matter with this person. Her looks were wild, her features sunk, her hands were cold, her feet colder still, she felt a heavy pressure on the chest and in her stomach a repugnance to every kind of food. All her blood, so it seemed, had flown to the chest. My first task consisted in regulating the circulation, in restoring equal vital heat and activity of the whole organism. To this effect the patient stood in cold water to above the calves of the legs, twice for 2 minutes every day, then she took a brisk walk to thoroughly warm her feet. The arms up to the shoulders were treated in the same manner. Twice a day she had back, chest and abdomen vigorously washed with water mixed with vinegar. For this ablution she lay in bed. These comparatively easy applications were continued for a fortnight. The violent agitation gave way, although the devil was still active in the confused head. Her features began to revive. After 2 weeks the patient commenced to make use of the lower bandage alternately with half-baths (only for $\frac{1}{2}$ minute and followed by ablution of the upper body) and the Spanish mantle; these 3 applications were continued for about 3 weeks. After the third week the applications were limited to 1 whole-ablution and 1 short bandage of 1 hour, weekly. Thus the supposed devil was driven out, and the excitement was changed into great calm and undisturbed peace.

20*

Poor parents brought their boy of 10 years of age and related as follows: "As often as the bells ring for church, the boy begins to rave and to utter the most horrible blasphemies such as we have never heard before. He continues cursing as long as he sees a person on the way to church. Then he ceases. As soon as the first person leaves the church after service, he begins to swear and continues as long as he sees any one come from church. Whenever we pray, he curses; when we cease praying, he also stops cursing. Father, it is really dreadful. Nothing has yet brought him any help, and speaking to him makes him worse. He once took hold of his mother with both arms as with claws and shook her so violently that nobody would believe a boy to possess so much strength. Physicians have been consulted, but without result. He was also blessed by a priest, and on that occasion he cursed more dreadfully than ever."

The boy had a very strange appearance: a livid complexion, distorted features, and his hair standing on end like a hedgehog's spines. I ventured to touch his hand whereupon he was about to spring at my face. Two priests who had seen him in this terrible condition said: "Whoever believes in possession by the devil must say: Here it is."

I treated the complaint from the beginning as a natural one nor was I deceived; in 6 weeks the poor child was completely cured. The boy had to put on a shirt dipped in water (with some salt) for 1 to $1\frac{1}{2}$ hours daily. He likewise took a whole-ablution of water with vinegar once daily. Both applications were continued for a fortnight. In the third week he put on the shirt as aforesaid on one day, the next day he had a warm bath (28° R.) for $\frac{1}{2}$ hour followed by a cold one, ($\frac{1}{4}$ minute) the third day he took a whole-ablution. He continued to make use of these practices alternately during the third and fourth week. In the fifth and sixth week one wet shirt, and one warm bath with rapid cold ablution, respectively, were sufficient to complete the cure.

The cure was quickly accomplished. The perfectly cold boy became warm again, the lost appetite returned.

and he relished his meals chiefly prepared from milk and flour. The devil was blown away, as it were.

Perhaps some of my readers will ask: "Why does not the pastor apply gushes to such patients since in our madhouses maniacs are especially treated with douches?" In my humble opinion a sportsman who wants to entice the fox out of his hole would not do well to stand at the entrance of it and discharge his gun there. It would be more advisable to invite master reynard by means of a fowl or a sucking pig placed before his hole. Now listen, dear reader! Where there is a disease, there is also injurious matter. To dissolve and evacuate this, means enticing and catching the fox. A douche, however, does not dissolve, nor does it evacuate. When the dissolution and evacuation of morbid matters has been accomplished, then a light douche has a meaning and then I, too, agree with its use.

4 years ago, a girl came to me and related as follows: My brother has been in a mad-house for more than a year. He was pronounced incurable. Now I have some of the symptoms which preceded my brother's disease. I have been in a situation till now, but I had to leave because I am unable to work. If I get no help, I shall soon follow my brother to the mad-house.

On various questions which I put her, she replied that her appetite was constantly changing, being sometimes good, sometimes entirely wanting, that she suffered from a racking pain in her limbs which whenever it gave way was followed by severe pain in the chest, that more than half of her thick long hair had fallen off. It was evident that very bad juices were the cause of the girl's condition and that the surest sign of their evacuation would consist in a renewed growth of the hair on the half-bald head.

The patient made use of the following applications: daily the wet chemise dipped in salt water or water mixed with vinegar, likewise daily lukewarm half-baths with vigorous cold washing of the upper body (duration 1 minute). It was summer. Every day she walked much barefoot with good result, especially in the dewy grass. She

continued these practices for 3 weeks. Then she took
warm baths followed by cold ones, the lower bandage
(the patient used a sack) dipped in an infusion of hay-
flowers. The whole cure lasted 3 months. Then the patient
was completely restored, and her hair grew more luxu-
riantly than before. The person married later on and enjoys good health to this day.

A pastor greatly respected and loved by his parishioners
came to me and told me that he felt discouraged on
seeing himself unable to attend to his duties. This condition which was accompanied by great sadness, ill-humour and inability for study, had induced some of the
pastors in his neighbourhood to take the poor gentleman
to a medical establishment where he remained for several
weeks. On his return he was quieter but not cured. He
asked me what he should do whether leave his parish, or
remain where he was. The gentleman had that healthy
appearance which so often deceives in such cases and
causes so many rash, unjust, and uncharitable judgements.*
Looking at him more closely, one could notice that his
eye was dull, his colour pale, his hair withered. The
applications were of 3 kinds: head and foot-vapour, cold
upper and lower showers, frequent walking on wet stones
or standing in water for 3 to 4 minutes. After some days
he began to take warm baths alternately with cold upper
and lower showers. On the sixth day a bluish eruption
appeared on the whole back. The more this eruption
came out, the more the patient felt relieved. When the
morbid matter was all led off the pastor was well. The
whole cure lasted 14 days. With new courage the zealous
priest returned to his parish.

Itch.

This horrible complaint can cause much havoc on,
and still more in, the body. It is greatly to be lamented

---

* It is the same folly to judge from a person's corpulence
that he or she indulges in eating and drinking too much (such
sorely tormented people are generally the most easily satisfied)
as to judge from the healthy appearance of a mentally diseased person that his or her sufferings are only caused by
scruples about their health.

that people, in order to cure this disease, have recourse to remedies which harm the body instead of healing it. Who knows all the greasy ointments containing sulphur, brandy, and other admixtures. One thing these disgusting smeary remedies bring about: they thoroughly close the pores of the skin, they obstruct through greasy crusts the air and water canals so indispensably necessary for the health of the body, they force the perspiration back into the body there to poison blood and juices and to cause serious diseases, for many perhaps fatal ones. This is no exaggeration, but it must grieve everybody who knows how easily and quickly itch can be cured.

Once there came to me for help a man of 28 years of age, he was well built but his appearance made me think of a piece of worm-eaten wood. He had found help nowhere; it could not be ascertained what was the matter with him. I asked him: Have you perhaps had itch in your youth? He answered affirmatively to my curious question and added that he had been cured in 3 days. — God forbid that I should cure like that!

It is just with regard to such disgusting maladies which better than any thing else reveal the presence of morbid matters in the body, that the cure must be based on the principle: Any matter in the body that ought not to be there, must be expelled. To do the opposite of this would mean planting insects in clothes and hair, and mice in the ploughed field. According to this principle the water-applications must tend to entice, extract and remove unhealthy and poisonous matters and to strengthen the whole organism that it may aid in the proceeding.

First our patient took on 3 consecutive days a warm bath (33° R.) of a decoction of pine-twigs* with three-fold change.

Soap did him good service in opening the pores and removing the dirt. I cannot help calling things by their

---

* Extract from pine-leaves would serve as well. For me, for farmers, and for the poor the pine-twigs are quite sufficient.

proper names although it may unpleasantly affect the
nerves of some of my readers. These baths were followed
by strengthening applications: in the first week he took
whole-ablutions from bed in the night and a fourth warm
bath with cold ablution; in the second week he took a
warm bath followed by a cold ablution and a cold half-
bath with ablution of the upper body; in the third week
he took a cold whole-bath, later on a few warm baths
every month. Should the cure not be accomplished by
these applications, the 2 latter practices may be continued
for some time. A warm whole-bath taken weekly will
be of good effect at all events.

In six weeks our poor patient was cured and was
now able to embrace a vocation. His good health continues to this day; he has never again had the least
attack of the former troublesome disease.

Thus itch is treated when it has been suppressed
and forced back to the interior of the body.

If any one suffers from external itch, he should take
a warm bath (33° R.) and rub the skin with sharp soap.
The so-called green soap, which can be had at any
chemist's, is best. After a bath of 15 minutes' duration
he should wash with clean water (cold or warm) and
ordinary soap. It would be of excellent effect if the
patient could have a second similar bath of fresh warm
water directly after the first. Also this second bath
should be followed by a cold or warm ablution.

Since itch is very often taken by contact, through
clothes, linen etc., it is of the greatest importance to
change linen and clothes after the baths. Without this
precaution all applications would be of no avail.

In this manner itch can be cured in 3 or 4 days.

Jaundice.

The gall-bladder is situated in the liver, and thence
the gall flows into 2 canals. Sometimes concretions are
formed in these canals; they proceed from the liver and
are called gall-stones. Through these indurations the
flow of the gall is obstructed; the same effect may be
produced by pressure, shocks, and other accidents. When

the gall is thus obstructed, it enters the blood-vessels and causes the disease called jaundice. It appears also after other serious diseases as typhus, fever etc. If the complaint, however, is the consequence of a diseased liver, the blood becomes morbid or even poisoned, and in this case jaundice is often fatal. It is of less importance when it is caused by disturbances or proceeds from other maladies. The first symptoms of jaundice are seen in the white of the eye, in the skin itself, in the stools and the urine. There is generally loss of appetite and change of taste. If the liver is not affected, this complaint is easily cured. For interior use I recommend especially: daily 3 to 4 times, each time 3 to 4 spoonfuls of wormwood tea or 3 times a saltspoonful of wormwood powder dissolved in 6 to 10 spoonfuls of warm water. Sage- and wormwood-tea will do excellent service.

To swallow 6 pepper-corns daily with the food is likewise a means for improving the digestion. Temperance in eating and drinking is to be recommended. Milk is the best food. The best water-applications are: Twice to 3 times a week a short bandage and an ablution from bed in the night. The yellow colour remains often for weeks, but this is of no consequence. If the yellow hue, however, changes gradually into brown, if the appetite continues decreasing, if great irritation and burning is felt in the skin and the emaciation is progressing, there is much reason for fear of the liver being incurable and cancer or induration of the liver setting in. It is of a particularly good effect in cases of jaundice or a diseased liver to take every morning and evening a cupful of milk with which a spoonful of coaldust and sugar has been mixed.

Kidney complaints.

A farmer relates: "I am just as sickly and miserable as I seem strong and corpulent. I can no longer work, am constantly puffed up, breathing is often so difficult, that I believe I must suffocate. I toss about in bed at night without being able to sleep. The urine is mostly very thick and mixed with blood, and I have often a very

violent burning in the bladder. I have had several doctors.
One said I was suffering from a liver complaint and gall-
stones. Another declared that my kidneys were in a bad
state and that suppuration of the kidneys would set in.
A third thought my stomach digested nothing and that
I was, therefore, always obstructed with phlegm, because
there is always a great deal of sticky phlegm in my mouth."
The following applications were prescribed for the comfortless man: 1) In the week 2 warm baths with boiled
oat-straw, with threefold change, 30 to 32° R. (10 minutes in the warm water, 1 minute in the cold). 2) In the
week 2 short bandages, likewise with oat-straw water,
for 1½ hours. 3) To drink daily 2 cups of tea from
shave-grass and juniper-berries, brewed for 10 minutes.
In six weeks the man was perfectly well. His unnatural
corpulence had disappeared, the yellow-brown colour of
the skin was removed, and as the fresh and healthy colour
had returned, so also had his strength.

A poor workman writes: "I became ill with complaint of the kidneys in November 1887, but I kept to
my work until the middle of January 1888. In the
meantime my strength had become so low that I was
obliged to keep my bed for 11 weeks. The doctor who
attended me, declared that my complaint came only from
colds and suppressed perspiration, and that it would be
a tedious case. In the urine was always a great red-
brown sediment. The urine was chemically analysed, and
it was discovered that this sediment consisted of blood.
Through this constant loss of blood I became so weak
that the doctor feared dropsy. He, therefore, examined
the feet and heart day by day; but there never appeared
any thing like dropsy. As after a time I felt better, I
went back to my work again, but after 20 weeks the
suffering returned, and I had to give it up once more. As
I had already taken so much medicine and all kinds of
things without any permanent result, I resolved upon the
advice of a few friends, to go to Wörishofen. I now
turned to the cold-water-cure which I liked exceedingly."
The man was cured by the following applications:

1. The first day in the morning upper shower and knee-gush, in the afternoon half-bath for $\frac{1}{2}$ minute.

2. The second day very early in the morning to rise from bed for a whole-ablution and return to bed immediately, then walking in water; in the afternoon upper shower and knee-gush.

3. In the morning upper shower, later shower for the thighs; in the afternoon shower for the back and walking in water in the afternoon. So alternately for 3 weeks further.

4. Daily morning and evening to drink a cup of tea made from 10 crushed juniper-berries and a little shave-grass, each cup taken in two portions.

Knee, tumour on the.

A person, 30 years old, suffers from a swelling from the ankle to above the knee. It was very painful, quite firm and hot. The patient used medical remedies for 6 months and among others a bandage of plaster of Paris for 12 weeks and a second one for 8 weeks. Her condition was so aggravated that the foot could not be allowed to touch the ground; the joint of the knee was especially painful. Since nothing had brought her relief, she used infused hay-flowers by way of trial and bandaged them round the leg from above the ankle to the middle of the thigh. — The pain gave way, the swelling decreased and when it was reduced to one half of its former size, showers were applied to the suffering part (every second day). After about 8 weeks the whole foot could be used again, and after some time the person could resume her very hard work.

Lumbago.

Lumbago is a severe pain at the small of the back. The best application is lying on a cloth that has been dipped in hot water mixed with vinegar. It is generally sufficient to renew the cloth twice or 3 times, each time after 1 hour.

Lungs, complaint of the.

A house-wife relates as follows: "The physicians say
that I have catarrh of the lungs and of the throat, that
my lungs are much affected, and two physicians declared
there was no help for me. I should like to make a last
attempt with water; if this brings me no help, I resign
myself to the will of God. For 20 days the woman
received 2 upper showers daily and directly after a knee-
gush, she also had a short bandage twice a week. She
took daily 2 cupfuls of tea from boiled fennel-seed, common nettle and ribwort. After this time the cough had
disappeared, the obstruction with phlegm was removed,
the appearance healthy and the strength restored.

Lungs, emphysema of the.

It very frequently happens that people who are still
in the prime of life, suffer much from difficulty in breathing, and not seldom their condition becomes so painful
that they constantly fear to suffocate.

Generally such people are rather corpulent, and their
mode of life helps too, as a secondary cause, to make
their condition worse. The chief cause of the evil is
generally, that the organism is suffering from a general
weakness, is feeble and inactive, has little blood, and on
account of the inactivity and torpidity the increase of
blood does not take place in such a manner as to supply
the wants of the body. I should like to compare such
people with a machine, each part of which is in good
order, while the whole is too weak for the demands put
upon it. A further cause are almost regularly the gases,
which accumulate in the abdomen, and exercise a pressure
on the organs of the upper part of the body. A greater
strain is thereby put upon these than their task otherwise demands.

They suffer under this pressure, and a universal contraction takes place. The evil is removed first by banish-
ing the gases out of the body, and secondly by hardening the whole body and strengthening it by means of a
simple, good, and nourishing fare. My experience of more

than 35 years teaches me that exactly in people afflicted in this manner Bright's disease readily gets the upper hand, i. e. that the already weakened body by this disease becomes fully broken down, fully destroyed.

A gentleman, rather corpulent, not yet 40 years of age, had from time to time such attacks of suffocation that he was firmly convinced — the doctor too confirmed him in it, — that, were the attack to return twice, he would succumb to it. The difficulty of breathing was so great that his struggles for breath could be heard on the ground floor of the house. At every attack this sense of suffocation lasted for a considerable time and so exhausted the body that after each he felt quite ill. When, after a short time, he had recovered again, he felt well and fresh. The attacks often kept off for some days. but then their violence increased all the more.

The said gentleman possessed the greatest dread of water and could only then make up his mind for the water-cure when no other remedy was left to him. For six weeks he used different applications. The cure was such a perfect one that the attacks never returned and the gentleman has always since then — it is now about 21 years ago — enjoyed the best of healths.

The patient took for several days together tea made from blackthorn - blossoms, which produced a very mild but copious evacuation of the bowels; then he made use of the short-bandage, of lying on wet sheets and covering with wet sheets, and lastly, of half and also whole baths, of one minute's duration. Among the applications the Spanish mantle was also of good service. They proved of greater effect in the following order.

First the short-bandage; it begins to expel the gases and to loosen the causes of the gases;

then the covering with wet sheets and lying on wet sheets, a continuation of the first application, which also serves to strengthen the body;

further the Spanish mantle; this leads out the corrupted matters through the skin;

lastly, half-baths, to brace the organism.

Another gentleman suffered from difficult breathing to such an extent that the doctors declared dropsy of the heart had set in. This gentleman, although well nourished, was not particularly corpulent; nevertheless he could only with the greatest exertion ascend the stairs. Appetite he had almost none, sleep very disturbed; he was never without anxiety and fear. In his former profession he had had plenty of exercise, but afterwards he came into the chancery and this sedentary, inactive life brought him by degrees into the described painful condition. For his cure quite a few and easy applications of water sufficed. They are also of help still, as soon as ever the evil begins to show itself anew. It has often announced itself during twelve years, but each time it has been quickly removed. Besides the water-applications the gentleman used tea as well, of which he became fond on account of its excellent effects. This tea alone effected the regularity of the bowels and the leading out of the gases from the stomach, and at the same time spared more numerous and stronger applications of water, which the gentleman feared, and for which the time often was wanting. This tea was the mild "Tonic laxative," and applications were the following: If the complaint appeared in a lesser degree, lying on wet sheets three times in the week, vigorous ablution of back, chest and abdomen, every morning when rising, were sufficient. If the evil appeared in a stronger degree the gentleman used the short bandage, or also a half-bath. — To these applications were united ablutions in the night, which were always of good service.

It is remarkably strange, and I am often astonished that people should use the strongest remedies against such conditions, remedies which can never have good results for the health; the tormented patient is, alas! often treated with poison even.*

---

* There is now a letter lying before me in which the patient complains of, and enumerates, the poisons he has had to swallow in different diseases. I will reserve the enumeration for another time.

The latter was always, and is still to this day, an unsolved riddle to me. I have always to exert myself in order to preserve my interior calm, when I hear of such things.

A priest got inflammation of the lungs in a high degree, after this emphysema of the lungs (expansion of the lungs, inflation of the lungs,) and with it came such a cough, that it was hardly possible to listen to it. With hardly any appetite, with a countenance of sadness and ailment, he appeared to be in a very low condition. The lungs were still pronounced as curable by the doctors.

The applications were the following: For fourteen days together: 1. every day two upper showers; 2. twice every day to walk in water for three to five minutes; 3. three times a week a shawl; 4. every second day a sitting-bath of 1 minute's duration. The patient took a decoction of Fœnum græcum boiled with honey, if possible, every hour a spoonful.

The effects were: the showers strengthened the upper part of the body. The cough became in the beginning still stronger, but very much phlegm was thrown up. After three days the cough and expectoration decreased, and in twelve days there was only a little remainder of the phlegm left. — This was removed by further applications of upper showers, knee-showers and tea from common nettle and ribwort. After about three weeks, perfect restoration took place.

Lungs, inflammation of the.

Margarita is lying in bed. She has a violent dry cough and much tendency to vomit; the heat increases from hour to hour. Acute pain and burning torment her chest and one of her sides. The physician declares that inflammation of the lungs is coming on. How can the patient be helped? Every child knows that a sponge can absorb and retain a great deal of water. Should there be nothing to absorb heat as a sponge does the water? Every woman in Germany knows the *Topfenkäs* (cheese prepared from curdled milk).* Take some of this *Topfen-käs* and some of the *Topfenwasser* and mix it to a paste, spread this paste on a linen cloth and put the plaster on the burning spot whence the fire of inflammation threatens to spread. I do not know a better means for absorbing heat; I have seen the greatest inflammations checked and extinguished by this remedy if it was applied twice to 4 times a day according to the degree of heat. I know many persons who owe their life to the application of this simple compress.

As interior remedy the patient should take a spoonful of Provence-oil twice a day.

Should these two remedies prove inefficient i. e. should the inflammation not be checked by them, then water may be applied. The patient should make use of the lower bandage twice a day. Instead of the lower bandage both feet to above the ankles may be swathed in cloths dipped in water and vinegar; they must be renewed as often as they become very warm. Wet socks may be substituted for the foot-bandage and dry ones put on over them.

If the sick Margarita makes use of the plaster for 3 to 5 days in the beginning of the illness, she will be well again in 6 to 7 days or at the longest in 9 to 10 days.

Other parts of the body may be inflamed as well as the lungs. We speak of inflammations of the diaphragm, abdomen etc. All these are to be worked upon according to the above mentioned principles: diversion of the blood, cooling of the inflamed part i. e. extraction of heat through the influence of cold.

I was once called to a patient at midnight. He was almost unable to breathe. He coughed dreadfully and had a great tendency to vomit. In the chest especially on one side of it, he had a sensation as though he was pierced with knives. The patient's whole body was glowing hot. Instead of preparing him for death, for which

---

* Sour milk is put on the warm hearth. Here the curd of the milk coagulates and forms *Topfenkäs*, the liquid part of the milk is called *Topfenwasser* (whey).

purpose I had been called, I had a lower bandage applied to him and a *Topfen-plaster* placed on the painful spot. To effect interior cooling he took a spoonful of salad-oil. This did him good. For 6 days he continued thus, and then the man was out of danger.

If somebody dies from inflammation of the lungs or any other interior inflammation, what has there been going on in the body? The interior is reflected in the exterior.

You have, no doubt, seen little ulcers or perhaps you have been afflicted with such yourself. How are these ulcers formed? First you perceive a red spot on the skin, then you feel burning inside. The swelling increases, and after some time you see the upmost part of the cone become white. Then, people say, the ulcer is ripe, and it is time to lance it or to squeeze it so as to remove the matter and with it the bad blood which has gathered there.

Such a little ulcer (carbuncle) generally causes great pain not only in the part where it originates but in the whole body. This is the best proof for the truth that the whole body has to share the sufferings of the individual part, that it is for the good of the whole body if such things are well healed but in like manner turns to its disadvantage if they are neglected.

If a greater ulcer of this kind does not become mature, the affected spot will soon assume a blue or red-brown colour, the blood decays, and the decayed blood has an effect similar to that of poison. If it mixes with the sound blood, blood poisoning will set in, which, when not arrested, always ends fatally.

The same process takes place in cases of interior inflammation, but there the poison produces its effect more quickly, its ravages are more terrible and more detrimental.

Martin, a handsome strong man, gets violent fever. First he feels chilly, then hot. His head is so hot that the physician declares his illness to be inflammation of the brain. His whole inside is in flames, as it were. The forerunners of the evil were headache, lassitude, and a sensation of chill. The patient felt no particular pain in any part, except the fever. After 10 days the man died, and at the dissection of the corpse it was discovered that the poor man's brain was intact, and that he had died of inflammation of the lungs.

How would you have treated this case? I was asked. This case shows clearly how easily the diagnosis (the discriminating knowledge of a disease obtained by the examination of its symptoms) deceives. The ordinary symptoms of inflammation of the lungs are: a piercing pain and burning about the lungs, cough and tendency to vomit. Our patient had not one of them. How great a difficulty such a case presents to the allopathist. And often it is the highest time, the fire has already assumed great dimensions. The fire-engine must not fail to quench it, otherwise there is no help, nor would applications of drops and spoonfuls be of avail; the fire would instantly consume them.

My simple maxim for such desperate cases (and I hope it will not be opposed by any one) is: Whenever there is a fire, try to extinguish it, check the mightiest flame first; if the whole body is on fire, extend your proceeding to the whole body. Perhaps you will become master of it; at all events, you will weaken it and obtain time for further consideration.

As to the above mentioned patient, I should have had his chest, back and abdomen washed every hour for 3 or 4 consecutive hours; these ablutions would have checked the fire. Then I should have continued quenching the fire with lying on wet sheets and covering with wet sheets, with wet socks, foot-bandages, the latter to be renewed every hour. If the patient's lungs had been otherwise healthy — and such seems to me to have been the case since he felt no pain in the highest stage of inflammation — his cure would, humanly speaking, have been certain i. e. if God in his infinite wisdom had not decreed otherwise.

Megrim. (Migraine.)

Megrim or migraine is a disease to which the weaker sex is particularly subject but which sometimes also attacks

the strongest men, especially those who are much given
to mental labour. To comfort such patients, you sometimes hear physicians say: Be quiet, a stupid head never
gets migraine. The complaint originates either in a
disturbed circulation or in some derangement of the stomach
or the bowels. (Entire want of appetite and repugnance
to all food.) If the lower body is, on the whole, weak,
if there is much wind, if the bowels do not move regularly, these complaints re-act on the head and cause pain;
or the blood may have a determination to one particular
spot. Migraine often announces itself by a sensation as
if a veil were spread over the eyes; some have great pain
in the corners of the eyes, and in some the sight itself
is impaired.

Migraine often appears after illnesses, when nature
has not yet recovered its strength and the activity of the
organs is not yet a normal one. It may also be inherited.

Migraine is easy of cure. If it proceeds from gases —
and these are in my opinion the principal cause — it will
be sufficient to wash the abdomen with cold water twice
to 4 times daily for 2 or 3 consecutive days. Not only
the gases will be expelled by this simple application but
it also works on the bowels and not seldom it alone will
restore everything to order. The effect will be stronger
still if the water is mixed with some salt or vinegar.

Should these applications prove inefficient, 2 or 3
half-baths may be taken within a week. These should
suffice. Moreover the patient may take tea to evacuate
the gases. Caraway or fennel is of excellent effect. Five
drops of lavender-oil taken on sugar every morning and
evening will render the same service. Many have been
relieved by chewing 6 to 8 juniper-berries during the day.

Effervescent powders are thought to be an unfailing
remedy against this complaint. I admit that they lead
off gases but their effect must not be exaggerated. They
are not unfailing remedies. Such people always remind
me of the amusing story in which a hare is killed by
means of a rocket. The *Migrainestift* is nowadays considered as the *"non plus ultra"* for Migraine. It consists
of a finely worked piece of wood containing the wonder-

21*

acorn which has a strong smell of camphor. No real
gentleman or real lady goes out without this little "*Vade
mecum.*" The root of the complaint is, as we have seen,
in the abdomen. With the *Migrainestift* the forehead is
stroked a certain number of times. I will not take the
liberty of judging any further about this; but I should
not be able to help smiling if a patient, to whom a
clyster has been ordered, wanted to have his ear syringed
instead.

Melancholy.

"For several years I have suffered from distemper of
the mind, headache, cramp-like pain in the face, rheumatism, and profuse perspiration of the whole body. Several physicians have endeavoured to cure me, but in vain."

In 14 days this sad condition was removed and to brace
the system for the future one half-bath and one whole-
ablution weekly were sufficient. The applications of the
first fortnight were: 1) Twice a week a wet shirt dipped
in salt water in order to lead off morbid matters; 2) twice
a week a half-bath to strengthen the lower body; 3) twice
weekly a whole-ablution to rouse the whole organism to
activity.

"I come to consult you about a person suffering from
melancholy. A house-wife, 38 years old, has a great dislike for all occupation, nor is she able to do any thing.
She lives a sad life and cares neither for her husband
nor for her household. She avoids all company and never
leaves the house. She is already rather emaciated, and
the remedies prescribed for her have been without effect."

Applications: 1) To wash every evening when warm
in bed with water mixed with vinegar; 2) twice daily a
warm foot-bath with ashes and salt, for 14 minutes;
3) to take 20 drops of wormwood extract in water twice
daily. After 3 weeks she was in a pretty good condition.
Further applications: 1) 2 short bandages weekly; 2) 2
whole-ablutions weekly. These applications were to be
continued for a fortnight; from that time forward the
patient took one whole-ablution and walked in water 3 to
5 times every week.

Through over-exertion and harassing cares a gentleman contracted the following complaints: humming in the ears, continuous sensation of pressure in the head, debilitation of his reasoning faculty and his memory; he was, therefore, utterly unable to perform the duties of his vocation. Moreover he suffered from great depression of spirits, from fear and alarm. He seldom slept well. The bodily strength of the once robust man was dwindling fast, and there was a considerable loss of weight. The greatly dejected patient submitted to the following treatment: Upper shower, shower for the back, walking in water, 2 bandages a week, once a Spanish mantle, and for interior use wormwood drops either pure or mixed with arnica or centaury. These extracts had a particularly good effect. After an 8 weeks' cure he felt perfectly well and able to work; his temper was raised and cheerful and has remained so ever since. His bodily weight has gained 22 lbs.

Mucous Fever.

If catarrh is compared to an infant, mucous fever is the grown-up child. Mucous fever always owes its existence to catarrh and both are sources of innumerable other complaints, as mentioned on a previous occasion. The cure, and consequently also the applications, are the same for both. Whoever wants to cure catarrh easily and quickly, should lie in bed, wash his chest and abdomen every hour and have his back washed by someone else. Three or four such ablutions cure catarrh in its first stages in one night. If parts of the throat, head, or chest become inflamed in consequence of the catarrh, we have developed mucous fever which is nothing else than catarrh tormenting the whole body. Those parts which were first attacked by the catarrh, be it throat, chest, or any other part, remain always most sensitive until the patient is completely restored.

Nervous complaint.

A priest relates as follows:

"In consequence of great excitement, fear, and fright I got a complaint which in its beginning consisted in frequent palpitation of the heart, constant difficult breathing and general weakness. The attacks of palpitation ceased after some months; but other complaints appeared in their stead: now and then very violent and alarming attacks of asthma, frequent painful pressure and a feeling of contraction extending also to the abdomen. I felt the pressure especially in the neighbourhood of the ribs, sometimes also in the spinal marrow. I often felt great weakness and lassitude in my limbs and pain in the joints. The bowels are constantly tormented by costiveness and gases. My voice is much weakened so that even simple speaking causes me pain and asthma; moreover it is utterly impossible for me to continue speaking for any length of time. My head is troubled with giddiness, pressure and violent headache in such a degree that I am sometimes unable to think. Every trifle irritates me and increases my sufferings in chest and head. My mind is plunged into unspeakable melancholy which drives me almost to despair. The physicians declare my disease to be a nervous complaint. Two of them, an allopathist and a homoeopathist prescribed me several remedies (douches, particular diet, bromkali, Zincum oxydat., Natr. phosph. etc.) none of which had the desired result, but rather increased my sufferings. Cold whole-baths and much exercise in the open air, which were ordered by a third physician, seemed to have a better effect. This lasted for 6 months when I resolved to have recourse to cold water only."

Thus related the patient. Let us look at him a little more closely. His appearance is unusually red, the eyeballs are somewhat yellow, ears and lips red mixed with blue. The gentleman, who is hardly more than 30 years old, has lost almost all his hair. What must we conclude from these symptoms? Certainly a very great determination of blood to head and chest. The pain in the forehead shows the violence of the afflux of blood to the head and the blood causes distension of the veins. How is there a cure to be effected? The two principal places of suffering, head and chest, require our first attention. Both are overwhelmed, as it were, by the super-abundance of blood. This must be led to the extremities. Then I may proceed to dissolve whatever be abnormal in chest and head (conglomerations, distensions of veins, etc.), and finally I must work on the whole system.

A course of applications in the following order will be most suitable: foot-vapour, head-vapour, short bandage, Spanish mantle, walking on stones, upper and lower showers, Spanish mantle, walking barefoot, in winter best in newly fallen snow. Within 3 weeks the patient's condition was much improved. It required months, however, to effect the complete cure of so deeply rooted a disease.

The patient will learn to judge from the more or less good effect of every individual application which of them should be oftener repeated. General applications i. e. such whose effects extend to the whole organism should, however, always accompany those that aim at the cure of one particular part.

A priest from Bohemia relates: "Eight months ago I got, in consequence of over-exertion, violent palpitation of the heart, sleeplessness, rising of the stomach, swelling of the abdomen, and difficult breathing. I suffered from pain in feet and hands, restlessness and great lassitude. At last my appetite also failed, and there was no evacuation of the bowels."

At his arrival the patient seemed very much exhausted, his complexion was pale yellow. After a seven weeks' cure he was in the full possession of health and good spirits. Also sleep had come again.

The water-applications of which he had made use were the following: In the first 3 weeks 1) a half-bath from bed in the night; 2) in the morning upper shower and walking in water; 3) in the afternoon shower for the back and half-bath; 4) daily much walking barefoot in the grass. Later on upper shower with knee-gush, half-baths, and twice a foot-vapour; as internal remedies he took 8 to 10 juniper-berries daily and drank tea from wormwood and sage.

Nervous disorder.

A gentleman of position had so injured his body and mind through an unusual amount of business, that one could no longer judge which was the most disturbed, mind or body.

There was reason to fear that the disturbance of the mind with its sad consequences might take a lamentable end. For months together he could take neither rest nor sleep, the most painful sufferings tormented his whole body; all medicinal remedies were without effect. The water was to rescue here, and really after thirteen weeks the patient, fresh and healthy, was able to resume his profession and begin work anew.

Such a condition can only be treated by the most simple applications: 1) Twice daily to wash the upper part of the body with water and vinegar. A knee-gush (for 1 minute) follows this washing. The second application is to be repeated in the afternoon. The 2nd day: A mild shower on the upper part of the body with half a can of water. Directly afterwards to take exercise on wet stones, besides a can of water poured on the knees; in the afternoon the same. The 3rd day: An upper shower (one canful) Afternoon: upper shower (one canful), directly afterwards to stand in water (for 3 minutes). This application was so painful that tears came into the patient's eyes. Thus he continued for about a week. In the second week upper showers with increased knee-gushes were ordered every day alternately with standing in water, in so far as the sensitive feet would allow; these gushes were increased during the week from one to three cans. Also the standing in water was extended as far as the knees, but always only for two, at the utmost three minutes. In the third week the upper showers, together with knee-gushes and standing in water were further increased, and every second day a sitting-bath taken, generally in the afternoon. In the fourth week: upper shower with standing in water every morning; in the afternoon a half-bath. In the fifth week in the morning a shower for the back with standing in water, or a knee-gush. In the afternoon an upper shower. This was continued, every half day an application: a) upper shower with knee-shower, b) half-bath, c) shower for the back, until perfect restoration was effected.

Interiorly were taken: a) white powder, daily a salt-spoonful, alternately with, b) 6 to 8 juniper-berries daily, c) tea from wormwood and sage.

Nervous exhaustion.

A pastor is suffering from unbearable headache which is, whenever it gives way, followed by a sensation of fatigue and pain in the throat which renders him almost unable to speak. Also in his back he often felt a painful contraction. According to a certificate brought from his physician, he was suffering from "developed nervous exhaustion, brain and spinal marrow were in great danger of being affected." Moreover there were great irritability and sensations of fear.

Applications: A light upper shower in the morning and in the afternoon; walking in wet grass and on wet stones for 4 minutes daily. Thus to continue for 5 days, then a more vigorous upper shower, a knee-gush and twice walking in water, daily for 5 other days. He also took sitting-baths alternately with the aforesaid applications.

To complete his restoration to health he made use of the shower for the back, the half-bath, the upper shower and walking in water daily for some time. These applications removed all complaints and the pastor went back to his post in perfect health and as cheerful as ever.

Nervous headache.

Two students had to leave college before the end of the term. Both suffered so much from headache and rising of the blood to the head that they were not only unable to study but even to read for a few minutes. All remedies applied had been without effect. I advised them to spend the greater part of the day in walking barefoot especially in the dewy grass, on their rambles in the wood to stand in a rill for some minutes every hour and finally to take 2 upper showers and, in warm weather, 3 of them daily.

The two boys followed my advice and did even more than I required. The visible improvement of their health gave them courage, and at the close of their holidays they returned joyfully to their college.

Would that so wholesome a practice as walking barefoot in wet grass might find a place among the numerous drill-exercises taught in schools many of which cause great heat and excitement whilst walking barefoot on a wet meadow is unsurpassed in its calming effect.

A man, of 45 years of age, came complaining to me and began: "The doctors describe my disease as nervous head-complaint. I am never without a head bandage; I sometimes feel an unbearable pressure on the back of my head, first on the right side, then on the left. If the pain extends to the back, I get violent palpitation of the heart not seldom for hours together. Appetite is often entirely wanting, and I suffer so much from giddiness that I can no longer walk alone, my wife had to accompany me hither. My mental sufferings, however, are far worse than those of my body. The depression is sometimes so great that I wish for death." The gentleman was rather corpulent, his complexion yellow and dull, his body much inflated.

In 13 days the patient was completely restored. His bodily weight had decreased; headache and giddines had disappeared; good spirits, appetite, and sleep returned in their stead.

The applications were the following:

1) On the one day upper shower and knee-gush in the morning, shower for the back and walking in water in the afternoon.

2) On the second day shower for the back and walking in water in the morning, shower for the back and knee-gush in the afternoon.

3) On the third day upper shower and knee-gush in the morning, whole shower and half-bath in the afternoon.

The natural strength of the patient allowed so many applications daily.

Nervous over-excitement.

Two students came during their Easter holidays and related: "We have head-complaint, determination of blood to the head, impaired sleep and appetite, and great lassitude: we are, therefore, unable to continue our studies.

Could we not make use of our holidays to restore our health by water applications?

I advised them to spend their holidays as much as possible in the open air, in the woods or fields walking barefoot. As it was yet rather cold I told them to take brisk exercise, especially after walking in water which they should do from time to time for 2 or 3 minutes in a ditch filled with water. They also held their arms in water twice or 3 times a day. The young people liked these applications very much. Filled with new courage and strength, they returned to their studies and joyfully looked forward to the autumn holidays which should offer them the welcome opportunity for another course of water-applications.

Be it observed that the walking in the wet cold grass must be performed at such a rate as to produce sufficient vital heat; for the same reason the standing in water ought to be followed by rapid exercise.

A seminarist came to me with the following complaints: I have such a pressure in my head that I often scarcely know where I am, and what I do. I suffer also from giddiness and am unable for any mental occupation, I had to leave the seminary 3 months previous to the time fixed for my ordination.

There was warm August weather, and the young man spent the greater part of 10 days in gardens and woods walking barefoot from morning to night. Moreover he had 2 to 4 upper showers daily. Within 12 days all symptoms of the complaint had ceased; he had recovered both his strength and his good spirits and for further bracing of the system he needs only to spend his autumn holidays in the same manner.

Perspiration.

There are people who perspire easily and profusely; at the slightest exertion they are bathed in perspiration which condition, besides causing weakness and weariness, renders them liable to all possible colds and inflammations.

An official came to me one day and lamented about his impaired health, his difficult breathing etc. The doc--

tors, he said, pronounce my disease to be liver and kidney complaint. "My greatest misfortune, however, is that my stomach will retain no medicine; every spoonful causes me vomiting." "Your good fortune, you mean to say," I replied to the gentleman whose complaint betrayed itself through an offensive smell of perspiration. "You perspire much when walking, also in the morning when getting up." "Yes, so it is! How do you know?" Instead of answering his question, I advised him to take a half-bath with ablution of the upper body (of 1 minute's duration) as often as he came home bathed in perspiration, after the bath to dress quickly without drying and take exercise in his room for ¼ hour. "What!" the official exclaimed, "your reverence are joking! God forbid! I should be stricken by apoplexy at the first attempt! How often have I been warned against cold and dampness, and you tell me to enter a bath of cold water!" I remained calm but it required all my eloquence to convince the gentleman of the harmlessness of the proceeding. Amongst other things I asked him whether he ever hesitated to wash face and hands, when he came home and the salt water was running down his forehead? "No," he answered, "I do that each time." "Has your doing so ever had any disagreeable consequence?" The gentleman, fearing the inference I should draw from his negative answer, reflected for a moment, then he pronounced a decided "No." "Well," I replied, "let your whole body enjoy the same benefit; promise me to do it only once." He gave his word. After a fortnight I met him again. "Are you still alive?" I asked him. "How grateful I feel for your advice, Father," he said, "all my fear of cold water is gone. Shall I continue the bathing, it does me so good?" Yes, it did him good and gradually cured all his complaints. The gentleman is still alive; he must be nearly eighty years old now.

So simple an application is often sufficient to give good humour and to destroy diseases in their germs. Many will laugh at this assertion. Never mind! Their derision will not impair its truth.

Another remark may find its place here. There is

scarcely any thing so much feared even by intelligent people as the application of water when perspiring. Their opinion may be founded on the truth that he who, bathed in perspiration, exposes himself to cold or draught endangers his health and even his life. I fully admit all this. The result depends here, as in other things not so much on "what" is done but on "how" it is done.

My maxims based on long experience and practice, are the following:

a) Whoever is wet through perspiration, rain, etc. must not expose himself to cold or draught; this would be dangerous.

b) Whoever feels chilly should not attempt any application of water.

c) Who is wet through rain etc., should change clothing as soon as possible.

d) Who perspires, be it through disease, through work, walking or in consequence of any exercise whatsoever, should take a cold bath or a cold whole-ablution, dress without drying and take exercise until the body is dry. (Rapidity of proceeding is indispensable.) I hope this will calm and satisfy the most hot-blooded sanguine.

A gentleman of position perspired every night so profusely that the whole mattress, the pillow and featherquilt were every morning dripping wet, a heavy nightly cross which made the gentleman dread the hours of rest. To add to his misery, he suffered from catarrh during the whole winter and no wrapping and muffling could protect him against it.

A rapid cure cannot be expected in such cases; it can only be effected by gradual strengthening and bracing of the system, so much weakened through sweating, and by a continued leading out of morbid matters. Such a patient must practice great patience. Our gentleman is a proof of the astonishing effects of water-applications when made use of with punctuality and perseverance. As reward he regained his complete health. But that is not sufficient for readers afflicted with a similar complaint; they will desire to know how the cure was effected and what they should do if they happened to be in the gentle-

man's case. This is my answer: Put on the Spanish
mantle 3 times a week. Should your duties prevent you
from doing so during the day, use it as a night-shirt for
1½ to 2 hours. Take a whole-ablution from bed twice
or 3 times weekly, or if you have sleepless nights, as many
times every night. Whenever you are perspiring, wash
yourself more vigorously, but rapidly and go to bed without
drying, covering yourself well. If possible, have your bed
not in a cold room. Do not forget that you must begin
the applications with the Spanish mantle. When you have
experienced its beneficial effects you will not fail — were it
but out of gratitude — to wear it at least once a week for
1½ to 2 hours, nor would a weekly whole-ablution impair
your appetite for water. I could mention the names of
many who, after having renounced to prejudice, have become
great friends of water.

A particular and most loathsome kind of abnormal
perspiration is sweating of the feet. It consists in nothing
else than in foul secretions which corrupt the vessels containing them. This is the cause of the extremely offensive smell which makes men and even animals shun the
presence of such poor sufferers.

The suppression of sweating of the feet is not seldom
followed by sad consequences. I know of a gentleman
who was advised to wash his feet with cold water several
times a day in order to put an end to the troublesome
sweating. The feet, indeed, ceased to sweat but a tedious
and dangerous malady set in instead. Could it be otherwise? Whoever wants to entice the fox out of his hole
must not stop the issue of it. Such a sportsman would
be laughed at by the sparrows and mocked by the hares.

How is sweating of the feet cured? All foul and
decaying matters, however far they may have penetrated,
must be dissolved and led out. The skin and the vessels
must be healed and strengthened.

The best and safest way of curing sweating of the
feet is the following. Both feet are bandaged in cloths
dipped in an infusion of hay-flowers or pine-twigs. These
bandages absorb the foul matters and have at the same
time a strengthening effect which is particular to these

two plants. Five or six of these bandages should be taken
within 10 days; after this a warm foot-bath (reaching to
the calves of the legs) with threefold change (the cold
ablution not exceeding 1 minute's duration) of 10 minutes
each should be taken daily for a fortnight. Either of the
2 above mentioned applications made use of once a week,
will secure the result of the cure. When this has been
completely effected, walking in wet grass for $\frac{1}{4}$ hour from
time to time will be of good service. Those who cannot
do this should walk barefoot in the room for some minutes before going to bed.

Rheumatism.

Who would attempt to enumerate all the various
rheumatic conditions under which people are suffering.
now in the head, and in the chest, then in the toes, in
the arms, in the back, etc.

The hard-working peasant, the wood-cutter and all
those who literally eat their bread in the sweat of their
brow know little of this complaint, and if rheumatism ever
troubles these people, it is sure to be quickly removed.
It may make its appearance in the morning; in the afternoon it will flee, chased by healthy exercise.

The latter observation affords useful hints for the
cure of rheumatism.

A veterinarian came to me lamenting that he was
no longer able to pursue his profession because a fearful
rheumatism had got hold of his right shoulder-blade and
was obstinately clinging to it like a cat whose claws
caused him piercing pain. He had imprudently exposed
himself to cold when perspiring and expected to carry
this troublesome cat for 6 full weeks, since the same
thing had happened to him several times previously. "You
will be free from pain within 24 hours," I replied, "provided you allow me to set my dog on your cat." He
laughed, and we laid a wager on the subject. He gave
me his word that he would punctually execute whatever
the strict master should please to order. He went home
and had his back vigorously rubbed with a dry cloth,
then an upper shower was applied to him. After about

8 hours he had a head-vapour with succeeding cold shower. The twenty fourth hour had not yet struck when the cat was beyond the mountains, and I had won my wager.

The reader probably desires to know why dry rubbing was applied in this case. When rheumatism is caused by sudden transition from cold to heat or vice-versa, the pain is generally occasioned by a disturbed circulation, by conglomerations, slight inflammations etc. Applications tending to dissolve, evacuate, and strengthen the suffering parts will restore the circulation to order again. Friction aims at assisting the water in producing heat and in effecting the diversion of the blood. If the affected part were rather cool, a shower would cause the rheumatism to change its place in the body but not to leave it altogether; it is, therefore, preceded by dry rubbing.

A peasant got such violent rheumatic pain in both feet that he was no longer able to walk; his thighs were especially painful.

He took twice daily a lower bandage dipped in a decoction of hay-flowers and went to bed for 2 hours each time. Ten such applications effected a complete cure.

Another peasant could not be swathed on account of excessive pain in the hips. He was, therefore, put in a bath of oat-straw decoction (33 to 35° R.) with three-fold change and took 2 such baths of 25 minutes daily. In 3 days he was cured.

I could mention numberless cases of rheumatism in the head in which the cure was effected not by applications to the head itself but chiefly by foot-baths and foot-vapours.

Cold applications to the head would make things worse; warm ones would cause a conflux of blood in the affected part. The best sequence of applications is the following:

the warm foot-bath with ashes and salt,
the shawl,
the foot-vapour,
the head-vapour followed by a cold gush, and again
the shawl

These applications will cure the most violent head rheumatism, if one of them is made use of daily.

No kind of rheumatism should be neglected because each one can develop into many and serious diseases of the lungs, eyes, ears etc., into inflammations, blood poisoning, ulcers etc.

A student had indulged in much drinking, and in this condition exposed himself to the cold air. He got rheumatism in the chest. Thinking that such a trifle could do him no harm, he neglected the complaint. When a dry cough of a malignant character set in, it was too late for human remedies, and in 2 months the promising young man died. Had he only vigorously washed chest and abdomen 4 or 5 times a day, his chest would have been free from rheumatism, and he himself out of danger, in one or two days.

The head of a college relates: "I suffer unspeakably in my arms, shoulders and feet; I am quite enveloped in rheumatism, as it were, and if the pain gives way in one part, it becomes worse in another. My respiration is so difficult that I often fear to suffocate; I am also troubled with congestions. I have been magnetized and electrified, I have used many other remedies but without effect. The water-cure has freed me from pain in 10 days; I am convinced that a continuation of some easy applications will restore me to perfect health."

The applications were: An upper shower and 2 thigh-gushes daily; on the second day the Spanish mantle; from the fourth day a half-bath instead of the upper shower daily, and a head-vapour weekly.

A gentleman comes. His appearance is sickly. His features are stamped with an expression of deep melancholy. At the first glance I recognize in him a man of great suffering. His unhealthy complexion is of an ominous yellow hue; the hair is very scarce. The gentleman is not yet 40 years old.

His own report of his health is as follows: I frequently suffered from abdominal pains, violent attacks of colic and diarrhœa. Later I got disease of the kidneys, as the doctors called it. After years these complaints left me, and I got this rheumatism instead. It seems to me as if a compendium of all my former pains were now torturing every separate limb. I employed a great many medicaments; the result, however, was never the wished for help, but my old suffering. It cost me a great effort to perform my duties till now. I never complained to any one since nobody understood me. My sufferings are only known to Him who has promised a crown to those who suffer. One remark I might add: I was affected with dry perspiration of the feet, the remedies employed against it, were effectual but my general health was impaired. I have made use of mineral baths, and they increased my complaint. My bodily pains, however, were far exceeded by my mental sufferings caused by the observation that others thought my sensitiveness to play a great part in the matter. Suffering without sympathy is double suffering.

The story is a long one, dear reader, but I trust a very instructive one, too. Let us never be hard and unjust to those who suffer!

Who will be able to detect the root of all this suffering, to disclose to us the interior of this sorely diseased body? The problem is less difficult to solve than it seems at first sight. The patient has given the premises in his account, we have only to draw the conclusion. The yellow complexion, the frequent attacks of colic, the suppressed sweating of the feet reveal the presence of poisonous matters, nor can the impaired growth of the hair be without a deeper cause to account for it. A thorough cure can only be effected when this poisonous matter is dissolved and expelled, when the whole system is strengthened in such a manner as not to allow such fatal juices to gather afresh. Is the antidote for this poison to be found in a chemist's shop? It would be well paid for if it were. Artificial means, especially when they are of recent invention, are readily purchased at a dear price whilst He from whom are all good gifts, is scarcely thanked for the natural remedies which prove the best after all.

In the limpid rivulet, in the clear fountain, there flows the efficacious remedy which I mean.

The patient had first to put on the Spanish mantle. This was followed by a head-vapour with vigorous cold ablution, then a foot-vapour was taken. I allowed the use of these vapours only at rather long intervals; for the more leniently the body is treated, the easier it is for nature to endure the applications and the more readily it will second their action in order to expel the morbid matters. Then the patient took a short bandage and, to strengthen the system, an upper and a lower shower. He made use of all these applications alternately, taking one daily for 3 weeks. In the fourth and fifth week he had weekly 2 half-baths, 1 head-vapour, 1 foot-vapour and once the Spanish mantle; finally in the sixth week, he had 2 warm baths, each followed by a cold one, 1 half-bath and an upper and lower shower. As future applications I recommended the patient to take every week an upper and lower shower and 2 or 3 whole-ablutions, and every month a warm bath without change.

Water did not belie my confidence even in this difficult case. The serious complaint which would, in all probability, have proved fatal, disappeared. Healthy appearance, and lost strength returned, and the patient's broken courage was replaced by renewed enthusiasm for his profession.

A man, 40 years old, had such rheumatic pains in his right leg that he could only walk short distances with the help of a stick. Sometimes he had also pains in his arms and his shoulders. Having employed various remedies without result, he had recourse to water and in 6 days he was almost free from pain. He continued the applications and was completely cured.

The applications were the following:

1) For 6 days 2 upper showers and 2 thigh-gushes daily, once a week a lower bandage, twice daily walking in water to above the calves of the legs for 1 to 3 minutes, every day a shower for the back and walking in the grass.

2) After these 6 days he took an upper shower with knee-gush alternately with a half-bath of 1 minute's, duration.

22*

Count N. has been suffering from rheumatism for 35 years. In the year 1854 he resorted to Aix-la-Chapelle and obtained relief by a course of bathing. Much bivouacing during the Franco-German war (1870—71) brought on the old complaint, and again he used the Aix-la-Chapelle baths with good result. Only for a short time had he enjoyed his restored health, when a relapse took place. The patient consulted physicians of renown but without receiving effectual aid. After having tried in vain the baths at Aibling, he went to Aix-la-Chapelle and returned not cured but much weakened by hot baths of long duration. Seeing the fruitlessness of all his attempts, he resolved on trying the water-cure.

On the 20th of June 1887, the patient arrived here after having been confined to bed for 2 months. His whole body was tormented by rheumatic pains, especially the joints of the knees, the feet, the hands, and the shoulders. The right hand and the arm to above the elbow were greatly swollen, the joints inflexible; the knee was likewise swollen and could not be used. The general health of the stately, strongly built gentleman seemed to be impaired through long suffering.

The treatment was as follows:

1) Twice a week, a lower bandage dipped in a decoction of oat-straw, hay-flowers, and pine-needles (duration 1½ hour).

2) Every morning and evening, a bandage dipped in the same decoction was applied to the swollen arm for 1 to 2 hours.

3) Two herbal whole-baths with threefold change weekly.

4) Three times weekly, the shawl for 1 hour.

After a fortnight the patient's health had considerably improved. He left Wœrishofen and continued the applications at home. He took

1) the above mentioned arm-bandage;

2) 1 herbal whole-bath with change weekly;

3) a cold half-bath of ½ to 1 minute's duration 3 times a week;

4) a sitting-bath of 2 minute's duration 3 to 5 times weekly.

These applications had the effect that the swelling of the diseased arm and knees gave way, and the joints became flexible **again.**

To complete the cure, count N. used the following applications in the September 1887:

1) The warm hand-bath, a hand-bandage of infused hay-flowers immediately followed by cold ablution of the hand;

2) the half-bath 3 or 4 times a week;

3) 1 herbal whole-bath with threefold change weekly;

4) 1 upper shower 4 times weekly.

The result of this course of applications was a most favourable one. The joints became perfectly free from swelling and pain and recovered their flexibility, and count N. has ever since enjoyed excellent general health and good spirits. He is able to walk for hours without a sensation of fatigue and, after he had been obliged to renounce for years to his favourite sport, the chase, he indulged in it for 9 consecutive days in the autumn of this year, a fact which caused great astonishment among his noble friends.

To prevent a relapse count N. employs one of the means of hardening every day: a half-bath, a whole-bath or walking in water.

Rupture.

A complaint very frequently met with in our days are the various kinds of rupture. They often appear over-night like mushrooms in the wood; sometimes they announce themselves through a sensation of pain. All persons thus affected may be membered among the invalids on account of their incapability to do certain kinds of work; for every greater exertion would expose them to violent suffering and even to death.

Rupture is chiefly met with in weak natures, hence its frequency in our age of effeminacy and indulgence. I have the firm conviction that a rational hardening from childhood, and plain nourishing food would prove effectual means against the further spreading of this complaint.

Fifty years ago, there were few such "broken people" to be found in a village; in a small town they could be counted on the fingers. Now-a-days among 20 persons, 3 or 4 will be affected with rupture. To add to the evil rupture is regarded as a disgracing defect which no one likes to own; therefore many a rupture is, in its beginning, left without the necessary. treatment, and the small evil becomes a great one. Rupture is not only met with among those who have to earn their bread by means of hard labour; it also occurs frequently in the higher classes. How quickly a rupture may be got! A. jumped over a ditch and got rupture; B. suffered much from gases, and got it thereby; C. brought it down from the pulpit after an enthusiastic sermon.

I feel deeply afflicted whenever I hear that an otherwise healthy and strong man has become invalid by rupture. How many must leave their profession at the age of 40 or 50 on account of the sufferings and inability caused by such a defect. I have already spoken of a rational water-cure. If water had but the power of preventing this one evil, even then the small trouble connected with its application could not be compared to the benefit derived from it.

Rupture is, as a rule, neither innate nor inherited. It is a consequence of general weakness of the system either natural or brought on by disease. Hardening by means of water-applications would have prevented this weakness or effected its cure. Will the so-called "civilised world" ever become wise? I doubt it. But you, good countryman, who read these lines, follow my advice: Take 1 or 2 half-baths or sitting-baths every week (any tub may serve as bath). You will soon experience their strengthening effect. Any time of the day is suitable for the purpose and the whole proceeding, undressing, bathing, and dressing, will not take you more than 4 to 6 minutes. You can take the bath when coming from work, and return to work immediately after; perspiration is no impediment. After 3 or 4 such baths, you will not require to be encouraged to continue them; they will become almost a necessity to you.

A peasant once complained to me of great pain in the groins. The physician had declared that a rupture was about to appear. I advised him to make frequent use of lying on wet sheets and covering with wet sheets. The pain soon gave way. The peasant suspended for some time the hardest labour and remained free from rupture. The case was a warning to him, and he was, henceforward, a zealous water-man.

Can rupture never be cured? I myself have cured several cases in adults where the rupture was of recent formation. The spot was vigorously rubbed with camphor-oil and a plaster of pitch spread on wax-cloth applied to it. Fox's grease has always been and is still regarded as one of the best remedies for recent ruptures. The afflected spot should be rubbed with it every 2 or 3 days and each time again covered with the pitch-plaster. In this manner I once cured a rupture which was 7 weeks old.

Children are comparatively often affected with rupture. The cause is generally to be sought in the distention of the intestines by food. Such a child should have an oat-straw-bath daily and likewise lie on wet sheets and be covered with wet sheets every day until the cure is effected. The affected spot should be gently rubbed with camphor-oil or, which is better still, with fox's grease. Unless a rupture has already assumed large dimensions, it will be cured in a short time by these remedies. If the former is the case the cure can hardly be expected and for such sufferers the only resource will be a truss which must be worn according to surgical directions.

Mothers should do everything in their power to prevent such defects in their children from the beginning. The happiness of their children and their own depends upon it. If God spares my life a little longer, I soon hope to offer them a little book containing some hints on rational hardening of infants. May they not be afraid of the cold water-man: his heart beats warmly for children and for all those engaged in education. I do not intend to address myself to those mothers who by muffling and wrapping in velvet, silk, and wool prevent their "angels" even from enjoying the fresh air. My advice is only for those who desire to contribute to the bringing up of a healthy and strong generation.

A gentleman of about 40 years of age, complained of giddiness, congestions, and violent headache. His appetite was good, but he could not satisfy it without causing himself pain. His complexion was as unnaturally red as his body was stout whilst his arms and feet were disproportionately thin. According to medical direction, he wore a truss because two ruptures were about to appear. The chief complaint consisted in inflation of the abdomen by gases.

As soon as the gases were expelled and the organs strengthened through water-applications, the protruding beginnings of rupture disappeared; congestions and headache also ceased, and in 4 weeks the patient was restored to perfect health.

The treatment had been as follows:

First day: Upper shower and knee-gush in the forenoon, upper shower and walking in water in the afternoon.

Second day: Upper shower with walking in water to the knees in the forenoon, upper shower and standing in water in the afternoon.

Third day: Upper shower with kneeling in water in the forenoon, shower for the back in the afternoon.

Fourth day: Upper shower and kneeling in water in the forenoon, shower for the back in the afternoon.

Fifth day: Half-bath, later upper shower; in the afternoon upper shower and 2 hours later sitting-bath.

Sixth day: Upper shower and 2 hours later half-bath; in the afternoon bath reaching to the arm-pits.

Seventh day: Walking in water to above the ankles and 2 hours later shower for the back.

In this manner the applications were continued for 4 weeks, when the patient was restored to perfect health; it is especially remarkable that his bloated face and his

SAINT VITUS'S DANCE. — SCARLET FEVER.   345

unusually inflated body had resumed their normal shape
and that the ruptures had completely disappeared.

Saint Vitus's dance.

A father relates: "I have a daughter, 10 years old,
who has never been healthy from her infancy. Teething
was so hard for the girl that we believed she would die.
Moreover one of her legs became thinner than the other.
Now the girl has Saint Vitus's dance; she can neither
eat nor sleep and is terrible to look at when the cramps
come. I have sought help from many doctors; but her
condition has always become worse."

"Good man, boil aftermath in water for $\frac{1}{2}$ hour, take
rather much so that the water may become thick and
add some salt to the decoction; then dip a coarse chemise
in the water, wring it out, and put it on the child; then
wrap her well in a woollen blanket, and let her remain
in it for $1\frac{1}{2}$ to 2 hours. If the girl falls asleep, do not
wake her, when the 2 hours are past. Do this twice daily
for 8 days; then report!"

After 8 days the man came and related: "The girl
has got a dreadful eruption on the whole body, especially
on the back and the chest, but she is becoming quite
cheerful; the cramps have ceased, sleep and appetite have
returned. What shall I do further?"

Answer: "Give the child the wet chemise every third
day, for a fortnight; then the child will be well. Let her
also take 20 drops of wormwood extract in water as
hitherto."

Scarlet Fever.

Scarlet fever is an epidemic which generally breaks
out once or twice in every year and not seldom demands
many victims. It usually attacks the children, but adults
are not always spared by it. The symptoms with which
it commences are headache, pressure on the stomach and
chest, lassitude and alternate sensation of heat and chill.
The cure of scarlet fever by water is very easy. Children
are generally out of danger after 2 days, for adults it
will take a little longer. As soon as the symptoms of
the disease appear in a child, be it still carried on the

arms or going to school, it should put on a shirt dipped in hot water, with which some salt has been mixed, and lie in bed. The covering must be of such a kind as to shut out the outer air, and the child thus wrapped up should remain so for 1 hour. Then the shirt is taken off, and the whole body will seem strewn with crimson red spots or patches. Should the heat be very great, a rapid whole-ablution could be applied before the child is put to bed again. In serious cases in which the fever reaches a high degree, the shirt may be taken twice or 3 times a day; if the heat gives way, the intervals between renewing the application may be longer. Later cold water (mixed with vinegar) is used for the shirt. By such treatment scarlet fever can be cured in 4 to 6 days, at the utmost.

A patient ill with scarlet fever has seldom appetite; it would, therefore, be imprudent to force him to take food. (The eruption is not only on the outside of the body but also in the inside.) There is generally a violent thirst which is best satisfied by water; some sugar or a little wine may be mixed with it. Children in the country who prefer milk may take it. I do not believe that a child thus treated will die of scarlet fever.

Louis, a boy of 10 years of age, can scarcely speak with heat. His face is red, and he complains that everything hurts him. Since heat and anxiety are great, Louis is washed every hour for 2 days. On the third day he begins already to eat; the ablution is only applied twice a day. On the fifth day Louis feels well, on the sixth day he walks about in the room, and soon he will play in the open air with other children.

Mary, 20 years old, can no longer walk. She has violent headache, a sensation of great fatigue in her limbs, a dry cough and pressure on the chest. Her uneasiness and restlessness are extremely great; she feels disgust for every kind of food, but her thirst is insatiable. Mary will get scarlet fever in a high degree. Every hour she should have her back, chest, and abdomen vigorously washed with cold water mixed with a little salt. After the ablution — which must be performed as quickly as possible — she should be carefully covered, but not too much.

For 2 days the patient was washed according to the aforesaid direction. She ate nothing but drank the more. Her neck is still burning dreadfully. The eruption begins to disappear, the thirst is less violent. The patient should still be washed twice or 3 times daily for 2 to 4 days.

After 3 further days Mary was completely cured.

John, a boy of 13 years, seems less lively, he has lost his former love for occupation, his cheerfulness is gone. Suddenly his whole body begins to swell, especially head, feet, and abdomen. The boy will get dropsy. Six weeks ago, John has had scarlet fever; the eruption appeared only sparingly, and this is the consequence of its imperfect development.

The patient put on a shirt dipped in warm salt water 6 times within 8 days. In 10 days he was perfectly well again and had also recovered his good spirits. When scarlet fever is not thoroughly cured and morbid matters remain in the body, dropsy often follows; but even suppressed scarlet fever can be cured by the abovementioned course of applications.

A girl, about 24 years old, who had always enjoyed good health, got scarlet fever. The eruption increased within 8 days in such a manner as may be rare even in the most serious cases. The patient directly required that water should be used as remedy. Her confidence was chiefly based on the fact that her sister had been cured by it from grievous illness. She was advised to have back, chest, abdomen, arms and feet washed every hour. The interval of 1 hour was too long for her. The heat became so violent that during 5 days the washing was not suspended for more than ½ hour. The girl ate almost nothing and drank little in small portions. Only on the eleventh day after a continual application of water the heat gave way, the eruption began to die; on the fourteenth day it had entirely disappeared, and the girl was completely restored to health.

Sciatica.

An official suffered for more than three months from violent pain in the left thigh and the whole leg down to the ankles. He had employed all possible remedies, at

last he was advised to make use of two only: warmth
and rest. Hence the gentleman sought to warm the suffering
parts by warm wrappings and warm baths. But the pains
increased, his strength gave way, he had lost more than
50 lbs. of his bodily weight, and he could seldom sleep
for a whole hour at a time.

At last he took courage to use the remedy which
he had shunned more than all others, the cold water.

He received 2 or 3 applications daily. First day:
shower for the back in the morning, upper shower in the
afternoon. Second day: upper shower in the morning,
shower for the back in the afternoon. Every second or
third day he took a half-bath, he also walked barefoot
sometimes.

Directly after the first shower, the patient slept 4
hours in the night. As he slept better, his appetite and
appearance also improved. In 6 weeks he was completely
cured.

A professor from Hungary had been afflicted with
neuralgia in the hips for 7 years and had visited various
bathing-places, Buda, Teplitz, Heviz and others, but without
success; he had also used vapour-baths. For 2 years he
had suffered from sleeplessness, his appetite was good,
his bowels irregular; the patient further complained of
inflation by wind, pressure on the head, but especially of
extreme sensibility for changes in the weather and constant
sensation of chill, in spite of woollen clothing. Moreover
tallow-like secretions of the skin took place, and his hands
were always moist.

He had the following applications: Every night whole-
ablution, in the forenoon upper shower, in the afternoon
shower for the back, every 2 days a half-bath, knee-gushes
and sitting-baths. The result of the cure was excellent.
Already after the fourth day, the patient slept calmly
during the whole night, and he enjoyed good sleep ever
since. The tedious sciatica has completely disappeared.
His skin is also in a normal condition. The gentleman is
overjoyed at his recovery and praises his light clothing in
the following terms: "The clothing I wear is so light,
also on cool rainy days, as other people's in midsummer;

I feel perfectly warm in my linen shirt and light stockings, and I am no longer susceptible of the influence of temperature. The water has effected a wonderful change in my system."

Sleeplessness.

A pastor had suffered from sleeplessness for 9 weeks. His strength decreased from day to day, and he became more and more incapable for mental labour. Depression, lassitude, despondency took the place of his former diligence and cheerfulness.

Great exertion and worry had caused violent agitation in the mind of the good gentleman: his condition was that of one in continuous fever. He was reduced to complete calm by the head-vapour, the Spanish mantle, the upper shower with knee-gush, the foot-vapour, the short bandage, by lying on, and covering with, wet sheets which practices were continued for 12 days, 2 or 3 being taken daily. Already after the third day the gentleman slept for 3 hours. He enjoys the best of healths to the present day.

Sleeplessness may be caused by irregular circulation, by suppressed or insufficient transpiration, by gases which torment stomach and bowels.

People who spend the whole day in mental exertion are particularly subject to this complaint.

I have had occasion to dwell on the aforesaid causes and their remedies more than once in this book; it remains only to suggest a soporific for those engaged in head-work.

I know a gentleman who is much given to intellectual labour. He would prefer to have neither stomach nor feet. It is generally difficult to make such gentlemen listen to reason. In this case, however, I was successful. The gentleman made up his mind to bestow a little more care on the poor companion of his soul. He made it a habit to use the Spanish mantle once or twice a week. The sleeplessness soon gave way and with it all the little complaints by which it had been caused.

Another gentleman had a basin with fresh water put near his bed every night. If sleep, the longed for friend, did not appear after ½ hour, he got up, took a whole-ablution and returned to bed without drying. He became drowsy, but the next hour perhaps found him awake again he then renewed the proceeding once or twice, if necessary The effect of these nightly ablutions was so good that the gentleman had never again to complain of sleeplessness

If children are wakeful and fretful at their usual bed-time, it is generally because they have received too much food. The poor little body sighs under the burden, and the gases will not allow the little head to rest. Apply a short bandage to the child, and it will soon fall asleep.

I often heard country people say: a warm foot-bath closes the eyes when exertion and fatigue fail to do so; but in cases of mental fatigue, it will rarely produce the desired effect. One or two cold sitting-baths during the night would render better service there. I recommend these also to such as suffer from hemorrhoids, gases and other complaints of the lower body. The duration of a bath should be from 1 to 2 minutes.

Sleeplessness may finally be caused by an unequal degree of vital heat in the different parts of the body. There is generally too much blood in head and chest and too little in the extremities. It has been explained on several occasions, how this is to be remedied.

I caution against artificial soporifics. They seem to me unnatural and whatever is unnatural, can never be conducive to health.

Small-pox.

Small-pox is one of the most contagious and virulent diseases, whether it appear in its milder form (varioloid) or as the dreaded confluent kind (variola). The treatment for both cases is identical. It is generally believed that the patient must die if the eruption does not appear, hence the importance of remedies which tend to promote it.

Six persons who were ill of the simpler form of small-pox were cured by ablutions applied as often as great heat and uneasiness was felt. In the beginning the washing was required every hour, later every two hours, then twice or 3 times a day. On the seventh day the 6 patients were perfectly well. They ate nothing and drank much which can do no harm, when little portions only are taken at a time. Would that all patients observed this rule. Much drinking does not appease thirst thoroughly and increases the sensation of anxiety.

I have often been astonished on seeing the eruption so quickly produced by the aforesaid treatment. Wash without the least fear. The more promptly and the more punctually this is done, the more quickly the small pustules will form, the sooner the poisonous matter will be secreted by them.

One remark more: Do not fear to admit fresh air to the sickroom. A window should always be open in order to allow the infectious breath of the patient to escape.

Four persons got small-pox. They were cured by applying twice or 3 times daily the wet shirt instead of the ablutions; the former might also have been substituted by the Spanish mantle. The shirt was taken off after an hour and renewed when heat and uneasiness became great. On the sixth and seventh day it was only done once or twice. The whole cure lasted 8 days, and none of the patients were disfigured by those dreadful scars so often occasioned by this disease.

Fred can no longer walk, he feels tired unto death, his appearance is frightening. He suffers from violent headache, frequent attacks of nausea, and pressure on the chest. The physician is sent for. He declares that the symptoms are those of small-pox, that the eruption will not appear before the fourth day, that an aperient medicine will do the patient no harm, and that nothing else can be done. Fred is not satisfied by this verdict; he has a bath, filled with water, put near his bed. Every hour he descends into the water and washes himself with a rough towel; the proceeding takes him not more than 1 minute each time. Within 18 hours the patient has applied 18 of these ablutions. Before the return of the physician Fred was well again. He ate nothing during this time, and water was his only drink.

Whilst I am writing this, I hear from a friend of mine that he, following my advice, has succeeded in curing by the same application 4 or 5 persons who were suddenly attacked with fever, and whose condition gave much ground for fear of small-pox.

If the feverishness that precedes the eruption appears in any person during the prevalence of small-pox, scarlet fever and other eruptive diseases water should be applied directly. Mere waiting and observing "what may ensue" is always dangerous. The fire will spread and consume the patient's strength only too rapidly. To quench it in its first beginning will prove an easy task whilst a few days hesitation may render all help unavailable.

As soon as a child or an adult complains of headache, uneasiness, difficult breathing, cough, broken courage and lamed strength, one may be sure that the time for water-applications has come. They will do no harm even in cases in which the abovementioned symptoms prove deceptive.

In conclusion I give the following rules for the treatment of those affected by small-pox:

The ablutions should be performed as rapidly as possible and extend to the whole body.

The covering (closing to the outer air) after the application should be performed with care but should not be so as to be troublesome to the patient. The air must be kept pure by proper ventilation; the latter must be so arranged as not to allow a draught of cold air to fall directly on the patient.

Never urge a patient to eat. The stomach itself will not fail to announce the time when it is disposed to work. Food forced on it without the previous claim of appetite remains undigested. Such food is sometimes the principal impediment of recovery, sometimes the sole cause of a relapse.

If there is a desire for food, the simplest and most digestible kinds should be chosen and administered to the patient in small quantities. I specially recommend good preserved fruit. Water, water mixed with wine, and milk are the best beverages for such patients.

In some places water has already been employed for the cure of small-pox, but alas! in too rugged a manner.

It is to be wished that it should be universally used and more gently applied; numerous lives could thus be saved. I venture to assert — and my assertion is based on experience — that death of small-pox would be of very rare occurrence if water were promptly resorted to wherever it shows itself in its commencement. Is it not a deplorable fact that every year hundreds and thousands succumb to this epidemic and to the fever which precedes and accompanies it, whilst the remedy is close at hand, and not a drop of it is employed to cool the fever and quench the heat. Who can understand this? Would that the efficacy and salutary power of the water were at length fully appreciated.

The treatment of small-pox by water has the particular advantage that it never allows the poisonous matter to do its corroding work on the surface of the body in such a manner as to cause disfigurement by scars.

The ablutions prescribed in the aforesaid cases may be substituted by the Spanish mantle which is taken for 1 to 1½ hours twice or 3 times a day. The mantle must be carefully washed out after each application, since it will contain much poisonous matter.

A further application consists in a twofold piece of coarse linen dipped in water and laid on chest and abdomen. In a similar manner the same cloth can be used as a compress on which the patient lies down (s. Lying on wet sheets). This application may be repeated twice or 3 times in a half day, if the heat is great.

Spine, complaints of the.

An officer had injured a vertebra of his spine when driving and, according to the verdict of several physicians, the spinal marrow was affected. The gentleman suffered atrocious pains, and only at times was his condition less unbearable. These severe sufferings had also affected his mind, and medical attendance was of no avail although the most celebrated physicians of the city had been consulted. Finally he was pronounced incurable, the comfortless declaration being added that his complaint would develop in consumption. The water cured him in 6 weeks, and the gentleman enjoys good health even to this day although his recovery took place 20 years ago. His mental sufferings ceased with the bodily complaint.

I cannot tell exactly which applications I prescribed in this case; but if you, dear reader, should be similarly affected, I should advise you to make use of the following practices: Take the Spanish mantle 3 times a week; take a half-bath with ablution of the upper body 3 times a week, and an upper and lower shower twice a week. Continue thus punctually for some weeks. The whole organism must be strengthened and the complaints originating in the local injury will gradually disappear. The disturbed vertebra, too, will be restored to rest. I repeat: if one part of the body is suffering, the whole body is affected. The whole organism participates of the pain of the individual member.

A boy, 16 years old, was affected with curvature of the spine. He had been treated by several celebrated physicians but without result. They sent him to a medical establishment where he was bandaged in various ways. After 17 weeks he left the hospital on two crutches, the doctors having given the verdict that nothing else could be done for him. A friend presented the diseased boy's father with "My Watercure." Through ablutions with water and vinegar the condition of the patient was so much improved that he could walk pretty well with the aid of a stick; then they brought him to me expecting me to complete his cure. After a 17 days' course of applications, the boy walked like any one of his age, if not with the same vigour, yet with great safety without the help of a stick and without pain. The treatment had consisted in the following applications: A waistcoat of very coarse linen was made and dipped in water in which oat-straw had been boiled. The patient had this waistcoat put on, and another dry one over it; finally he was enveloped in a woollen blanket. He slept in these wrappings first every second night, later every third night. Every day he received 2 upper showers and a knee-gush or a half-bath; the 2 latter applications were sometimes substituted by walking in water. As further applications, to prevent a relapse, he used 2 half-baths, 2 upper showers and once the waistcoat, weekly.

Stomach, acidity of the.

Crescentia relates: "I am 45 years old, my stomach causes me almost daily much suffering. From time to time I feel better, but these intervals are always very short. I have sour and bitter risings of the stomach, and very often I do not know how to warm myself; the more acidity and bitterness, the greater is the sensation of chill."

The appearance of the person was very ill. She was emaciated, her features were sunk; there was, no doubt, great poverty of blood caused by defective digestion.

The applications prescribed to her were the following: 1) To pour boiling water on hay-flowers, to fill with them a small bag and place this on stomach and abdomen. The hay-flowers should be as hot as can be endured and the bag bound round the body with a cloth; the application is to last 1½ hours and to be taken for 3 consecutive days. 2) To take every night for 3 days a warm foot-bath with ashes and salt — 14 minutes — and later every third or fourth day. 3) To take a whole-ablution from bed in the night 3 or 4 times weekly. 4) To take twice daily 4 to 6 spoonfuls of wormwood tea. Continue thus for a fortnight; after this time it will be sufficient to take a foot-bath and a whole-ablution from bed or a half-bath weekly.

Stomach complaints.

Poor stomach, of what mischief and evil art thou supposed to be the cause! Next to heart and nerves, thou art truly the chief scape-goat. Ask a hundred people if they be not troubled with stomach complaint! Very few will answer with a decided "No." And yet in most cases the stomach is as innocent as a new-born infant and as healthy as a merrily playing boy. Examples may prove the truth of my statement.

For a whole year Amalie vomited most of what she took. Her stomach would retain nothing but 3 to 4 spoonfuls of lukewarm milk. Several celebrated physicians were consulted. The apothecary at last declared that in his

23*

whole apotheca he had no remedy which she had not tried
The patient was brought to my dwelling in a cart. Although her coming had not been previously announced to
me, I could not send the poor people back. The patient
was emaciated, her features sunk, her voice broken, a
picture of misery. There was, however, no cough (the
most important thing for me), only a dreadful stomach
complaint and I was asked to give her something for the
stomach. I told them to be quiet and not to complain
so much about the stomach which was one of the healthiest organs of this person. Some of them grew angry,
others laughed; the sick woman herself seemed to be
doubting as to whether I was speaking in earnest. To have
travelled so far, she may have thought, under such pains
only to hear this pitiless declaration! But this made no
difference to me.

What brought me to such an opinion?

The person did not cough but the air (gases) forced
itself out of her mouth. Stomach and abdomen were filled
with gases to excess. The otherwise so patient stomach
would no longer bear these surroundings and suspended
his activity entirely, or at least the greater part of his
functions. The evil was aggravated by the dryness of the
skin and a complete want of transpiration.

The sequence of applications was the following:

Lukewarm lower bandages, ablution of the upper body,
short bandage, whole ablution, knee-gush ($\frac{1}{4}$ minute), again
lower bandage, upper shower, kneeling in water up to the
pit of the stomach ($\frac{1}{2}$ minute), whole ablution, covering
with wet sheets, and lying on wet sheets. Every half
day the patient should make use of one application in the
above mentioned succession and moreover walk on wet
stones several times a day.

Through the lukewarm lower bandages I first sought
to make the skin warmer, moister and softer, then I acted
on the lower body by means of whole ablutions and other
practices. I succeeded; the air, the gases sought their
proper outlet, and the skin resumed its normal activity
(perspiration). The gases were expelled, the appetite

returned, blood and juices were improved, and in 5 weeks the patient was well again.

For long years Rose has suffered from stomach complaint and for some months especially from stomach cramps. She has often to keep her bed and can only with great difficulty attend to her duties. Several physicians have declared that her disease was nothing but stomach complaint. The poor sufferer used a great deal of remedies, liquid and solid, powders and pills.

Her appearance tells of great suffering: her features are sunk, her complexion is pale, her body only consisting of skin and bone. The lower body was greatly inflated, and even the touch of the dress caused her pain. She had often been troubled with vomiting, and her feet and hands were always quite cold.

My opinion of the case was the same as in the preceding example. The complaint had its root in the lower body and had been caused by frequent rapid transition from great heat (near the kitchen fire) to extreme cold (ice-cellar). The girl bore what seemed to her a small discomfort as long as she could until finally the pressure of the bowels on the stomach became so violent that the latter, confined and compressed as it was, was literally forced to return whatever food was conveyed to it.

Besides the general applications, which had to rouse the whole body to activity, partial ones had to be used for the purpose of dissolving and evacuating what had collected in the abdomen, especially the gases. Each day one of the following applications was used ·

The Spanish mantle (general application).

Compresses of infused hay-flowers on the abdomen, every day for 2 hours.

The lower bandage (dissolving and evacuating).

Covering with wet sheets and lying on wet sheets.

Cold whole-ablutions twice every night from bed and again the Spanish mantle.

Walking on wet stones or in wet grass and sometimes a knee-gush served as secondary applications. After 4 weeks an alternate application of the Spanish mantle and the short bandage, every second day, was sufficient. Moreover the patient continued to brace her system by walking barefoot. She became quite well and has been so to the present day. I met her not long ago and she assured me that she enjoyed such good health as never before in her life.

Frederick vomited in the beginning much acid matter; later whatever he ate or drank. No remedy was available and the doctor defined the complaint as induration and obstruction of the stomach.

The appearance of the patient was by no means bad, his features were somewhat aged, his complexion yellow. Much air was expelled from the stomach, the abdomen was so inflated that it often resembled a drum, and this symptom was regularly accompanied by violent headache. Here we have again inactivity in the lower regions, indolence of the bowels.

Hence the irregular stools, the accumulation of gases, the pressure on stomach and head. The patient had to lay a cloth, dipped in water and vinegar, on the abdomen for 2 hours daily; to take, likewise daily, a warm foot-bath with ashes and salt, and to have his back washed with cold water twice every night. After 6 days the patient's condition had improved. After 10 days he employed twice weekly the short bandage, once the Spanish mantle and every second day a foot-bath with ashes and salt. The third prescription ordered for the last 2 weeks 3 upper showers, 3 lower showers, and 2 half-baths (to the pit of the stomach) weekly. In 6 weeks the patient was completely restored.

I could quote innumerable such cases; these few, however, may suffice.

I readily admit that if such complaints are not cured in time, if the continuous pressure on the stomach and its inseparable attendant, the inflammation of the stomach are not removed, then, of course, the dreaded and dangerous stomach tumours will form and finally degenerate in the terrible stomach cancer.

Even with regard to this, deceptions and errors may occur. I was once told that according to the verdict of several professional men, a person had developed stomach cancer. The people only required me to indicate to them the best means of precaution to be taken in order to prevent the disease from attacking other members of the family. I gave them some rules among which there were also some for the patient. In 4 weeks he was completely cured. The remedies consisted in simple infusions from common yarrow, wormwood and sage and in short bandages used alternately with foot-baths.

A woman, 64 years old, has violent burning in the stomach, rising of the stomach and vomiting, often cold fever and sometimes profuse perspiration. The evil increased in spite of all remedies applied. The best effect will be obtained by the following remedies: 20 drops of extract of wormwood in a small cup of hot water, twice daily; lying on sheets dipped in warm water, for 1 hour daily; every second day a twofold cloth dipped in warm water and laid on the abdomen for 1 hour; every second day a warm foot-bath with ashes and salt for 14 minutes.

A person, 40 years of age, complained of frequent pain in the stomach and the abdomen, want of appetite, rising of acid, and enervation. Especially hands and feet were always cold. The applications were as follows:

1) Every morning and every evening to rub chest and abdomen vigorously with water and vinegar (mixed in equal quantities).

2) To take 6 to 8 juniper-berries daily.

3) To take a whole-ablution from bed 3 times weekly.

In 14 days the patient was completely restored; in order to preserve her good health, she would do well to take a whole-ablution once a week for some time.

"For a long time I have suffered from a severe stomach complaint. After food I become dreadfully inflated, and often I am obliged to vomit under great pain. My feet ache frequently, my lips are always white, my whole body is emaciating. I have had several physicians; they gave me nothing but laxatives which have reduced me to a state of great weakness.

Applications: 1) Three times weekly to apply a compress of infused hay-flowers to the abdomen for 1 hour. 2) To take a whole-ablution from bed every second night. 3) To take 25 drops of extract of wormwood in water every morning and 25 drops of extract of rose-hips every afternoon.

A housewife complains: I am never free from pain in the bowels, the abdomen is often inflated and when it is very bad, I feel a pressure on the stomach, much acid matter rises from it, and often I am obliged to vomit. I also suffer from pressure on the head and great giddiness. There are days when I have to make water every ¼ hour, and then again days when I cannot do so but once. Three physicians declared my disease to be stomach catarrh.

This patient was cured within 4 weeks in the following manner:

In the first week she had only 2 upper showers and 2 knee-gushes daily; she took daily 1 cup of tea from juniper-berries and shave-grass.

In the second week: 1 upper shower and knee-gush daily and twice a lower bandage.

In the third week: Once the Spanish mantle, 3 times a sitting-bath and once a half-bath.

In the fourth week half-baths, 3 times the Spanish mantle and walking in water daily.

Stomach cramp.

Mr. N— suffers from pains in the abdomen through catching cold; an accumulation of gases caused him frequent vomiting. When much air had been expelled, and he had had violent vomiting, he felt well again and had very good appetite. In the course of time the evil increased, and after every meal his pains became so violent that they made him scream. His hands and feet were ice-cold and the whole body chilly.

In such cases the stomach is generally quite innocent, and it is only the pressure of the air on it which causes a tendency to vomit and actual vomiting. By the latter the sufferer is relieved but only for a short time. The complaint can only be completely removed by restoring to the whole body equal warmth and transpiration and by regulating the circulation. In our case this was effected by the following applications: On the first day the patient took 3 whole-ablutions of hot water and vinegar in bed and, without drying, was well covered after each ablution. On the second day it was done only twice and from thence once daily. This proceeding is sufficient in all cases when a person through cold has got a fever combined with rising of the air and vomiting.

Stomach tumours.

Much vomiting, burning in the stomach, etc. are not always positive signs of the existence of stomach tumours, although such cases occur sometimes.

Such sufferers should avoid salt, pepper, and spices or spiced food in general. Very simple diet and especially simple beverages have proved the best remedies for the beginning tumours; milk is of particularly good effect.

The treatment of external tumours gives us excellent hints for the cure of internal ones. A boil on the finger is easily cured by wrapping it in a little rag frequently dipped in water; the water cleanses and heals. Why should not internal tumours heal if a spoonful of water is taken every half hour for some time, or if from salutary herbs tea is prepared and taken in the aforesaid manner instead of drinking the usual cup at a time? Only try this simple remedy; you may take tea from wormwood or from sage or from both herbs (mixed in equal quantities). Or take a small saltspoonful of aloe powder, dissolve it in half a pint of water, and take of the medicine a tablespoonful every hour. The latter remedy should only be taken for a half day at intervals of 2 or 3 days.

An excellent house-remedy, easily to be got even by the poorest, is the water obtained from Sauerkraut (pickled cabbage). A sufficient supply of it can be taken from the water which rises above the cabbage in the tub. This water cures the oldest sores. One spoonful of it should be mixed with 6 to 8 spoonfuls of ordinary water and 1 tablespoonful of the mixture taken every hour. As a rule this remedy will be efficacious, and should it not be so, it will never harm any one. Such medicines are always much more safe and advisable than those which contain poison.

Tea from ribwort is also not to be despised.

As exterior application I recommend to such patients a twofold compress of linen to be worn on the abdomen for 2 hours every second day. Water is sufficient for the compress but a decoction of hay-flowers, shave-grass or pine-twigs is greatly to be preferred.

Large and malignant tumours in the stomach cannot be cured. They will do their work of destruction until the ruin of the whole system is accomplished in death.

Stone complaint.

It often occurs that gravel and stone form in the bladder and in the kidneys. Whoever has seen a person afflicted with this complaint or suffered from it himself knows how fearful these pains are. The cure by water is infallible and painless; it is. therefore, the easiest and best.

Among the various remedies for this disease, oat-straw-baths hold the first place. Oat-straw (if this cannot be had, shave - grass or sour hay may be taken instead) is boiled for ½ hour and the infusion poured into a warm bath (30° R.). In this bath the patient remains for 1 hour. The bath should be followed by a vigorous cold ablution. Three such baths may be taken in the week. Two or three short bandages or compresses on the affected parts (a fourfold linen cloth and the usual covering to prevent the entrance of the air). It is understood that both applications are only to be taken in bed. They dissolve gravel and stone in the bladder and the kidneys and expel them. There are also several kinds of tea which occupy a prominent place among the remedies against this disease. Tea from oats is prepared by boiling oats for ½ hour in water. Two cups of the infusion are taken daily. If the tea is prepared from oat-straw, it is of still greater efficacy. Shave-grass tea is scarcely excelled by any other. Rose-hips, too, will make a very efficacious tea; this, however, must be taken for some time. Experience taught me that it is particular to the latter kind of tea to prevent further formation of such stones. The above mentioned applications should be taken in the given number for 2 or 3 weeks; then they should be made use of half as frequently for 3 or 4 more weeks. The blessing of the heavenly physician will be the most powerful medicine also for this malady.

A gentleman who proceeded according to my direction, told me that he had expelled many thousands of small stones within a few weeks.

Another gentleman suffered so much from gravel and stone that the acrimonious juices penetrated even to the feet where they produced innumerable small boils. Sometimes a sensation of itching and burning tormented his whole body. Thirty baths within a year, the Spanish mantle twice or three times a week, tea of the aforesaid kinds, completely cured the disease and all its painful consequences.

In conclusion I wish to say a word to the younger generation who, ever ready to do away with what is old just because it is so, or because they suppose it to be based on prejudice and ignorance, grasp with eagerness whatever is new as the only good.

For all sufferings of particular frequency and painfulness — and among these the one in question must be counted since the number of those tormented by its maddening pains is legion — remedies have been provided by the all-wise and all-kind Creator. The whole earth is strewn with herbs great and small, to relieve pain and heal disease. Men have cancelled the names of many of these salutary plants from their dispensatories as unscientific and obsolete, but they preserve their place in the book of nature and will never be effaced from it. They are made for man and destined to afford him pleasure and relief. Led by its instinct, the irrational creature, especially the wild animal, finds the salutary herb for

every pain, for every wound. Our ancestors, and many
who will soon descend into the grave and whose opinions
are regarded as old-fashioned, did the same.

I rejoice in the progress of science but I do not
call progress everything that bears this appellation of
modern sound.

My book has been written chiefly for the poor, for
patients in the country and to them I say: "Thank your
Creator for these good gifts, and do not envy the rich!"

Keep quietly to your innocent herbal remedies. Whether
they be applied internally or externally you have (even
if by chance they were not chosen rightly) the assurance
that they can do you no harm.

It would grieve me if you also would tread under
foot the gift of God, the salutary little plants, which
grow near your house, in your field, or your meadow.
Then, even I who love you so well, should be no longer
able to help you.

A gentleman in his best years became ill. He had
violent pains in the kidneys and could not make water.
The doctors declared that there was a stone in the bladder
which could only be removed by operation. To this the
patient would not submit himself.

The gentleman was visited by a friend who inquired
about his complaint. When the patient had described
his condition, he received the following advice: To take
in the morning, at noon, and in the evening a warm
sitting-bath of shave-grass decoction, and to drink a cup
of shave-grass tea before each bath. In 36 hours a stone
of the size of a hazelnut was expelled. Suddenly all
pain was gone, and the man was cured.

Mr. K— in D— writes: "For 6 months I had been
very ill and was treated for stone and kidney complaint,
I also suffered much from piles. The three physicians,
who attended me, could not help me. As I was absolutely unable to see to any business I got somebody to
take my place for 6 months. Meanwhile I learned by
others that the doctors had pronounced me incurable.
Another physician advised me to go to Heidelberg in

order to undergo an operation for stone; but I thought, I would rather die at home than in another town. My sufferings increased, and instead of urine 2 pints of blood came from me.

I was quietly looking forward to my end and resigned myself to my hard fate. Often when dreadful pains did not let me sleep in the night, I longed for death to release me from so much suffering.

At length God heard my prayer. After I had spent £ 5. 13 s. 4 d. in medicines and mineral waters, I heard of your book, ordered it and commenced the cure immediately. In 8 days I no longer felt any pain, my urine was as clear as spring-water (it had been as dull as bad beer before) and to-day after 4 weeks, I am, in spite of my age of 60 years, as healthy and merry as a youth of eighteen. Although the physician despaired of my recovery I am perfectly well. If your book had not fallen into my hands, I should now be in my grave."

Tetters.

Thousands of men are tormented by tetters, whether they own it or not. These troublesome parasites and vampires like to lodge themselves under the hair, on the back, the chest, etc. Sometimes they do not shun the light of day and fasten themselves like leeches on the arms, the feet and more especially between the fingers. These eruptions may be either hereditary or caused by bad food and beverages which corrupt the juices; they may also be consequences of a disordinate mode of life.

It is very dangerous to attack this unclean guest with sharp remedies, be they for exterior (green soap) or for interior use (quicksilver, arsenic, etc.). Tetters are easily suppressed, but in that case the last things will be worse than the first, not to mention the destructive influence of corrosive remedies on the skin.

I give the following rules for the treatment of tetters:

Externally nothing should be applied except lukewarm water to wash away the dirt. Everything else can be of evil consequences.

Food and drink for such patients should be digestible
and simple, but yet so as to increase and improve the
juices. Sour, salt or spiced food as well as all ardent
drinks should be avoided since the blood already contains
plenty of acrimonious substances. The water-applications
to be made use of by such patients are the following:
On the first day, a head-vapour and the Spanish mantle;
on the second day, a foot-vapour and a lower bandage;
on the third day, in the morning the Spanish mantle and
in the afternoon a short bandage. Then the applications
may be suspended for a day. On the fifth day, the patient
should keep his bed and take a cold whole-ablution every
two hours. If he cannot remain in bed, he should take
the whole ablution out of bed in the morning, at noon,
and in the evening; it must then, of course, be followed
by excercise. The applications should decrease in number
in proportion as the secretion of impure juices ceases and
the formation of a new skin progresses.

One further remark may find its place here. Tetters
may be wet or dry according to the amount of moisture
secreted by them. Dry tetters secrete so little of it that
it readily forms a crust on the surface of the skin, whilst
wet tetters are running constantly and are, therefore, more
troublesome, more dangerous and more difficult of cure.

The consequences of suppressed tetters are incalculable. Serious diseases, the immediate result, often
lead to slow decline and an early death or, which is worse,
to insanity.

A student had on his left cheek a round crust which
covered the raw flesh like a lid and opened very frequently to let 2 or 3 drops of matter flow out. The
face of the gentleman was full; on his head several little
pustules could be perceived. The patient had consulted
several physicians and applied various remedies but without effect.

He answered my question, whether the injury had
been caused by an accident, in the negative and said it
had come spontaneously. Now everything was clear to
me. The pale sickly complexion, still more the quantity

of matter flowing from the spot on the cheek left no room for doubt. The poisonous matter came from the body.

Till about 15 or 20 years ago, people made for themselves artificial openings in an arm or a leg. These so called fontanels were never allowed to close, and they were indeed, what their name indicates, little fountains from which bad humours of the body flowed keeping the spot in constant suppuration. In our case vigorous nature itself had formed the aperture and supplied it with a suitable lid.

For a fortnight the patient applied the head-vapour and the foot-vapour every second day. He also took the short bandage and the Spanish mantle so that he had 2 and often 3 applications a day. Tea from sage, wormwood and mint helped internally to promote the cure. Under the crust a delicate skin began to form, the surest sign of the accomplished dissolution and evacuation i. e. of the cure. After 3 weeks it could not even be seen on which cheek the crust had been.

A girl, 25 years old, relates: "My whole head is covered with eruptions, I have numerous little pustules under the hair, my ears are full of large flakes, and when they fall off from time to time, the place remains without skin. I have also violent headache sometimes, my eyes burn like fire and secrete a sticky fluid. I can no longer breathe through the nose and a sensation of violent itching and burning extending to my whole body disturbs my sleep in the night.

Applications: 1) Weekly 2 warm baths of oat-straw decoction, 30° R. with twofold change, the warm bath of 15 minutes' duration, the cold one not exceeding that of 1 minute; a cold whole-ablution may be substituted for the latter. 2) Two head-vapours of 20 to 25 minutes' duration weekly. 3) Two whole-ablutions weekly. 4) 25 drops of wormwood tincture in 8 to 10 spoonfuls of water twice daily.

In 4 weeks the tetters and the unhealthy matters in the whole body were removed and to complete the cure, it was sufficient to continue the applications for a fortnight halving their number.

A tradesman rather corpulent and about 40 years old, relates: "I have tetters on my arms and hands, the fingers excepted, also on the thighs, on back and chest. I spend many nights in which I can only sleep for 1 or 2 hours at the utmost. I have good appetite and strength.

The applications are the following: 1) Every night whole-ablution from bed. 2) Weekly 2 warm baths of oat-straw decoction, 28° R. with twofold change. (The rest as in the previous example). 3) Every day an upper shower immediately followed by a knee-gush. 4) Two saltspoonfuls of white powder daily.

After 4 weeks the man returned in perfect health; to prevent a relapse I advised him to take a whole-ablution in the night twice a week and every month a bath as aforesaid.

A peasant's daughter related: "For about 2 years I have always eruptions on the head, also in the face, now more, now less; under the hair many smaller and larger boils form and secrete a corrosive fluid. I have frequently violent itching all over the body and great heat in the interior. I have taken a great deal, especially purgatives, but without success.

The water-cure restored her to health in 6 weeks. She made use of the following applications: 1) Three whole-ablutions from bed weekly. 2) Twice a week the wet chemise dipped in salt water. 3) A head-vapour weekly. 4) Twenty drops of extract of broom in a glass of water twice daily.

Throat complaint.

Andrew begins to relate as follows: "I can scarcely speak; sometimes I am quite unable to utter a word. I had a very bad finger. It was then that I first lost the power of speech; now my finger is getting bad again. My appetite is very good, and there is nothing else the matter with me. The doctor says the uvula is too long and must be cut; but I will not let him do that.

The man's head is somewhat inflated; the left side of it from the ear downwards is a little swollen. Greater is the swelling inside, hence the contraction of these parts, hence the throat complaint. No doubt, the diseased finger has not been thoroughly cured, the poisonous matter has not been expelled. He who now strives to lead off the morbid matter and to purify the juices will bring the most efficacious help to the throat. First the whole body must be acted upon, then the head particularly. The former is done by the application of ths sack (lower bandage) and the shawl. A sack is always at a peasant's command. Let him slip into it after having dipped it in a decoction of oat-straw. The sack should be taken for 1½ hours on 3 successive days, and after these only every third day. The shawl should be worn for 1 hour daily. These applications having been made use of for a fortnight, others should be substituted for them. The patient may take 2 whole-ablutions and once the Spanish mantle weekly and, if necessary, a few head-vapours. The complaint was thoroughly cured.

A priest relates: "In the course of the summer of 1887, I sometimes felt a slight passing pain in the throat combined with a tendency to cough. Whenever I had to speak at length, in school, on the pulpit, or in the confessional, my voice became gradually weaker and threatened to refuse its service altogether. The evil increased during the months of September and October, I got violent catarrh of the throat, and the doctor declared the lungs to be affected. A 3 months' stay at Meran, gargling and painting the throat, mountain-climbing were of no avail against my complaint. About new-year's day one of the doctors proposed a little operation but it was never undertaken. On the 25th of January I left Meran to seek help at Wœrishofen. The water-applications, walking in water and 2 upper showers daily, soon brought relief; the pain gave way, my voice grew stronger and more sonorous, and on Candlemas day I was able to sing High Mass and to deliver a short homily at D—. But the tone of my voice was still hoarse and a slight sensation of pain followed the exertion. From week to week I felt improvement. After 3 weeks my voice was as strong and as clear as formerly, and I was able to perform the duties of my vocation."

Typhus.

As in small-pox the morbid matters penetrate the skin and appear as external eruption, so in typhus eruptions form in the interior of the body. According to the seat of this disease, we speak of typhus of the head or of the abdomen. In some cases of typhus tumours form on the outside of the body but these do not attain development. This kind of typhus has a peculiar name which I do not give, because it is of no importance for country people to know it.

Regarding the treatment of typhus 3 points are to be observed:

1) Do not let the heat of the fever reach too high a degree.

2) Tumours, if already existing, should be dissolved, or their formation prevented.

3) Poisonous matters should be expelled as soon as possible.

No remedy will be more efficacious for this threefold object than water: it cools, it dissolves, it cleanses.

John went near the corpse of his brother who had died of typhus. He imprudently put on some of the clothes that had belonged to the deceased and got typhus in its highest degree. Great was the heat, greater still the uneasiness of the patient. He had a tub of water put near his bed. As soon as heat and anxiety became very sensible, he went into the water for 1 minute at the utmost. He sat in the tub, the water reaching as far as the pit of the stomach, and rapidly washed the upper body with a coarse towel, put on a clean shirt and returned to the warm bed. These baths made him feel like one born anew. For 3 days he continued thus, taking 3, 5, or 6 baths daily. The fever-heat was his clock; on the first day it indicated the necessity of a bath 6 times, on the second day 3 times, on the third day once. In 5 days all danger was past. Now the wife of the convalescent was attacked by typhus. She employed the same remedy, the same tub, as her husband and in a few days she, too, was cured.

The beverage of both patients consisted in water and curdled milk. They ate nothing until brisk appetite set in. Then they took bread-soup, milk-soup, and a few potatoes. After a few days they were able to partake of their usual fare.

Max, a man of extraordinary strength, visited his brother-in-law who was ill of typhus; such a disease, he thought, would not attack him. After 8 days he felt his strength broken as well as his courage. "I can no longer stand, nor walk, I feel pressure and pain all over my body." He had caught typhus.

Max did not possess a bath but he had a large wooden vessel. In this he knelt and washed his whole body with a coarse towel and the coldest water as often as the heat reached a high pitch. He continued this cure for 8 days. Already on the sixth day he asked for soup, on the tenth day he got up, and in a short time he recovered his former strength. He was later an experienced teacher for others likewise attacked with typhus.

At a time when within 5 weeks 20 persons were cured through the aforesaid applications, an infant 2 years old, also caught the disease. Nobody believed that the delicate little creature would escape death. As often as the baby began to cry the mother plunged it in water which had been warmed a little, washed it quickly and swathed it in linen dipped in lukewarm water. After 12 days the little one was perfectly well again.

Although I willingly permit the use of lukewarm water to patients who would be caused too much fright by the cold element, I cannot help asserting again that the coldest water is generally the best for applications.

A girl is sent home from a boarding-school. She complains of violent headache, rapid change of heat and chill and diarrhœa; the child is unable to work or to walk.

On the first day the sick girl had back, chest, and abdomen washed 3 times, and a wet towel was applied to the latter for 2 hours. On the second day she took

24*

half-baths with ablution of the upper body as often as the fever-heat demanded it. On the third day two such half-baths were sufficient, on the fourth day one sufficed. The child was out of danger and soon completely restored to health again.

I could quote more than a dozen cases of patients who treated after allopathic and other methods, eventually became so weak, so poor of blood and juices that they never recovered their former health.

I generally advise such extremely weakened typhus-convalescents to take 3 or 4 times a day a little cup of tea from wormwood; this remedy will assist the formation of good and abundant stomach-juices; besides this they may have back, chest, and abdomen vigorously washed with water and vinegar 3 or 4 times a day.

Great anxiety befalls the head of a school if typhus or any other contagious malady breaks out in his establishment. Without exaggeration, I assert: If of 10 children sleeping in a dormitory one is attacked with typhus and treated according to my system, no other child will catch the disease. Contagion is generally caused by unhealthy exhalations of the sick body. Where my method is adopted these exhalations are absorbed by the wet cloths; the breath of the sick person will do no harm if the air is kept pure by ventilation. It is self-evident that the excrements of such patients must be removed as quickly as possible and emptied at a place where no danger of contagion can arise.

Ulcers.

A poor day-labourer had for many months an open sore on a leg, the opening being of the length of a finger and 3 times as broad. The man, still in his best years, had always great pain and could seldom sleep for a few hours. His appearance was very ill and all his courage gone. I advised the patient to spread boiled fenugreek on a rag and apply this to the wound like a plaster, to bandage the leg from above the ankle to above the calf of the leg in fresh leaves of colts-foot and then to put on the stocking to cover the whole. Every morning and every evening plaster and bandage had to be renewed;

besides this the patient had to take every two hours
2 spoonfuls of tea made from fenugreek. He could attend to
his work without interruption. A fortnight after he commenced the applications 2 thirds of the sore were healed;
the man had a healthy appearance, had no longer pain
and slept well. Three weeks later the foot was completely healed. Tea from fenugreek is prepared by boiling
a little spoonful of it in ½ pint of water for 1 minute.

An official complains of an open sore on the calf of
the leg: "It is rather large and secretes much dirt; the
colour of the leg which is of a blackish blue seems even
more frightening than the sore and the inflammation. I
consulted several doctors. Besides other remedies they
prescribed much mineral water, but all in vain." The
man, about 45 years old, is strongly built and pretty
corpulent. His rather flushed complexion reveals the beer-
friend. The corners of the eyes were dull, the eyes themselves somewhat yellow, the ears red. On my question
about his general health he answered: "There is nothing
the matter with me: I have the best of appetites, nor
am I a drinker, but I relish 2 or 3 glasses of beer daily.
My complaint is a purely local one."

All patients of this kind — an exception is as rare as
a white raven — complain of the one painful or ulcerating
spot believing that, if this be healed, their health must
be perfect. Only the reverse treatment will cure them.
First cure the body, expel all impure matters, and the
sore will heal spontaneously. In my opinion there can be
no blindness more dangerous, no folly more laden with
consequences than healing an aperture, closing an issue
through which alone the body can be saved. Nature
shows how it will and can help itself. We bind it, so
to speak, hands and feet by obstructing its safety-valves.
Is it to be wondered at if such proceedings lead to the
destruction of nature?

I advised the official to take a lower bandage 1½ hours
daily for a fortnight, to vigorously wash the upper body
twice a day and to apply the head-vapour once a week
for 20 minutes. These applications were intended to purify
the body and strengthen it for the secretion of the morbid

juices. After a fortnight the patient came back. His first
words were: "At our last interview I told you I was not
ill, but now I know that I have been very ill. I could
only with difficulty mount the stairs, so heavy was my
breathing; I was always unusually inflated. When I told
the physician so, he ascribed everything to my becoming
always older. Now, however, I feel like born anew. My
respiration is easy, and I feel so well. Formerly I suffered
very much from ill-humour, now I am always in good
spirits, and I enjoy my meals more than ever. During
these two weeks," the patient concluded, "I discharged
much urine. I feel much easier especially in the lower
body; the pains in the leg give way, and the sore begins
to heal. What must I do in order that it may be completely healed like the body?"

The official took twice weekly a lower bandage for
½ hour and daily a vigorous upper shower. To the sore
he applied a linen rag, which was 3 or 4 times daily re-
dipped in lukewarm water. Nothing else he was allowed
to employ for its healing. Two weeks had passed again,
when the official returned to me. His leg was healed.
He has never since ceased to praise the salutary power
of the water. A person thus cured should (this is of
great importance) continue one or the other of the tested
applications for some length of time. He may select the
practice whose effects have proved most beneficial for him.

Agatha suffered for years from a sore on the leg
which from time to time opened and healed again spontaneously. On the inevitable ointments I forbear to speak,
it would only irritate me. A physician promised to cure
her if she consented to faithfully follow his advice for
some time. The leg was brought in a position (in bed)
somewhat higher than the rest of the body. Almost immediately the pain gave way. Some trifling remedy, I
don't know what, was applied to the sore, then it was
well bandaged. The patient felt no longer pain in the
diseased limb, and the cure progressed in an astonishing
way until the sore was closed. Suddenly Agatha feels
heaviness in the head and giddiness, but she cares little.
In the night, however, her weakness became so great that

the doctor, who had been speedily called, declared marasmus would set in and bring the girl to an early grave. The last sacraments had to be administered to her that very night, and for 5 days she lay motionless. On the sixth day she recovered her senses and spoke with difficulty a few words. Of her own accord she applied wet bandages to the body and the diseased leg. On the second day the leg swelled considerably and began to pain violently, whereas the head was relieved. Agatha continued bandaging abdomen and leg. One half of the leg was inflamed and opened after 5 days. The cure, as described in the case of the official, was an easy task. Agatha regained her former health.

But how had the attack in the night been caused? If a boy stands on his head, the blood naturally flows to that part. The morbid matters led away from the leg (by the higher position) found their way to chest and head and effected those frightening symptoms. The bandages led them down again, the water opened the sore, and the morbid matters, finding their former passage and exit reopened, left chest and head.

I know that many physicians of the new school hold a different opinion, but that will not alter mine nor that of many others. I call every open sore caused by vigorous nature in order to throw off what is unhealthy, a health-preserver and life-guard. Who does not know that the healing of such sores has often been fatal, and that spontaneous healing of them in old age is always regarded as a sign of approaching death?

In a letter which is lying before me I read literally: "My sore leg begins to grow worse again. The rheumatic toothache and headache which greatly tormented me, have entirely ceased since my leg commenced to be more painful. These two complaints continue to trouble me alternately and whenever neither of them causes me particular suffering, I feel a decrease of general health."

There are complaints that leave one part of the body only to attack another. Gout and one kind of erysipelas are such wanderers. The complaint in question also belongs to their number with the difference, however, that its wanderings lead through hidden paths which prevent it from being so easily recognized as the two aforementioned maladies.

A successful attack against these wanderers can only be made by the use of threefold applications.

In our case the lower bandage removes all unhealthy matters which are on their wandering from the head to the feet and vice-versa. Often applied it deprives them of all inclination for a wandering life. As a secondary means it acts on the suffering part impeding the return of matters that had left it. The foot-vapour followed by a lower shower is directed against the painful spot. It dissolves morbid matters and expels them. Cold ablutions or the Spanish mantle are destined to strengthen and invigorate the whole body in order that it may lend ready aid in the healing process.

Hence the sequence of applications would be the following: The short bandage, 2 whole-ablutions from bed in the night, again the short bandage, the foot-vapour and finally the Spanish mantle.

As internal remedies tea from centaury, sage, and mint will render good service: the two former act in a purifying manner, whilst the latter improves the stomach juices.

I will indicate two other kinds of treatment for open sores, one of which may be useful to people who have no accomodation for bathing.

A peasant short of stature and rather stout came and said: "Your reverence, I have such an open sore on the leg; have you no water-remedy for me?" "O yes, my friend," I replied. "Look here, peasant, go home, and spread over your bed a woollen carpet or any other coarse cloth. Then, take an old worn out sack, dip it in water, wring it out, and slip into it. Then jump into your bed and cover yourself well first with a woollen blanket and over this put the feather-quilt." The peasant's eyes the curious twinkling of which had amused me till now, looked at me with astonishment; my prescription seemed to cause him considerable fright. "And this," I continued, "must be done daily for a week and each time you will stay in the sack for 2 hours." The peasant was perspiring with fear of the proceeding as he went; nevertheless he did as he was told. Within 50 days he slipped into the sack no less than 25 times, and then his sore was healed. Joy made him jump not so much on account of the cured leg as on account of the good spirits obtained in the sack. I advised him to make use of this practice from time to time; but this was not necessary with him. "Out of gratitude and for my own pleasure," he exclaimed, "I will continue this sack-proceeding for a whole year." And he kept his word.

Another course of applications for the healing of open sores is the following:

Take: 1) Twice weekly a warm bath of oat-straw decoction with threefold change; 2) twice weekly the lower bandage for $1\frac{1}{2}$ hours or the Spanish mantle for the same time.

As a warning I give the following case.

A gentleman pretty corpulent but very healthy received an open sore on the leg which was very troublesome to him. He had recourse to the water-cure and made use of it for 12 days, after which he felt remarkably easy and well. "But this troublesome open sore," he said, asking me to heal it. "Whoever cures your leg will shorten your life, I shall not do it," was my decided reply. My answer vexed him, and he went away. This had happened in autumn. In spring he went to a bathing-place and took mineral baths; on his return home he employed several other remedies and succeeded in closing the sore. Six or eight weeks he enjoyed his healed leg, then a great tumour began to form on his upper back. The physicians thinking it to be a carbuncle opened it, but instead of matter they found a hard substance. In 12 days blood-poisoning had put an end to the gentleman's life.

I could quote similar instances in great number.

I came into a house. A son of the family was just taking a foot-bath of hot water after the direction of the doctor. He was to take the bath as hot as he could endure it. His pains, very great already, were considerably increased by the hot water. The leg from the ankle to the calf of the leg was dreadfully swollen, and the swelling was so coloured and inflamed that the bursting of it seemed imminent.

It is incomprehensible to me how such a thing as hot water can be ordered as remedy for a limb already containing so much heat, hot water, which would almost scald a healthy leg. The gentleman grew excited during the bath, declared that he could bear it no longer and required that the water should be removed from his sight. His order was obeyed, and I advised him to apply a soft rag dipped in Krautwasser (water from pickled cabbage) to the most inflamed spot, to bandage the leg from the ankle to the calf of the leg in a larger very soft cloth dipped in cold water, and to cover the whole with a dry wrapping. Both compresses should be repeated as often as heat and pain are felt in the leg. The young gentleman followed my advice; in 2 days he was able to walk. The boil burst. To promote its healing he applied a bandage (a small linen bag) of infused hay-flowers. In 10 days the leg was completely healed.

A gentleman of distinction relates: "Every year I get a complaint from which I have to suffer for 2 to 3 weeks. First I feel heat and a piercing pain in my legs, then they begin to swell as far as the knees. When the swelling appears the pain gives way, but I am unable to do any work. Can this not be prevented?" The answer is: "Yes, by the following applications." 1) Once or twice a week put on a pair of linen stockings dipped in warm oat-straw decoction. Swathe the feet in a dry cloth and keep this foot-bandage for 2 hours. (This can be done in the evening.) 2) Once a week take a short bandage for 1½ hours.

A countryman comes and shows his swollen legs, which feel quite hard up to the knees and are covered with blackish-blue spots. He suffered great pains so that he spent whole nights without sleep. Since his legs were thus affected he had also been subject to great mental suffering, and so low-spirited was he that he often wished for death. He had no appetite, and his appearance was very ill.

The applications were the following: 1) In the first week 2 foot-vapours and in every succeeding week, one. 2) Twice weekly a shirt dipped in oat-straw decoction for 1½ hours. 3) Twice weekly a lower-bandage for 1½ hours. 4) During the night the foot should be swathed in a cloth dipped in water in which 2 spoonfuls of fenu-greek have been boiled. It was just this bandage which brought great relief of the pain and effected the necessary dissolution. As internal remedy the patient took 2 salt-spoonfuls of fenugreek boiled in ½ pint of water, in 3 or 4 portions during the day.

Urinary difficulties.

I was once hastily called to a carpenter, 70 years of age, to prepare him for death. He suffered, I was told, terrible pain and was unable to make water. When I arrived at the patient's house I saw that I could do nothing in my capacity as pastor; for the man was running about in the room and screaming with pain; his wife was like-wise crying and lamenting. I told her to boil a handful of shave-grass in water and prepare a close-stool. The physician lived at a distance of 6 miles and, had he been called, would certainly not have found the man alive. The woman came and poured the boiling water in the close-stool. The patient sat on it and allowed the shave-grass vapour to fumigate the painful spots. I ordered him to remain on it for 20 to 30 minutes and then go to bed. In an hour, I added, I should come back and prepare him for death. On my return after an hour I found the man quiet in bed and bathed in perspiration. He had discharged 4 pints of urine and felt no longer the least pain. The preparation for death could be omitted. On the following day the man took again a vapour for 20 minutes; on the third day he rested and on the fourth day returned to his usual work.

The man had caught cold, and this had caused the complaint. It is incredible what help so simple a herb can bring in hours of bitterest suffering, if promptly and rightly applied.

A day-labourer had a similar complaint. He applied shave-grass vapours but they failed to produce the desired effect. They had to be assisted by another application. Shave-grass was boiled, a fourfold linen cloth dipped in the hot decoction, wrung out a little, and laid on the suffering part. One shave-grass vapour and one such compress for 2 hours daily sufficed, and in a few days the man was cured. In this case also the complaint originated in a cold although there were other secondary causes. The discharged urine showed that a deal of morbid matters had been dissolved in the interior.

In a similar case I employed warm water mixed with vinegar instead of shave-grass with the same good result. Besides the external applications I recommend tea from shave-grass a cupful of which may be taken in 2 or 3 portions daily.

A housemother had been confined to bed and under medical treatment for 19 weeks. The physicians declared her disease to be cancer of the bladder. Her pains were so great that her cries could be heard by the neighbours. All hope for her recovery had long been given up. I advised the poor woman to have shave-grass boiled, to dip a cloth in the decoction, to place the decocted shave-grass in the cloth (previously wrung out a little) and to apply this compress to the painful spot. The patient felt relieved even after the first application. She continued making use of it 3 or 4 times daily for 5 days, the duration of each application being 2 full hours. On the fifth day a salt-stone was expelled under unspeakable pain. The complaint was thoroughly cured; the fatal cancer had been caught.

A man, 64 years old, otherwise strong and healthy could no longer discharge urine. The physician used the catheter and declared that there was no remedy for this disease. Indeed the doctor had to be fetched every 24 hours for this unpleasant operation. After 4 days the man's whole body was glowing with fever-heat, but he was not allowed to drink. Thus the poor man was tormented by twofold suffering. The physician gave little hope for recovery. I was consulted and advised the patient to lie on a wet sheet folded several times and dipped in warm water, for ¾ hour. The same sheet was then to be re-dipped and applied to the abdomen for 1 hour. After the first application 3 pints of water were discharged. In the beginning it was renewed twice a day, later once daily. The patient took daily a cupful of tea from shave-grass, juniper-berries or dwarf-elder (boiled in water for 5 minutes). Rosmary-wince or even juniper-berries only, boiled in water and taken as tea would have, likewise, rendered good service. The first complaint with its pains gave way, the fever, too, disappeared. The man felt much better after this cure than previously to his illness.

A peasant, about 42 years old, relates: "I have been suffering for 4 years, and my sufferings increase from month to month; I have difficulty in making water. Every half hour I get violent cramps followed by a very scanty discharge of water. I have consulted many physicians; according to the direction of a medical man at Munich I drank 80 bottles of mineral water, this relieved me a little, but the disease is not removed. During the night I have to rise every half hour to make water and if I omit this, it makes my sufferings worse. I am otherwise healthy, have, as everyone says, a good appearance, and I seldom drink beer. What is to be done?

Applications: 1) In the week 2 warm baths of oat-straw decoction (30 to 32°) with threefold change, 2) On the remaining days of the week a short bandage likewise dipped in oat-straw decoction, for 1 hour; these applications are to be continued for 12 to 14 days. 3) Daily 3 small cups of tea from shave-grass and juniper-berries, boiled for 10 minutes.

A man-servant had great difficulties in making water. Under great pain a small and slow discharge took place. The physician declared it necessary to draw off the urine by means of the catheter which was done every second day for some time. The evil, however, increased and with it the pain became greater.

The man-servant took twice daily 25 to 30 drops of tincture from juniper-berries and rose-hips in a wineglass-ful of water. He immediately noticed an improvement;

in 10 days the complaint had almost disappeared. Every other day he took drops of wormwood tincture before taking the aforesaid remedies and in a short time he was completely freed from the complaint."

For all complaints of the bladder, gravel etc. an infusion of black currant leaves is very recommendable. Such tea has rendered excellent service in the most difficult cases.

Vaccination, bad effects of.

A gentleman relates: "I have been healthy all my life. Ten years ago when smallpox was raging in my neighbourhood I had myself vaccinated. I got no pustules but the vaccinated spot on the right arm remained of a somewhat reddish hue and a slight eruption appeared round the openings made by the lancet. Through 8 years I only noticed that the inflamed spot grew in extension, and now after 10 years the eruption has the appearance of wet tetters and is so troublesome that it sometimes deprives me entirely of my night's rest. These eruptions are stronger now on the one arm, now on the other, and the same change takes place in the feet. I have employed a great deal, even the most poisonous ointments on the surface of the skin; I have also taken much medicine but without success."

Applications: Here blood and juices are evidently corrupted and the eruption only serves as outlet for unhealthy secretions. It is therefore necessary that the whole body should be acted upon in order to dissolve and evacuate the morbid matters.

1) Weekly 3 whole-ablutions from bed.

2) To wash the eruption with an infusion of fenugreek twice or 3 times daily. Instead of infused fenugreek, aloe may be used. (1 teaspoonful of aloe dissolved in 2 pints of hot water.)

3) Twice a week the Spanish mantle. These applications are to be continued for a fortnight or 3 weeks.

Further applications: Every week or every fortnight a warm bath followed by a cold one (See Part the first.) It would also be good during this cure to drink wormwood tea, 3 or 4 spoonfuls twice daily.

Voice, loss of the.

It frequently occurs that people lose their voice partly or entirely, without apparent cause.

Twelve years ago there came to me a priest who was obliged to carry about with him paper and pencil in order to communicate his thoughts to others by writing. Utterly unable to perform the duties of his vocation he had sought help everywhere. Gargarisms, magnetism, electricity, scarification had been employed in vain; 14 times lapis infernalis had been applied to his throat and caused so much havoc in it that a physician declared he would never regain his voice. At last cold water became the remedy to which the priest, next to God, owed his recovery. His complexion was rather sickly, but he felt particular pain in no part of his body; he was lacking nothing but his voice, so he thought. How can the organ of speech be unfit for use if it is not injured, if no pain whatever is felt? If I bandage a person's mouth, no organ is injured and yet he will be unable to speak. It would be folly to seek for the cause in the throat. I must remove the bandage and his voice will be heard. The organs of speech may be perfectly sound but various influences, bandages, as it were, may impede their action. Which are these influences?

When shepherd boys amuse themselves by throwing stones into the rill that flows through the valley they impede its regular course and force it to leave its bed and either to run in another direction or to fill with its water ditches and hollows that may be near. The same process often takes place in the human organism. If we could but look into this many-veined river basin we should see how often the circulation is disturbed by such obstacles and that agglomerations, swellings of mucous membranes etc., must be the consequence. Who has not seen a so-called kernel (a hard concretion in the flesh) on a hand or a foot? Imagine now what pressure such a swelling, or whatever it may be called, must cause if it is formed on an internal part. Must not the activity of a thus pressed organ be impaired and disturbed? Muffle the

most high-sounding bell and it will be mute and all burning and hammering will be of no avail.

Let us now return to our speechless gentleman. Already the first upper shower showed me the dreadful
agglomerations, almost tumours which had bound the
organs of speech like as many fetters. The removal of
the agglomerations was effected by dissolving and evacuating water-applications. Among the former the head-vapour
holds the first place. It produces perspiration over the
whole upper body; a cold shower immediately succeeding
it will wash away what has been dissolved, and strengthen the system. Since the patient is rather stout and
such persons generally suffer from determination of blood
to the head, a foot-vapour with following cold shower
should be applied to lead the blood downwards. These
2 applications may be taken once a week, and if the corpulence is very great, twice weekly.

A second application which acts in a dissolving manner
on the whole body is the Spanish mantle. To this are
added cold baths (1 or 2 weekly for 1 minute), half-baths
reaching to the arm-pits with vigorous ablution of the
upper body; one upper and one lower shower may be
substituted for the half-bath. These applications punctually
taken and combined with a regular mode of life, much
exercise in the open air, and light manual labour, restored
the whole machine to its proper motion and the little
wheel of the voice ran without burning and electricity
spontaneously and as well as it had formerly done. Nobody had believed that this priest would ever regain his
voice. In 6 weeks he was completely restored and to this
day, after 12 years, his voice has so sonorous and powerful a tone that it gives pleasure to all who hear it.

A priest had lost his voice and had consulted the
most renowned physicians for 5 years. He inhaled much,
he had the parotid glands cut, all in vain. The seat of
the complaint was always considered to be in the neck
until the last physician who examined him declared that
there was absolutely nothing the matter with his neck
but that he could not discover by what else the loss of
his voice might be caused. This declaration induced the

patient to have recourse to the much feared water-cure. He regained his voice before 6 months had elapsed, and it was of so mighty a sound that he thought half of it would have sufficed him.

Also in this case the loss of the voice did not originate in the organs of speech. The gentleman's neck, however, was unusually thick and the upper body disproportionately stout compared to the emaciated hands and feet. He had formerly often suffered from attacks of colic. Nature sought in this manner to help itself but failed in throwing off all morbid matters.

Later these attacks ceased and the patient felt from time to time contractions of the chest which, however, did not trouble him much. The tenant which had formerly dwelled on the ground-floor was now lodging in the upper story. No inhalations, no cutting of the glands or even of the uvula, would here effect a cure. If the whole organism is restored to order the voice will return spontaneously.

The patient took in the week a head-vapour and a foot-vapour, an upper and a lower shower. To contract the bloated parts of the body, he descended 4 times weekly into the cold water (to the arm-pits) remaining in it for one minute during which time he vigorously washed his upper body. He also took the Spanish mantle once a week. After 4 weeks the applications were reduced to 1 upper and lower shower and 1 half-bath weekly. The patient was not allowed to discontinue the applications suddenly. He had to make use of them for some length of time in the same succession as during the actual cure. It generally requires no urging on my part to induce patients to continue the applications.

The desire for, and the trust in, the application of water hold pace with the sensation of increasing strength.

Our gentleman's voice was restored to its former strength. The old complaint never returned although 11 years have elapsed since the cure.

A professor in his best years was unable to attend to his vocation of teacher; he had lost his voice. He first consulted the doctors in his neighbourhood, then other celebrated physicians who made throat complaints their special study. After inhalations and electricity had been applied in vain he was told that the vocal ligaments had lost all elasticity, that seeing the inefficacy of all remedies nothing could be done at present to cure him and finally that he should let his organ of speech enjoy rest from all activity for a whole year. This verdict did not satisfy the gentleman and he resolved on making use of the water-cure. In 6 days he regained his voice, in 6 weeks it was so strong and sonorous as it had scarcely ever been before. This happened 5 years ago and the gentleman need have no fear; his voice will remain as it is. I will now answer the question: what had there been the matter with the gentleman? His appearance was not sickly although his complexion lacked the freshness of health, his appetite was excellent, he possessed plenty of natural strength; should only the vocal ligaments have been treated so unkindly by nature as to lose all elasticity and refuse their service altogether? That is not probable. The gentleman was somewhat vexed at my assertion that nothing was the matter with the organs of speech and when the neck was entirely passed over in my examination, he was on the point of losing all confidence in my treatment. I, however, wished to prove to the gentleman that, the complaint not orginating in the neck, I was right in ordering no remedy to be applied to it. Where was the root of the evil? The gentleman had on the upper part of the back, on both sides of the seventh vertebra small elevations like little cushions. They exercised a pressure on the organs of speech. Vigorous showers were applied to the young gentleman, he received the shawl, half-baths and the Spanish mantle. Later half-baths with ablutions of the upper body were sufficient. The fear of water soon gave way to such a desire for it that the applications became a necessity to him. Not a week passed without some applications which preserved him in good health.

Countess N., 15 years old, relates: "Two years ago I had diphtheria in its highest degree. After this malady

I got a terrible headache and some weeks later, after a hot bath, I lost my voice and was therefore obliged to converse with others by writing. My parents consulted the most celebrated physicians. I had to inhale, to take divers mineral remedies, I was electrified every day for several weeks; leeches were applied to my neck which often caused me to faint: I can only think with terror of the details and will not even attempt to mention all the medicines I took. Thus I continued for more than 2 years and finally the doctors declared that I should die of consumption. On this they all agreed that I should never recover my voice. The whole year through my hands, my feet, and my head are ice-cold. I cannot eat nor does any food do me good; I am often tempted to despair. I am only 15 years old, but there can be no more unfortunate being than I am.

The girl is suffering from extreme poverty of the blood; this is proved by the sensation of chill; only in the chest she still feels a certain warmth. She must be swathed in order that formation of blood may take place and the circulation may be regulated. The patient should live on a simple fare and take twice or 3 times daily a cold arm-bath reaching to the elbows and a foot-bath reaching over the ankles or better still she should walk barefoot in wet grass or on wet stones. This may seem contrary to reason, but these are excellent means to produce vital heat in the system, especially in the bloodless extremities. To effect the same in other parts of the body, back, chest and abdomen should be vigorously washed with cold water twice daily. The first attempts cost a great effort on the part of the patient but the awakening vital heat gave her new courage. Duration and height of the 2 baths could be increased. These practices were continued for 8 or 10 days. Then followed light knee-gushes and upper showers; they were taken every second or fourth day, one in the morning, the other in the afternoon. After a fortnight these applications were replaced by a half-bath reaching to the pit of the stomach, taken for 1 minute, and an upper shower, daily. The diet should be of such a kind as to promote the formation of blood and juices, hence it should consist in simple food not spoiled by spices, etc. Milk is the best drink, but nothing ardent should be taken. To brace her system she had to continue the aforesaid practices for some time.

A girl, of 16 years, lost her voice without any apparent cause and could only with great difficulty make herself understood. She consulted physicians; these ordered medicaments, but they had no effect. The girl had a blooming appearance and good appetite; her head was full and round, her short neck rather thick, her breathing somewhat difficult. Her feet were always cold. In 6 weeks the girl was completely cured. By which applications? The blooming complexion, the full hot head, the cold feet showed clearly that there existed a determination of blood to the head. Hence the disproportionate development of the upper parts of the body, perhaps also agglomerations of blood. Equality of vital heat was the first object to be aimed at. The girl took twice or 3 times daily a cold foot-bath (of 1 minute's duration at the utmost) followed by brisk exercise in the open air; she also walked barefoot in the wet grass or on wet stones. The practices tended to draw the blood downwards to the extremities; others had to be made use of in order to dissolve and remove the agglomerations in the head, neck, and upper body. To effect this the Spanish mantle was applied daily during the first week, three times during the second week and twice during the third, later only once a week. After a fortnight 1 half-bath with washing of the upper body was taken in the week, to brace the system. The same result might be obtained by 1 upper and lower shower. Thus the three objects, production of equal vital heat, dissolution and evacuation of superfluous matters and strengthening of the whole system, were attained by the respective parts of the healing process. The girl increased in strength and her voice became clearer and more sonorous than it had ever been before and was thus excellently adapted for singing which art is the object of the girl's particular study.

Worms.

Among the vermin apt to weaken the human body and cause disorder in the organism the ascarides and other kinds of worms are especially injurious. Little children are frequently troubled with them and, if a mother be noth careful, they may do much harm. They form in the rectum; indigestible farinaceous food and especially black bread are particularly favourable to their formation and growth. Worms are generally expelled from the rectum, but sometimes also from the mouth. Symptoms of their presence in the body are: great appetite, uneasiness and pain in the abdomen. Children afflicted with worms are apt to put their fingers in the nose and have a sickly appearance due to the deprivation of nourishment through the worms.

Remedies against worms are:

1. Cut up an onion and put it overnight in 2 pints of water. In the morning the juice should be well pressed out of the onion and the water drunk fasting. If this remedy has been used for 3 or 4 days the worms will certainly be killed and expelled.

2. A spoonful of honey is boiled in 2 pints of water and this water taken. The worms drink themselves full of this water and a cup of wormwood tea, which is poison for them, taken later, will kill and expel them.

3. The strongest effect is produced by wormseed, the seed of a plant which has the property of expelling worms.

Three thick long worms came one day out of a woman's mouth. She had been ill for some time and was taking medicine. Two spoonfuls of wormseed taken 2 hours before breakfast on 2 successive days effected that within 3 days no less than 78 long worms were expelled.

Wormseed is not espensive and can be had at any chemist's.

Among all worms the tape-worm is the most dangerous. To expel this, a very safe remedy with directions for use may be obtained in every apothecary's shop.

Alphabetical Index.

Printed in the United States
16824LVS00001B/26

9 780766 136557